Sisu Mother

Sisu Mother

First Published as
Tyttö Maailmalla
by
Lempi Kähönen-Wilson

Translated from the Original Finnish
by
Richard Impola

North Star Press of St. Cloud, Inc.

Copyright © 2002 Lempi Kähönen-Wilson

ISBN: 0-87839-177-0

First Edition: June 2002

All rights reserved.

Printed in the United States of America
by Versa Press, Inc., East Peoria, Illinois

Published by
North Star Press of St. Cloud, Inc.
P.O. Box 451
St. Cloud, Minnesota 56320

CHAPTER I

"Can't I run any faster? He'll catch me now."

I was crying, running for my life. I stumbled . . .

I sat up wet with sweat. At first I didn't know if it was real or a dream. But it was only a dream, a horrible dream. My sister Anu was there, asleep in the other bed, and the clothing hung from the rafters, as it always did in our own *aitta*. (A general purpose storeroom, also used as a summer bedroom.)

It was the summer of 1939. In the dream I had seen myself walking by the Kuoppa house. The yard there was filled with bloody bodies, some of them still moving. A giant of a man, nearly naked, ran out of the house and began to hack at those who were still alive with a huge broadax. I watched in total shock, unable even to run away. Then the man noticed me and rushed at me, brandishing his ax and shouting:

"I've taken this house, and I'm going to take everything, the whole town."

Terrified, I dashed off for home as fast as my legs could go, with the ugly giant in pursuit, waving his ax. No matter how fast I ran, I could hear his panting getting nearer and nearer, and then I awoke. I never dared tell anyone about this dream. I was very quiet and shy and was afraid the others would laugh at me. Being the youngest child in the family, I was often teased, but I was my mother's pet.

The following morning my sister Anu and I went to Husus Meadow to do some spring chores. On the way, we passed the Kuoppa house. I was so afraid my skin broke out in gooseflesh, but Anu did not notice.

The meadow was known for its snakes. We had been warned about them, although I had never heard of anyone's being bitten. Soon a loathsome snake raised its head nearby, its tongue out, hissing. I froze in place, as the snake and I stared at each other, hypnotized. Anu broke off an alder stick (supposedly the best weapon for killing snakes), crept up behind the snake as it continued to stare at me, and crushed it with no resistance. Then she lifted it onto a fence where we could see if it escaped, for its tail continued to wriggle. According to old belief, it would go on wriggling until sundown. Soon another snake rose hissing, only to meet the same fate from the alder stick. It was springtime after all, and mating season. Even the fence posts stood in pairs on the old brush fence line.

There were about a dozen houses in the little community, plus a cabin or two. Everybody knew one another, knew their good and bad traits—especially the bad—all too well. The houses had been built close to each other along a winding road, and the fields, pastures, and patches of woods belonging to them were scattered far and wide.

Husus Meadow was so far away that we always took lunch with us, at least during haymaking. There was no need to carry water, for a clear spring bubbled up in the meadow. One needed only make a birch-bark cup, fasten it to the end of a stick, and dip up a drink of fresh, cold water on a sweaty July day.

Now and then a snake was clubbed to death during haymaking, but our heroic feat became the talk of the town. Some even teased us, saying: "Here come the snake-killing sisters." Mother even boasted that if it had been the neighbor's girls, they would have run off like field rabbits.

The name of the community was Lahnavalkama (Bream Landing). It was on the Isthmus of Karelia. As a child I was curious—why had the place been given such a funny name? The story was that the lake had teemed with bream, especially during the spawning season—the brooks were still full of the fish. One needed only lift them into baskets with dip nets. Hence, the odd name.

One could still get bream in Kelja Bay if one set out nets at the right time in the spring. Father was an indifferent fisherman, but Aunt Anni was always on the go. "Elsie, come and row for me, and we'll set out nets." I was always ready to go out on the lake, and soon Anni would be dropping the nets into the water.

Very early in the morning, still half-asleep, we would set out to check the nets. Sleep would soon take wing when I felt the sting of cold, wet grass between my toes. The glowing golden orb of the morning sun would already be well up in the sky. It was really something to hoist the big bream into the boat. Even a big pike had strayed into the net, and it put up a strong fight. "It does you no good to struggle. You'll be fish stew today. We've had enough of fried bream this spring. We'll salt this fish for the winter so we'll have something to go with the potatoes," said my aunt, busy with the catch.

I had just finished the four years of public school that spring, and I wanted to go on, but money was always tight for a small farm owner. There were four of us children in the house, besides Father's widowed sister, Aunt Anni.

I had often dreamed of being a teacher. Learning was so easy for me, really too easy. I would watch my sister drumming the lessons into her head for hours. I just went over them quickly in the morning, but still I was one of the best pupils.

The nearest advanced school was at Käkisalmi. To attend, I would have had to live there. No, it was out of the question: there was no money for it. Some people thought that it didn't pay to educate girls—they would get married anyway. A few rich people educated their daughters in order to improve their marriage prospects. Love was never even mentioned.

At thirteen I was already taller than my mother and helped her with all the work. Often I was terribly sleepy when she came to wake me up for milking or other pressing work. I loved it when she let me sleep on Sunday. Father went to church only at Christmas, but he never worked in the fields on Sunday. During the summer, I would go to church with Mother and Aunt Anni almost every Sunday. To get there, we had to walk three kilometers along the poor wagon road through Katila. It was often muddy, so we went barefoot, carrying a rag with us to wipe off our feet before arriving at the church. Only then did we put our stockings and church shoes on. Often we had *piirakkas* (a small Karelian rice or potato pie) with us for lunch, and they tasted delicious when we ate them alongside the church meadow. If there was time during the morning, we went to look at the graves, for after all, our grandparents lay there under the ground.

Viljo, my oldest brother, was already twenty. He was very patriotic, and belonged to the Civil Guard, had already undergone testing, and would have to go into the Army come autumn. My sister Anu was already seventeen. She sneaked off to dances and had boyfriends. My brother Samppa was three years older than I and had a bad temper. We could never agree on anything. Sometimes we got into real fights, which Samppa would always win. I didn't dare tell my mother about it; Samppa would have given me a licking for it. It would have meant being a tattletale. One just had to put up with things. Aunt Anni was father's sister. She worked hard at everything, but was also very sharp-tongued. She always managed to find fault with my mother, and then she would pour out her complaints like a storm at sea. Mother never argued with her but let things go in one ear and out the other. She was always the respectable lady of the house.

In early autumn, strange news began to circulate. The great powers were heaping up war materiel, and there was talk of negotiations. People whispered that our neighbor to the east was making demands on Finland. A black cloud fell over the community.

The threshing machine chugged day and night, moving from one house to another. Mostly the same work crew went along with the machine. The housewives set out their very best table, for the work was hard and dusty, and the men worked long hours, often late into the night by lantern light. They were trying to get the grain in directly from the field during dry weather. The sauna was warmed every day, and often it was midnight before the last of the men arrived home.

Matti, who owned and operated the threshing machine, was in poor health. During breaks in the work, he would go to listen to the only radio in the community. One day, when the crew was having coffee at the edge of a ditch, Matti ran up to them breathlessly and gasped out:

"It's started now."

"What's started?" a man named Sakari asked quickly.

"Well, the war."

"That's terrible. Where?" someone said.

"Somewhere out there. In Central Europe."

The first thing that entered my mind was my summer nightmare. Even though it was a sunny fall day, the sky seemed to darken, and the air seemed charged with thunder. People's faces grew serious, and they had little to say. A strange, gnawing fear governed everyone's thoughts, especially the older generation's. After all, the hardships of the War of Independence were still fresh in their minds.

In October a census was taken of every home to see what kind of family lived there. If there were old or ill people, or children, they would probably have to move to a safer place, depending upon how the negotiations with the neighboring country were going. I was barely thirteen and was thus a minor, but Mother said: "My daughter can manage as well as any grown-up. None of us is going to leave." Nothing more was said on the matter.

At the end of October, the army moved into the community. Soldiers and horses were lodged at the houses. Viljo was already in the army and had been sent to the non-commissioned officers' training school. There were still five of us left, and we all slept in one room, Father and Mother in a bed and the young ones on the floor. All spare mattress covers were taken into use and were stuffed with rye straw, as was the custom then. We even sewed new covers so that no one would have to lie on bare straw. The men had the *tupa* (all-purpose room, perhaps like a large farm kitchen) and another bedroom to sleep in. At night everyone had to tread cautiously on a trip to the outhouse to avoid stepping on someone's legs. In the morning, a line formed there for that purpose, but then the soldiers settled the matter in army fashion by setting up a pole to sit over behind the woodshed. Luckily the soldiers ate at the Ihalainens' house, which was in the center of the community. They had a field kitchen there, along with a large iron sauna pot to supplement it. The soldiers' headquarters was also at the Ihalainens'. They had the largest house in the village.

In early November, the old and the children had to leave for an unknown destination. It was the first evacuation. All this was done in case war should break out.

I stood watching those who were leaving as they waited for the bus to arrive. There was a family of my relatives among them: the grandmother, three boys under eight years of age, and the youngest, a girl, sitting in her mother's lap. They all wore name tags around their necks. The boys were excited about getting to go somewhere on a bus. None of them looked the slightest bit sleepy, although it was close to midnight. The woman from the Kuoppa house was also there with the little children and the grandmother. Her husband was away somewhere with the army reserves.

Again the summer dream flashed into my mind. The Kuoppa house was empty now. The man had shouted that he would take the house and the whole community.

"No, no, it can't happen. The negotiations must end well. Better to forget the matter. It was only a dream. I mustn't even tell anyone about it."

November 30th was rainy and cloudy. In the afternoon a soldier who had listened to the news came to our house. Russia had attacked Finland! The war had begun! Helsinki and other cities had been bombed. There had been fierce fighting at the front, and the Finns had had to retreat in some places. The enemy attack had come as a surprise, without even a declaration of war.

Everyone was depressed. We spoke only in whispers and prayed silently to the heavens above that the front lines would hold. Otherwise we would have to leave suddenly. We had been advised that we would have to be on our way within an hour after the order arrived, taking with us only what we could carry.

On December 1st, the evening was quite clear. Someone rushed in and said: "Come and see. They're shooting with cannons." We all rushed out to the corner of the house, for we knew which way the Taipale River lay. It was probably twenty to twenty-five kilometers away. We could not see the path of the shells, but there was a flash every now and then when one exploded on the ground. It may have been imagination, but we thought we heard a distant roar. This, then, was the thunder of cannon described in the tales of heroes.

Mother was from Metsäpirtti, which lay beyond the Taipale River.

That night six new visitors arrived, a woman and her family. They had had to manage on their own when the attack began. They had a pig, a cow, and two horses. Now the horses had to be housed in the threshing barn. I don't know where everyone got food from, but we went on from one day to the next. There was mutual understanding; everyone pulled together on the same unseen rope. In the evening we all discussed whether the front at the Taipale River would hold; if it gave way, we would have to leave quickly. No one mentioned the crowded quarters, although there were twenty-six people in the *tupa* and the two bedrooms.

The front had been stabilized in our area. The Finns took back the places that had been lost in the first days of the war. Stalin must have been disappointed that his army had not marched into Helsinki in two weeks, as had been planned. Soldiers were on the move almost every night, taking food and ammunition to the front and bringing wounded to the train, which took them to safer places to recover.

We lived every day under extreme tension. Dirty laundry piled up, but did we dare to wash in case we had to leave, and the clothes were wet? One morning Mother said firmly: "We're going to start washing now, no matter what. We have no clean clothes for sauna night. We can even heat the sauna to dry the clothes."

With all the women pitching in, the clothes were soon clean. Anu and I went to a hole chopped in the ice to rinse them. We even fetched the laundry water from the hole with a horse, for although our well water was clear, it would not get the clothes clean. We were forbidden to go out into any open spot during the day because bombing planes might surprise us there, but Anu and I didn't believe it could happen. The first trip went well. We stopped to warm our hands and set out with another load on the sled. Most of the clothes were already clean when we heard a suspicious droning in the east. Anu looked around. "Won't those darned hornets let us finish these clothes? Quick, get everything on the sled and go," she said.

The horse was lively, and trotted as fast as it could, but there was no chance of reaching the house in time. Anu turned the animal to shelter under the eaves of a hay barn on the shore. The planes were already overhead. Soon there was an earth-shaking roar, or rather three in succession. There were three planes, and each one dropped a bomb. The horse was frightened, and we both held onto the bit at the corner of its mouth. The planes went their way. There was a small brick factory nearby, the horse-drawn boom of it now pointing up at the sky. The bombers must have thought it was an artillery piece. But they didn't even hit that. The bombs fell into a field and did not even damage the road. They left a huge hole some six meters in diameter.

Under the cover of darkness, we made one more trip to the hole in the ice, and the clothes got washed in spite of our exciting adventure. A couple of days later five bombers came over, headed for the railroad station. They probably had it in mind to bomb the railroad, which was the lifeline of the army. Now the Finnish anti-aircraft guns began to fire. The planes turned back, but one of them was hit and dropped flaming into the lake. Although the ice was quite thick, the plane soon sank, men and all. No one was willing to go to their aid.

Christmas was near, but what kind of Christmas would it be? The war was bitter, and sorrowful tidings had already come to some homes. But our unanimity was strong, for we were fighting against our age-old enemy. Everyone did his best to preserve the independence we had gained so dearly.

The Christmas tree did not fit into the house, so we stood it up beside the steps. Its decorations were a small star at the top and snowflakes on its boughs. Candles glowed on the table inside—the windows had to be covered to prevent light from shining through because of the danger from bombs. We called the blackout curtains "Molotov curtains."

On Christmas Eve, the sauna was kept warm until morning, for everyone had to have the Christmas sauna. The soldiers went first because they might be called on to drive during the night.

Mother had begun to worry about everything under the sun.

"What will happen to us? Will the sauna *vastat* (bound birch twigs used to slap the skin in the sauna to stimulate circulation) last until spring? The woodshed is being emptied too quickly. What will we do if we run out of wood in the middle of the winter?"

"My dear, don't fret about it. If that happens, we have a house full of men here. We'll go into the woods and find dried pine trees. They make good firewood," Father consoled her.

In the evening when the day's rush was over—luckily none of the soldiers was called out to drive—father brought the family Bible to the table and asked a man named Ovaska, who had a clear, manly voice, to read the story of the birth of Jesus. After that we sang the lovely hymn, "Thus Spoke the Angel from Heaven." The war was forgotten, and that night at least everyone lay down on the straw contented.

Early on Christmas morning, the horses were hitched to the sleighs. The Christmas service began at six. The soldiers offered us a ride, and Father did not have to take his horse. A young blond soldier named Unto asked me to ride with him. I was so shy that I darted into Toivo's sled along with Samppa. I felt safer in the company of my brother. So Unto drove to church alone and in a sour frame of mind. Mother asked me about it later. "Why didn't you ride with Unto, girl? He looked so sad and alone there in the church. He's so quiet and shy that he doesn't talk much to the others."

Toivo, another of the soldiers, was one of those "bachelors" that we all liked. He spent all his free time taking care of his horse, brushing it down and feeding it well and probably telling it all his heart's sorrows.

The church was packed, mostly with soldiers. The Christmas hymns resounded mightily in the small building. On the way home, it was customary to race one another. A few of the horses had harness bells, but many people had fastened cowbells to the shafts. Someone even overturned a sleigh in the race, but everyone had fun and the clanking of the bells was very loud.

Someone had already started to make coffee at home. Plenty of *pulla* (a Finnish coffee bread) and cookies had been baked, for mother wanted to serve coffee to every one living under our roof. She started things off with these words: "I wish all of you a merry Christmas and a better New Year than this one. We've lived under the same roof now for two months, and it's all gone so well. I feel good about that. We're just like one family. Let us trust that this war will end well for all of us and that you soldiers will get back to your own homes. You are all longing to be there, especially Haltunen, whose little boy was born a few weeks ago. We don't have enough cups, but Elsie here will wash them as they are needed."

It felt as if unseen ties were binding us together as one family. Everyone came to clasp our hands and wish us a good Christmas. Even Unto seemed to have forgotten his sour mood of the morning and came to chat with me.

On the day after Christmas, we went for a joy ride, as the old custom was. Every visitor was offered a drink on that day. Little Antti was, of course, the first one. He had never grown much, was slight of stature, and in poor health. He was also glib-tongued and dropped in at least once a day to tell us the latest rumors. Father had a bottle in safekeeping, even though liquor was hard to come by. The state had provided the soldiers with a "Stephen's drink," which loosened the tongues of a few.

On the evening of St. Stephen's Day, I too went visiting at the other end of the community, at the home of my good school friend, Katri. Katri had had to leave with her younger brother and her grandmother. Her widowed mother, Hilda, had stayed at home with the cows, as we had. I learned that the others were in South Ostrobothnia, in Alavus. They were very homesick and were waiting to get back home. I got their address and decided to write to Katri.

After a pleasant chat, I started skiing home. In spite of all the prohibitions, I decided to take a short cut across an open field. Just when I was in the middle of it, I heard that unpleasant droning from the south and started skiing as fast as I could toward the nearest shelter, a threshing barn and straw shed without a door or threshold. I skied straight in and toppled face first into a pile of straw. At that instant, I heard the rat-a-tat of machine-gun bullets on the snow and even on the roof overhead. "Don't the devils have anything else to shoot at but a single skier?" I babbled to myself, brushing the dirt and straw off my clothes. The knees of my stockings were full of barley bristles, which would come off only by plucking them out one by one. I sat on a block of wood and cleaned up my stockings. There was plenty of time to do it, for I did not dare leave the barn until dark. At home the men talked about how someone had seen the burst of machine-gun fire and thought how stupid it was to shoot at an open field. I did not dare say that I had been the target.

I was a diligent and fast worker and whenever home chores permitted, I went to the doctor's house to help the Marthas (a women's organization) and the Lottas (the women's auxiliary organization for the army) to wash and patch the soldiers' clothing. Soldiers often asked to accompany me on my way home. *That's a nice-looking young soldier*, I would sometimes think. *But no, I still don't dare make friends with him. I don't even know how to talk to strangers.*

It was approaching evening on the 28th of December. It had snowed a little during the day and the temperature was twenty degrees. About seven in the evening, a breathless messenger arrived at the house. "You have to leave now and be on your way as soon as possible. You can take your livestock with you. They are to be driven to the railroad station." That was seven kilometers away.

There was a half-meter of snow, and the roads were plowed. Father and Samppa put bundles of clothing and food on the sleigh. The women began to free the cows, but the animals resisted going out into the cold and snow. Soldiers came to our aid, escorting us to the main road, and things began to go better. "That Ilona will get inflammation of the udders in this cold snow. She just calved last week," Mother lamented.

Neighbors were already on the move along the road, and in a herd the cows traveled better. When an army column of horses came toward us, there was a mix-up again. But that too was straightened out, and the cows again traveled in peace.

Toward morning, the train was fully loaded. They ran short of cars, and the men and horses had to go back home. Two cattle cars had been reserved for the people. There was a little straw on the floor, and we were packed in like sardines. Puffing heavily, the train lurched into motion. Slowly its speed increased; we had to get out of this danger zone under cover of the night. No one could know when bombers might surprise us.

No one complained much, although soft sobbing could be heard here and there. It was already late in the morning when Erkki, a boy to whom I was related, got the door pried open. The train had stopped. It was a typical gray December day outside. At that moment two pretty girls skied into view, wearing the most beautiful ski suits I had ever seen.

The train stopped in Savonlinna. It was time to care for the livestock, even to milk them. Some Marthas and Lottas appeared from somewhere with large baskets and gave us sandwiches, along with some kind of warm drink, which tasted heavenly. There was no heat in the cattle cars, and it was bitter cold outside.

Sisu Mother

The train started off again, and we rode slowly westward. Then it slowed down again and stopped. "Why the devil is it stopping now," someone said. "There's no station here."

There was a knock at the door and someone shouted loudly: "Enemy bombers coming! Quick, everyone out and into the woods. You'll be safe there if a bomb hits the train."

"There'll be nothing left for me to do if my Kaunikki (a cow's name) is lost," whimpered Varpu, our neighbor. Nevertheless, we all began to wade one after another away from the train through the half-meter-deep snow. The temperature was 15°. Mrs. Pennanen was ill and remained in the car with her daughter Mari. We stood gloomily under the trees. The frost was beginning to nip at our noses and toes; many were wearing only rubber-bottomed boots. We could not hear the planes. Slyly we began to creep back to the train, leaving behind many sorts of brown and yellow patches in the snow. It was a relief for many of us.

Mrs. Pennanen and her daughter were completely buried by robes. The car felt cold, and our clothes had been frosted over from being outside so long. To top it all, the train was already full, and there were still many people outside. "Make room for us. There's no place for anyone to lie down here. We can't leave people behind," said Mari Tahvo worriedly. Everyone tried to squeeze in more tightly, and we were all able to get aboard. It was so cold. Someone began to sing, and everyone joined in, even though our voices shook. "Is there a lovelier land in all of Finland / than our beautiful Karelia / the spacious land of song?"

The words brought a pang to our hearts. Were we losing our land forever? We sang a number of other familiar songs, and it warmed us. Color returned to our cheeks, and the words of the songs made us think of something besides our present plight. The train started off, but then it stopped again. Evacuation trains always had to give way to army transport trains.

Sitting in those dark and crowded quarters, my foot became numb. I groped around and felt the wall quite close to me. Supporting myself against it, I rose slowly and managed to stand up. I lifted up the numb foot, but when I tried to set it down again, the space had closed up. It was a long time before I was able to thrust my foot down to the solid floor again. Sitting down was out of the question, but I did have the wall to lean against.

The next time we stopped it was somewhere in Central Finland. We were again given good food and something warm to drink. Where could we have gotten food otherwise—the cows gave milk, but we couldn't live on milk alone, and besides, we milked the cows only once a day. One good meal and a cup of coffee a day, and everyone was satisfied. There were so many other things to think about that no one got hungry.

During the Christmas season, the nights are long and dark, which was fortunate under the circumstances. All army shipping had to be done under cover of darkness. The cloudy and rainy weather was also an advantage—there was no need to fear the bombers when visibility was lacking.

On New Year's Eve, the train stopped at the Keuruu Station. *Keuruu, Keuruu—it sounds familiar*, I thought. Yes, I once had to point out the road to Keuruu on the map in school. This was really exciting—what all else would I come to see on this famous sad journey?

Haapamäki had been bombed, and we had to stay there a long time before we could go on. We had no inkling of our final destination. After people cared for the cows, we were ordered into the station. It was really cold—someone said the temperature was sixteen degrees below zero.

The station building was large and high, really impressive looking. The people of Keuruu must have been very wealthy to have such a fine station. We were given a good, warm stew, as much as we could eat. If only I could stretch out on a real bed, I wouldn't need a lullaby to put me to sleep.

Many people lay down on the hard floor and fell asleep. At least one could straighten out his legs there, for a change. Some sat on a bench, nodding contentedly. Little Antti paced the floor, restlessly puffing on his roll-your-own butt, saying: "We won't get to melt the New Year's tin this time."

It was the custom to drip melted tin into cold water on New Year's Eve, which formed shapes as it cooled. The shapes were supposed to predict what the future would bring.

"Most likely we won't, just when we really want to know what lies before us. I would never have believed that we would be in a place called Keuruu for the New Year. God knows what corner of the world we're in," wailed Varpu.

The people were very friendly, but their speech was hard to understand. Naturally—it was the local dialect. Since we had always lived in Karelia and had never heard another dialect, it sounded strange to us. We had always used "*mie*" and "*sie*." (The "book" language is "*minä*" for "I" and "*sinä*" for "you." Other dialects have other variations.)

On New Year's day, we arrived at the Lapua station. This too was a historical place, for it was the site of the Lapua movement, a far-right political movement that at one point attempted to oust the elected government of

Finland. We heard that our train would be unloaded here. The people would be taken by bus to Alajärvi Parish, and the cows would follow on *Itikka* ("Insect" in book language) trucks.

"My God, insects here must be huge when they have trucks for them. What will we hear of next?" exclaimed Mari Tahvo. "We just kill insects without any trucks at all. No one can stand to have them buzzing around his ears. If the darned things get to bite you, the spot turns red and itches like crazy for days."

This "insect" matter was cleared up in time. It was another of the language difficulties. In South Ostrobothnia, cattle were called *itikat*. In Lapua, there was a slaughterhouse and sausage factory named Itikka. They had big trucks, which were used to transport cattle to the slaughterhouse.

From there we were taken to the Puumala School in the community of Kurejoki. Hot food awaited us, and a warm classroom to sleep in. There was straw to cushion the floor, and we lay right down on the *siskonpeti*. (In those days, in small farmhouses, for example, a common bed was made up on the floor for the children. It was called the "sisters' bed" "*siskonpeti*," or the "brothers' bed.") We had been traveling for four days, and now we didn't even have to take care of the cattle. The "insects" were taking care of everything. "Insects"—ha, ha, ha.

We awoke in the morning to a clear frosty day, with cooked oatmeal waiting for us. We needed no Uncle Markus (a radio personality who broadcast a popular children's program) to tell us that wisdom begins with oatmeal. With cold milk it tasted like food fit for a king.

Evacuees were parceled out into various houses. If there was a single room empty in a house, a family was sent to live in it. The people in the house were notified, and someone came to fetch us with a horse. A man named Aarne was organizing all this. He was fairly young, but there must have been something wrong with him because he was not in the war. Men were needed on the home front, too. On the second day, he took us to his home. I got the feeling that he was fascinated by Anu, although nothing ever came of it. Anu was seventeen, and a very pretty girl. Mother, Anu, and I got a very small room to live in, with one narrow bed. Mother slept in it, and Anu and I slept on the floor. There was a tile stove and one chair in the room; no more would fit into it. We were told that we could use the family kitchen for cooking.

Sisu Mother

The first night we had supper in the house. The *tupa* was large, dismal, and bleak. I had never seen such a huge, long table, which had benches around it. There were ten people in the family, and there were also two hired hands, plus the three of us. There must have been a big pot to cook the potatoes for all of us. For a while no one said anything. Then the master of the house asked in a friendly tone of voice, "How long have you been traveling?"

"It's six days ago tonight that we left at night, driving the cows before us," Mother said gravely.

"What a miserable thing for you, to have to leave home in such a cold winter. Are the houses there empty now?" asked the master.

"No, not at all. The houses are full of soldiers, and my husband and one son are still at home. There weren't enough railroad cars when we left," Mother tried to explain. It is doubtful that they understood her clipped, rapid-fire Karelian dialect. We had some trouble understanding them too, but it was easier for us because Ostrobothnians speak so slowly.

The stew was good, but the bread was hard, and Mother, who had poor teeth, could not bite off a single piece. Even the rest of us managed no more than a tiny bit at a time. It was the custom here to bake for six months at a time. The bread had holes in it, through which a pole was run, and then it was suspended from the rafters of the tupa for several weeks. After that, the bread was stored in a grain bin in the storehouse, where it stayed dry and did not mold. To mother it all seemed very strange. At home we baked *limppu* (round loaves) every week and *piirakka* on Saturday. Mother began to buy hardtack, since there was no chance for us to bake.

We were thankful that there was a real stove in our house. We heard that in some there was only an open hearth. There a blackened pot hung on the end of an iron rod, with a tripod on the side. Logs a meter long were usually burned in the fireplace.

Mother almost always prepared the food on the upright stove, which we fired up every day. "It was good that we got this little room," she would say happily. "If we had wound up in a corner of that large *tupa*, we would have frozen like cockroaches. This is such a cold winter. How do people stay warm in these drafty buildings?"

We got to know the people of the house. Their language seemed stiff and awkward. The word "*Joo*" seemed to serve for everything. When we said "Good morning" we would get "*Joo*" for an answer. "Why are these people so close-mouthed?" Mother said. "They can't carry on a conversation at all."

Anu began to explain to her what she had learned in school about the different tribes of Finns, that the Ostrobothnians, for example, were stiff and spoke little, that we Karelians liked to sing and talk. We tried our best to fit in with this way of life, but everything was so strange that we longed for the war to end so that we could go home again. This period was to remain in my mind like a nightmare.

Matti, the owner of the house, was blind, but that did not prevent his working. He went into the woods and felled trees with his sons. I often watched, holding my breath, as he held a block of wood with one hand and chopped with the other. What if it should slip? It was an empty fear on my part, for he did as well as those who could see.

The sauna was a *savusauna* (smoke sauna—a sauna without a chimney). While it was being heated, the smoke escaped through the door and a vent in the bathing room. In order to bathe in such a sauna, the fire had to be completely out. The only heat came from the huge heap of rocks over the fire bed. It took the better part of a day to prepare the sauna for bathing. It was an entirely new experience for us. The sauna was warmed only every other week in the winter. The building was far from others, probably because of the danger of fire. Everyone took hot water with him to the sauna, but cold water was carried in earlier to fill a huge half-barrel. The sauna was very high. We sat on the bench there as usual, but Good Lord, the soot was so thick there, and of course it stuck to our behinds. No matter how hard we scrubbed and washed with soap, it would not come off, and our water was running out. Luckily Miina, the daughter of the house, was on her way to the sauna, and brought us more hot water. It helped a little, but as we put on our clothes, Mother said:

"I feel as if I were cleaner when we came in. What a thing to call a sauna!"

"I've never put my shoes on when coming from the sauna, and I won't do it now," I said defiantly.

"I haven't either, but it's so cold," said Anu.

"What will it be like? It's at least three hundred meters to the house," said Mother.

So the three of us ran barefoot like the Jukola brothers (characters in Aleksis Kivi's classic Finnish novel, *Seven Brothers*) along the snowy path to the *tupa*. Darn, but it was cold. The next time we put on our shoes without grumbling.

Heikki and Martti, the hired hands, were from the neighboring house, and always went home for the night. Soon we made the acquaintance of other young people, and we were often out in the evening poking around in the dark. More of the neighbors' kids came over, and we played hide-and-seek or other games. Kalle, Martti's brother, was a regular evening visitor, indoors or out. Kalle always winked at me inside the house, or tried to pinch me if he had the chance. I became aware that Heikki and Kalle liked me. One evening, Kalle came suddenly around a corner and seized me in his arms. I broke away from him quickly so that no one would see us. On the other hand, a feeling of warmth surged through my heart, although I did not dare admit it, even to myself.

I came to know Kalle better when I went to get the mail, which he brought to Menkjärvi every other day. While we were waiting for the mail truck, Kalle, who was bolder, came to talk to me. We even walked home together. He asked me to go for walks in the evening. I wanted very much to go, but I didn't dare ask my mother. I thought I might slip off without anyone noticing, but I never did try. Somehow I was afraid, although I liked Kalle. "No, I won't go."—who knows, he might even try to kiss me. Kalle is a couple of years older than I am. I don't want anything like that.

Father and Samppa were still at home. The front had settled down in their sector, Father wrote. Anu waited for letters every day. Her boyfriend had stayed at home, and the separation made them love each other more and more. When she got a letter, she hid it cleverly, so that no one could learn her secrets.

There were rumors of peace negotiations, a story that Uncle Paasikivi (later president) had gone to work out a settlement. On the morning of March 13, it was announced that peace had come. At twelve o'clock, President Kyösti Kallio spoke on the radio. We all gathered anxiously around the big table in the *tupa* to listen to the president's speech. Sad to say, this was truly a day of misfortune. Karelia had been lost, along with almost the whole province of Viipuri. Hanko was gone, together with all the islands in the Bay of Finland, as well as Petsamo and other areas in northern Finland. "Let us be content that still the greater part of Finland remains free and independent. Now we must all try to live in harmony, all the tribes of Finland, and make do with what we have," said President Kallio.

SISU MOTHER

"Why was such a barbaric neighbor created for the Finns, to torment us from one generation to the next? Why was the blood of so many strong young men shed in vain? Will we have to live in the corners of strangers' houses forever? What evil have we done, since You, the God of goodness, will not help us? If You are in Heaven, why did You let this happen?" an anguished voice within me cried.

When you have lost all hope, pray more whole-heartedly.

CHAPTER II

Liisa, our former neighbor, came to visit us the next day. The talk did not flow, for Liisa, so lively and quick before, was now crushed with grief.

"What shall we do now? Do we have to start living in the corners of other people's houses?" she moaned in a voice broken with sobs.

"I don't know, I don't know, we've lost everything. All we've got is a small bundle of clothes and a few cows," said mother, her throat dry.

Father and Samppa came after a few days had passed. They had been allowed to stay that long. Now our room was too small for us even to sleep on the floor. Samppa slept on a bench in the *tupa*. Father found a somewhat bigger room, and we moved.

Anu had already found work on a large farm and was living there. I had nothing to do except for a little handwork. I was thirteen and a half years old, and a widow came to ask for me to help her during the summer. Delighted, I was ready to go, but mother was not entirely willing.

"You don't need to work, you're still so young. There'll be time enough for you to work." But I had already packed my bundle, and soon I left with the lady. "If you're not happy, you know that you will always have a home here, although it's so small right now."

I was accepted into this large farmhouse as if I were a member of the family. I shared a room with the daughter Lilja, which was bigger than her parent's room. The farm had ten milking cows, so every morning I had to milk four or five. My hands really ached at first, but I did not complain.

The oldest boy, Olli, was close to thirty. In my mind, I already thought of him as a bachelor. The lady of the house, Miina, was happy and playful. Once I came in from outside and saw smoke coming from in back of the curtains over the lower bed. I thought of picking up the water bucket and throwing it, but anyway I peeked in first, and found myself staring, frightened, at Miina. She was puffing on a stub of a pipe, and she whispered into my ear, "Don't tell anyone. My children know nothing about this. Sometimes I get so mad at this life and loneliness, and the pipe just seems to help. I can't do it in front of my children, since I have so many boys. It would set a bad example."

"I won't tell them. You can depend on me," I said, and I meant it.

The incident gave me a lot to think about. Did a person of that age, over fifty, still get lonely? Miina had been a widow for five years. She had eight children, three of whom were already away from home, and the youngest was eight. She wasn't by herself; there were six young people around her. There certainly was a lot in this world that I didn't understand. For example, that a woman smoked, and was lonely in the midst of a large family.

I had also become acquainted with a neighbor, and went to visit her along a trail that followed the river. Irja was a couple of years older than I was, and we had fun together. Lilja had gone to a dance, and I asked Miina if I could go to Peltolas', since it was such a bright, long evening.

Irja was home alone, and shouted happily when she saw me: "How nice that you came! Listen, let's go to Tohkula, they have an outdoor dance platform there. We can go straight along the river. I know the path well."

We started off nearly running, but the distance seemed awfully long. On the other side of the river, we skirted fields for ages. It was intermission time when we arrived. Irja began to chat with some friends. Then an accordion began to play. I drew back so that no one would come to ask me to dance, for I didn't know how. Irja was sought out, and she went gladly, although she didn't dance too well. She was out on the floor when, *Good Lord, someone had come up to bow before me! What shall I do?* I thought, petrified. I shook my head and refused to go, since I didn't know how to dance. When the dance was over, Irja grabbed me angrily by the hand and said furiously, "We're going home right now!"

"Why? We just came."

We ran back full tilt along the same trail we had come. Only when we had passed over the walkway to the other side of the river did we slow down and draw a breath.

"Why didn't you go and dance, stupid?"

"Well, I didn't know how. I didn't dare."

"Those boys might do just about anything bad to get even with us. You should have gone anyway. You would have learned."

It was late when I got home. The lady of the house guessed that we had skipped off to the dance. When we were alone, she asked, "Someone must have asked you to dance. You're a good-looking girl."

"Yes," I answered sourly. I did not whisper a word of how badly things had gone. I was sure I would never go with Irja again, no matter how nicely she asked. I was not ready yet for such nonsense.

The Bothnia dialect was beginning to sound familiar, although we stumbled sometimes. One baking day, the lady of the house asked me to get a flour *hulikko* from the storehouse. I ran off to get it. Looking around the storehouse, I wondered what it might be that was needed in baking, and picked up a big mixing stick made from a pine branch. Well, at least that was needed in making the dough. The lady of the house laughed fit to burst. Shamefaced, I tried to explain that I didn't know what a *hulikko* was. It turned out to be a wooden box for flour.

My wages were a hundred Finnish marks a month. With my first pay, I bought material, a soft, dark-green silk, and had a dress made. When I posed like a mannequin on the *tupa* floor, everyone seemed to like it. Even the bachelor came and took me by the shoulders and said, "You do have a fine taste in clothing, Elsie. Will you dance with me?"

The radio happened to be playing a waltz. Laughing, I tried to dance with him. When the dance was over, he bowed elegantly, "We have to dance more often. You have to learn to waltz so you won't need to be ashamed when you go to dances."

Autumn came too quickly; they needed help on the farm only during the summer. It was hard to part from my new family, where five months had flown by. There had been stumbling blocks, though. Perhaps the most difficult was learning to peel potatoes with a spoon, when they were small and hot and one had to hold them in her hand. There were no knives and forks in the house, except for visitors. We got butter only on Sunday morning and had to spread it onto the hard bread with our thumbs.

The bachelor escorted me when I left. My scant belongings were in a bundle on the bicycle handlebars. I felt as if he did not want me to leave, but it couldn't be helped. A hundred markkas was a lot of money then, even for a farmer. He squeezed my hand and said, "Come and visit anytime as if this were your home. We'll miss you. If you're free next summer, you will come back, won't you?"

"Of course, I will. Thanks for everything." There were tears in my eyes.

I began attending vocational school evenings, since I had not gone in Karelia. It was two evenings a week. My acquaintances from the first house, Heikki and Kalle, waited for me faithfully evenings and escorted me home, although the distance was two kilometers. Anyone seeing us would surely have had difficulty suppressing a laugh. I walked in the middle with a boy on either arm, as one of them pushed my bicycle. There wasn't much romance in it, for the boys were silent Bothnians. And what did we know about romance—we weren't fifteen yet. These were our first steps toward the other sex.

After a few weeks, a man from Lappajärvi came to ask if I would come and take care of his children. They had heard from relatives that a young and lively girl was free here. Mother objected again. "I'd like to keep you home for a while. You're still so young. But do as you like."

So I left with the man for new surroundings some twenty kilometers away. It was a small farm, only a few cows and five children, the oldest ten and the youngest eight months. I did not have my own room but slept in the *tupa* with the older children. It was a slight disappointment; I could not be by myself night or day. Nevertheless, the days passed quickly amid this hubbub.

Soon young people from the village began to stop in to see the new girl. It was such an out-of-the-way place that there were not even any refugees here.

Nearby was the Kuusela shanty, a place worthy of that name. Sixteen children had been born in it, half of them already out in the world. Mirja and Mimmi, two of the girls, became close friends of mine. We were all in the fourteen to seventeen-year range. During the long winter evenings we would get together somewhere out on the road, and would do ring dances and other kinds of dances. I was already so bold that I dared walk hand-in-hand with a boy named Tauno. He was interested in my home area, Karelia. I really liked him. At first he was shy, but once we got started, we had a lot to talk about.

I was home alone the entire weekend, with only the older children for company. One Sunday morning I had cooked barley porridge in the Bothnian style when a gypsy came in. "You really have a nice looking porridge there, and such a big pot. You look so sweet, let me taste a little of it. I'm so hungry."

I felt sorry for the wanderer and gave him some porridge. Now any number of his companions burst into the tupa, and all of them were hungry. I had cooked a lot of food since the rest of the family would come home in the evening. What should I do? I was afraid.

At that moment, some boys from the village entered the room. Kalle, Tauno's brother, was already grown up, and he said with a wink at me, "Hey, Elsie, I just stopped to tell you that the old lady's body will be here any minute." One after another, the gypsies slipped out. The whole crew climbed onto their sled, and the driver whipped up the horse. Away, at once, for bodies were coming—gypsies are superstitious and fear the dead. I thanked the boy who had saved me from a dilemma.

In the spring, a letter from Mother came, saying that they were being moved to Satakunta, where we would be given land to replace the farm we had lost in Karelia. She asked if I would come with them or stay and be a Bothnian. Of course I wanted to go. I didn't want to be left here alone, so far away, and besides, it would be interesting to see Satakunta now that I had the chance.

I spent a week or so at home getting ready to leave. My first friend, Kalle, came to see me one night. We walked outside, and he asked me to write, squeezed my hand warmly and said, "Don't forget me."

Olli, my employer from the previous summer, came to say goodbye too. "Write to us, Elsie, wherever you are," he said. "You're always welcome to us, as if to your home. I feel as if you're one of the family, and will always be. Carry your head high, you deserve to."

We moved to the parish of Kiikka, which is in the province of Turku and Pori. The Satakunta dialect was Greek to me. People spoke so rapidly that I had trouble distinguishing the words, and they ended almost everything they said with ". . . yes, always." I soon began to catch on, but mother and the people who worked on the place most likely did not understand each other. They were older people, and both spoke rapidly but in different dialects. Luckily we were able to rent a small red cottage in the woods. It had two rooms, and we made it really homey. Samppa and I fixed up a place to sleep in an outbuilding—after all it was summer and the weather was warm.

The Germans began to transport men and war materiel into Finland. The extra reserve was called up. My brother Viljo had served his hitch in the army, but after only a few weeks in civilian life, he was called up again. Father, too, was called up, although he was well over forty. And toward autumn, when Samppa turned eighteen, he too had to go.

In June of 1941, the war began again. The Finns advanced rapidly, with the aid of the Germans. The battle cry was: "A Greater Finland; Free White Sea Karelia!"

A few days after the war began, Mother's youngest sister arrived from Lappeenranta. Her husband had gotten a few days' leave. They had week-old twins and a two-and-a-half-year-old boy. The house was a beehive of activity. Luckily I had a bicycle, so I could get to the store and run errands to the church village, which was eight kilometers away. There were cards and ration coupons for all foods. We had to get ration cards for the newborn twins. The branch in charge of such matters was called People's Welfare. First we had to have a baptismal certificate; only then could we get a ration card. I had to go and look for the parsonage.

"I do have the time. I'll be happy to come. Seldom are there two at a time. How is Thursday at two?"

Mother began hastily to bake coffee bread, for there had to be a christening coffee to offer the pastor.

The pastor arrived on a bicycle, which amused us. At home the pastor had been driven elegantly with a team of horses, and later in an automobile. This pastor admired the lovely place and enjoyed riding the bicycle. He kept his car in the garage, since there was no gasoline.

My mother held the boy, who was named Aarne Akseli, and I held the girl, who was named Anja Anneli. My aunt tried to keep her lively son Antero quiet. At the kitchen table, the pastor was treated to real coffee, which my aunt had received in a package from America. One could not buy coffee in Finland, but we drank a substitute, for which rye, wheat, barley, and oat grains were roasted, and sometimes even peas.

There was no running water in the cabin, as was true of many farmhouses. Oh, what a time we had washing clothes, but luckily it was summer. I started to get delightful love letters from Kalle. Of course I read them secretly, my cheeks burning. It was certainly beautiful to be loved, I thought, but what was the result? Laundry to do, and a baby crying day and night. It was a good thing that Kalle was so far away. I would never get married, no matter how beautiful it might be.

The children slept badly, and my aunt was very tired. The children must have been ill, for their bowels were always loose. A doctor came to our home too, whistling as he rode his bicycle. "You do live in beautiful natural surroundings. No one can be sick in a place like this." But the children were. They had to be taken to the hospital at Tyrvää. There was nothing to do but drive them on a jolting wagon the fifteen kilometers to the hospital.

Now my aunt could rest and sleep. The stress had been too much for her. The children's father also got a short leave to come and see them. In a couple of weeks the neighbors received a call saying that Aarne was getting weaker. In the morning, my aunt went to call and ask about his condition. She returned in tears. Aarne had died, and Anja was getting weaker too.

Auntie and I set out immediately on bicycles for Tyrvää and arrived sweating at the hospital. Sad news awaited us there: Anja had passed away ten minutes before. My aunt began to weep uncontrollably and to stagger. I managed to catch hold of her and drag her to the nearest seat. Soon a nurse came to our aid, and we took her to an empty bed, where she lay and whimpered. "I can't go on living," she wailed. "I can't go on living. Let me die." The doctor gave her something to calm her and said: "She has to rest for at least two or three hours before she can even think of riding a bicycle. You go somewhere and rest for that time too."

I went out unwillingly, not even able to think. But I found a park bench, where I sat senseless. Not having a watch, I didn't know what time it was, but I started walking and asked people coming toward me where there was a funeral parlor. "Well, a couple of blocks away. Turn right there," an elderly lady said to me.

At the funeral home, they took me seriously when I told them the story in detail. They had no coffin small enough but would have them in a couple of days. It was arranged that they would be sent directly to the hospital.

When I returned to the hospital, my aunt was just waking up, and she did not remember where she was or what had happened. We walked in the corridor and she began to return to reality. "Now I'm beginning to understand why they were taken away. This world is too evil for them, for innocent children. Imagine, when they were two days old, they had to be afraid of enemy bombings. They have so much in common; they were born on the same day and they died on the same day."

A small group was gathered around the grave. The child's father had been able to come for the burial of the little ones. As he lowered the flowers into the grave, he burst into tears and blubbered, "They were too weak for this wicked world."

I was taking care of little Antero, who now became frightened. "Oh, Father will die now too, he's crying so hard."

"Father isn't sick. He's crying because he's so sad that Anja and Aarne passed away."

Their father had seen them only three times. It was hard to explain the situation to the lively boy.

The Finns took back the areas that had been lost and crossed the border into White Sea Karelia, where Finnish-speaking people lived. A letter came from Father, which read: "Yesterday we went through our home village. All the houses are still standing, except for Ihalainens', which was a burned-out ruin. We think it was used as an office, and since they had to take important papers out, they set it on fire. I think you can go back home soon. Bring a lot of cleaning material with you. I've heard that the houses are filthy."

We waited, excited, for the time we would get back home again. Mother was already beginning to fret when the permission did not come. "They could have let us go before it gets cold and the ground freezes, so that we could have gotten something from the ground. Winter is coming, and there's no food there. Father wrote that no grain or root vegetables have been planted."

We had planned to go together with the Hinkkanen family. They had a cow, and we had a horse. Mother went with the family in a regular coach and I in a cattle car with the man of the house. Hinkkanen's daughter was stationed near their home as a *lotta* and had cleaned up their house, so we thought we would go there first.

We were on a long train. It was an evacuation train again, but everyone was happy, for we were going home. The train itself seemed to be singing: home, home, to Karelia. We were no longer refugees, we were ourselves again.

The train was able to go only as far as Kaarlahti, which was one station beyond Käkisalmi toward Hiitola. The autumn evening was already growing dark when we got our group unloaded. Jussi Äitiä, who had gotten a leave, was there to meet us and acted as our group leader. We passed several empty houses, but at the edge of a woods we saw a light twinkling from a window.

In the house was a young woman who had just arrived with her in-laws a week or so ago. "Just come on in. As many as can fit on the floor can spend the night with us. It feels kind of safer with you here, when there are no neighbors close by." The woman made substitute coffee to warm us up after an evening snack. It really felt good to sleep on the "family bed," and we were refreshed when it came time to leave in the morning. We gave the woman milk to pay for our night's lodging.

The trip home was some forty to fifty kilometers. Jussi knew a shorter and quieter road through Rantakylä and a shortcut through the woods to Kelja. Even the cows seemed to sense something, for they marched along like soldiers without causing any great problems. It was already getting dark when we reached Kelja, where most of us stopped. Hinkkanen and I went on ahead a couple of kilometers to Lahnavalkama. My heart leaped up when I saw my white-painted childhood home still standing at the edge of the woods. The mountain ash was still there next to the wall, apparently filled with red berries. I said to Hinkkanen: "I'm going to cut across the field here to the yard of my home. I won't be long. I'll catch up to you on the road."

It was so dark already that I could not see the lake. I tied the cow to the fence and peeked inside. A nauseating stench wafted toward me, but I could really make out nothing inside. I did not go in, but I left the door open. It would be better to come during the day when we could see everything by daylight. It was warm and homelike at the Hinkkanens'. I got to sleep on a soft bed, and forgot all my cares. After all, we were home in Karelia.

We were not even allowed to go and live in our houses until a work crew had cleaned them. There was fear of bacteria and contagious diseases. We waited a few days; Mother grew nervous and complained: "Let's go and clean up there. God knows when they'll get to it. We could clean it just as well as anyone."

Now we were home again, even with some furniture. We had a table to eat from and a few chairs. Now we began to search for vegetables so that we could have something in the cellar for the winter. There had already been frost, but we found some potatoes, carrots, and on Varpu's land, at least a hectare of cabbage. Everyone's land had been joined into a *kolkhoz*, and now we too had everything in common.

Everything had to be heated by wood. There was no electricity in the entire area and the woodshed was empty. There were a few pieces of wood around the barn and the sauna. From a building alongside the threshing barn I got a few floorboards, and I sawed up a milepost set near our house. It had no significance, since the road had been straightened before the war. When the first snow fell, I went into the woods with the horse and found some dried pine trees to get us started. At the same time I checked the hay barn in Husus meadow, and it was full of hay. Now, if we could just get the cows home from Bothnia, all would be well. We got milk from the Hinkkanens sometimes. I went to their house with the horse to help them out with the firewood.

I was fifteen years old, and the only young person in the place. I was everyone's helper. Sometimes with the horse, sometimes on skis, I got the mail and went to the store, since they were so far away. Most of the inhabitants were old, and everyone had to help each other. All the young men were away at war.

Mother often sat at the window in the evening and looked out toward Husus meadow, where Kuoppas' empty house could also be seen. "Come and take a look with your younger eyes, girl. It looks as if something black is moving out there. I saw it yesterday and it disappeared into the Kuoppa house. I don't know if my eyes are playing tricks."

It was true. Something black did move out there and disappear into the shadow of the house. Early the next morning I ran to Tahvos'. Little Antti was an auxiliary air-raid watcher, as were the other men and boys. "Last week the Russians dropped some parachutists, and maybe they didn't catch all of them. I'll turn in a report as soon as I go there."

At twilight six soldiers appeared to find out what was going on. They saw with their own eyes a black bulk come from the woods. They waited about an hour, when smoke began to rise from the chimney of the empty house. They left their horse at our house, and I went to show them how to get to the house.

A man was warming himself at the stove when the soldiers went in. He put up no resistance, although he was armed. The poor man was cold and hungry. Mother gave him a piece of bread, which he immediately stuffed into his mouth.

"He's one of God's poor creatures, too," she said compassionately. "It was God's good fortune that you weren't killed when you went to cut wood close by here," she added thankfully.

Little Antti stopped often to chat and bring us news:

"The Pyhäkylä Youth Society is having an evening program and ring-dancing afterward at its clubhouse. If I had a partner I would go, but it's so lonely coming home at night, and it's about three whole kilometers."

I looked at Mother with an expression which said I'd like to go.

"The girl looks like she wants to go. It would be nice if she got to be with some young people. She's always with us old people, working like any man."

It was a fun program and a community sing. There were even a few young boys and soldiers on leave. It was so exciting when a tall blonde boy sought me out for the ring dance. He had laughing eyes and squeezed my hand warmly. I felt as if my head were spinning and my eyes shining like stars. He said he was from Alakylä, six kilometers away, and that a wagonload had come from there. He asked if I would come the next time, in two weeks. Of course I promised to come.

That entire night I dreamed of the ring dance and those laughing eyes. The eyes came to mind often during the day too, and I thought: "Is this love then, since I have no peace either day or night? And the days pass so slowly, in spite of all the work." When the evening came, Antti and I went, even though it was stormy. What a disappointment! He wasn't there, the boy with the laughing eyes. Antti said no one was there. The weather must have been too bad. Our trip home in that miserable weather lasted forever. That night sleep did not come, although I counted thousands of sheep. "Of all the things one gets into," I thought in my fifteen-year-old heart. "This is the first and last time I'll fall in love. This disappointment is too hard to bear."

To my sorrow, I did not see those laughing eyes again. Antti realized "where the shoe was pinching" and went to talk to others from the boy's village. I heard that he had had to go into the army.

After many months, he appeared again at the parties. Oh, how handsome he was in his uniform. My heart literally throbbed, and I could hardly breathe. Did he still remember me, or had he forgotten? The smiling eyes looked at me, warm and captivating.

I'm sure the program was entertaining , but I heard not a word of it. Why was it so long now? At last it was time for the ring dance—there he was coming to get me. My hands were wet and must have been shaking when we touched. We were whirling near the door and the boy said: "Let's go outside. There's so much to talk about. My name is Kaarlo. I have only a three-day leave. I may have to go to the front. I'm so glad you're here. I want to write to you if you give me your address. I don't even know where you come from."

Of course I wanted to, and I thought that now I would be like the big girls—I would get mail from the front. We were both very shy. We walked back and forth at the crossroads. A warm handclasp radiated to my very heart. Kaarlo pressed me to him gently for a few seconds, and we parted.

After a few weeks, I got a letter from him. They were on the way to the front in White Sea Karelia. I hid the letter, and sometimes read it in secret. This was my own, and I would let no one else hear about it. I answered immediately and waited again.

Weeks went by, and I waited and waited, but no letter came. Every day I ran to get the mail, which was now delivered to the village. Finally my letter came back. That did not bode well. My last hope was that his address had been changed, but why didn't he write? Perhaps he had been wounded and couldn't write.

I often went to church on Sunday, where they announced what soldiers had fallen, and I heard it there. Kaarlo had been struck by an artillery shell, and so shredded that there was nothing to put into a coffin. War is horrible!

Broken-hearted, in despair, I rode home on my bicycle. Mother soon noticed that something was wrong with her usually brisk and carefree daughter. Finally I unburdened my heart to her. She understood and tried her best to console me. "The world is hard, there is more sorrow than joy in it, Elsie. We just have to try bravely to get through the worst. Time is the best medicine. You're still young and your whole life is ahead of you. Next year you'll no longer remember him, and if you do, it will be the happy things. They make life better."

The patter of rain cleanses the soul.

CHAPTER III

In the autumn of 1942 the front lines of the war became fixed. Father got to come home for good because of his advanced age and his bad rheumatism. Anu was also at home and was planning to marry in the fall—Eka from the neighboring village. My brother Viljo was also engaged to Anna, and a double wedding was planned, of a type which could be arranged during a war when there was a shortage of everything.

There were still all kinds of vermin left by the Russians in the houses. I joined a work crew which went around exterminating them. There were three of us in the group. Katri was a good friend and a schoolmate of mine, and Saimi was from Yläjärvi, almost at the other end of the parish. Our duties were in and around Saappru and as far away as Kiskosaari. We stayed at Saimi's house, since it was the nearest.

The work was really interesting. We encountered all kinds of people and all kinds of housekeeping practices. We had to remove all metal objects from the houses, and the people had to stay elsewhere for two nights. The people were mostly old, since the young were away at war.

Soldiers were everywhere. One night I went to the store, and what a surprise—there was my former employer Olli, from Alajärvi! He had just gotten a rest leave from the front lines. We decided to ride our bicycles to my home on Saturday. I was pleased that I could show him my home; it was at least as nice as his. Olli confessed that he had often wondered if we had come back, and that he had often thought of me. I didn't know what to say—I was taken aback. To me he seemed very old, at least ten years older than I was.

After some weeks, I got to know Urho. He was from South Ostrobothnia. I would tease him by speaking in his Bothnian dialect, but he liked it. I would slip out often at night to meet him. We seemed to have a lot in common, and he made me forget Kaarlo completely. One night as we parted, he snatched me into his arms and kissed me gently. "I couldn't resist it," he whispered into my ear. My heart beat violently and a hot flush spread over my face. Luckily it was dark, so he could not see how I felt. My first kiss as a sixteen-year-old. Oh my!

Those little kisses gradually became longer and hotter. It was a wonderful time, in spite of the war. But still every time when I drew back from his arms, a little voice inside me said, *Don't play with fire, little girl. It's wartime, and you can only be hurt. Remember how you suffered when you lost Kaarlo?* A hard struggle was going on between my mind and my feelings.

Fortunately the work ended and I returned home. I missed Urho hugely. He wrote passionate love letters to me, even though he was already at the front. His kisses still burned on my lips, and I dreamed of him day and night.

Saimi and I possessed a spirit of adventure. Playfully we sent in work applications to Åland and received a reply. What should we do? I wasn't really needed at home, since Anu and Father were there. Mother objected, since my brother's and sister's weddings were coming up. I didn't even dare ask my father, but my desire to go and see the world was overpowering.

Father went off to a mill farther away, where he spent the night. Saimi and I took off, first by bus to Viipuri and then by train to Turku. This was a really plush ride, not in a cattle car, as on the evacuation journey. From Turku we went by boat, and this was something completely new to me. It was quite stormy, and the boat was tossed about precariously. I went on deck, and got a faceful of salt water. I staggered to the rail, and there went my supper into the Baltic Sea. I was pale when I came back inside, but I felt better. Saimi was dozing on a sofa, and I too sank down on it. When we awoke, we were in the harbor at Mariehamn.

As refugees we had learned to understand different Finnish dialects, but this "Swedish" was completely Greek to us. We were on a bus, and it was pouring rain. A woman was there to meet us with a lantern, and we walked along a narrow, rocky trail God knows for how long. Finally an impressive, two-story house stood before us. Electric lights blinded us when we got inside. The woman spoke a little Finnish. She gave us something dry to put on, and we sat down to a sumptuous table. I literally had to pinch myself to see if this was real. Compared to our meager wartime existence, it seemed overly extravagant.

Saimi's new home was somewhere nearby—these were large farmhouses. Every house had a telephone, an extravagance I had never had in my life. Saimi and I were able to phone often, and to visit evenings.

I don't remember at all how many rooms there were in the house, but in every one there was an upright wood stove. Since it was winter, my job was to warm the rooms once a week. In the large hall, I often stood admiring the impressive chandeliers and gilded borders of the ceiling. On the walls were huge portraits of previous generations. It was like a fairy tale for a farm girl like me to live in such a castle.

The owner of the place traveled a lot, so there were two hired hands to care for the farm. It so happened that the son Bengt's birthday was the same as my name day. The lady wanted to have a party for us. Young people came from the neighboring houses, Saimi among them. After being fed well, we went into a side room where the floor had been waxed just for dancing. Together we carried a gramophone and records into the room. Alas, how unlucky I was. The pair being celebrated had to dance the first waltz. I couldn't refuse—it would have ruined the party. I blushed a deep red and my heart pounded so that I could hardly hear the music, but to my amazement, it went quite well. Thanks to Olli, I thought, relieved. My tension eased, and I was asked for every dance. It was such fun that in my late years, I still blush when I think of it.

Bengt began to ask me often to go for walks, and I sometimes went. He spoke a little Finnish, and I tried to learn Swedish. He tried to get closer to me, but I remained cool. I did not want to be intimate with him, and said, "I like you, Bengt. You're fun to talk to, but I don't want a closer relationship. Let's just be good friends."

"Oh, if I could just get one kiss from you," he begged. I laughed and ran away. That made him angry, and he never asked me out again.

I often got beautiful love letters from Urho. I was also in touch with Tauno from Lappajärvi, who was also in the war. I wrote to still a third soldier whom I did not know. They were enough company for me. And I was not at all homesick.

In Åland, people knew nothing about the war. July parties were held almost every night in the neighborhood, and the help was always invited. We who had come from Finland almost forgot that the war was still going on. There were no shortages here: everything that was needed flowed in from Stockholm. There the men did not even have to go to war.

In time I would have wanted even to move to Sweden, but Saimi grew very homesick for Finland. When we were planning to go there, I received sad tidings from home. My brother, Viljo, had fallen in the war. The dreadful news brought me back to Finland. Viljo had been dearer to me than Samppa. As a little girl, I had always said that Viljo was my brother and Samppa was Anu's.

I wondered on the way home if the pastor would have to ride to our house in that carriage. When he was on the road, people always watched to see what house he turned into—that meant a death in the house. Viljo was the first-born—What would Mother feel in her heart now when the coffin was brought home. I thought of twenty-year-old Anna, who had been married only five months before, and whose entire future had been smashed. How small and confining home seemed after these high and spacious rooms, as if the whole house had shrunk. Everything seemed so strange, although I had been away for only seven months.

Poor Anna, a young widow, was pale, and her eyes swollen with weeping. Her mother had already died five years ago, and her father was an invalid. Her sisters were scattered around Finland. I remembered her as pretty and happy, always ready for some kind of prank. We had received her with open arms, and she must surely have felt at home, and as if she had found a mother. For years afterwards, she thought of our mother as her own.

Funeral preparations were under way. Mikko Kori's wife, Selma, was helping to prepare the food. This was the first war funeral in our village. A neighbor, Kalervo, had been lost, but not enough was left of him to bury. He had stepped on a mine and been blown to pieces. The whole village came to accompany Viljo on his last journey. He had been one of the best of the village boys, a Civil Guard member and active in all youth club doings. He had made violins and taught himself to play.

One evening surprise visitors appeared; Saimi and Urho drove into the yard. Everyone went to the window to see who was coming. Aunt Aino, too lived, with us summers with her son Antero. "That Saimi has really caught herself a good-looking boy," she said. I went out quickly to the yard and whispered something. Saimi introduced Urho as her own boyfriend. I was so shy that I did not dare introduce Urho as my own. We decided to meet on Saturday evening.

Something was gone from our relationship. His kiss no longer brought a glow to my cheeks. Urho noticed it, let me go, looked deep into my eyes, and said, "What's happened to my friend? That night when I saw you, it was hard for me to control myself. I wanted to take you in my arms and kiss you for a long time in front of everyone. You've brought me through many a hard time this last winter. Nothing was too hard to bear when I thought of you and read your letters. Have you found someone else or have I offended you somehow?"

"There's no one else, you can be sure of that. It's just that I'm so totally down in the dumps. Maybe my brother's death and all the uncertainty of life during a war when you never know what will happen tomorrow are the cause of it. I confess that your letters have helped me and made me look at the brighter side of life. I hope we can remain friends and that things will again be the same as last fall."

We parted, planning to meet again on Wednesday, if we had the chance.

I waited in vain at the arranged meeting place, and assumed that he had had to go back to the front. He was a non-commissioned officer, and their rest leaves were never long. His letters were no longer as passionate as they had been, but I was still happy that we were friends. I understood that the war was hard for anyone to bear.

It was autumn again, and we helped all our neighbors get their crops in. The war had gone on for years, and food was scarce in Finland, especially in the cities. There were Russian prisoners available for work. They had to be fetched each morning and taken back in the evening, a distance of some three kilometers. The prisoners were glad to come, and they were good workers. They got food from us, and Mother even prepared an evening snack for them. She pitied them: "They are people, too, but they are children of misfortune. They didn't start the war, their masters drove them all to it, gun in hand. They behave so well, and they work so hard. They're such poor skinny things."

Winter came early that year. My school chum Katri got me interested in joining her to teach Sunday school to the children of the village. Katri did not have a singing voice, so leading the music was left to me. I brought a violin with me as accompaniment. My brother had taught me to play a little. Sometimes we held a larger devotional service at our house, and then even soldiers came. Katri and I were the only young people in the village, and there was no gathering place for the young. Sunday school and correspondence kept our spirits up—thanks to Katri, the one who started things.

Sisu Mother

In the spring of 1944, we began to hear distressing news. Germany, which was helping Finland in northern Karelia, was beginning to collapse. Russia was beginning to take back the areas she had lost. Even on the Karelian Isthmus, the line was beginning to give way. The enemy had reached the Taipale River, only some twenty to twenty-five kilometers from us. We were instructed to be ready to leave quickly when the order came.

On June 20, a messenger drove hastily into the yard. It was time to go. Mother and Aunt Anni would go on a bus that was taking old people and children. Father began to pack what was needed onto a wagon. We had arranged with three neighbors to make the trip together. One didn't have a horse, so his goods were fitted onto the others' loads. Varpu, a neighbor's widow, was completely alone. I had promised to drive her cows, and she was to drive the horse. So the four neighbors—eight people, twenty cows, and three horses—began our evacuation journey on the twentieth of June at about ten o'clock in the evening. The journey west had begun. We had to stay on side roads and hold to the shelter of woods during the day, for bombers kept flying over us.

We traveled the whole night without stopping. The houses along the road were empty, their owners having set out on the same journey. In the morning, we saw a handsome house at the edge of a woods. Tahvo went to inquire if we could stop to rest there, and soon waved to us to come on. The house was empty. The cows got into a good field of clover, and we found a keg of salt bream. The potato plants were already in blossom, and I went to dig some new potatoes. The day was cloudy, so there was no danger from bombers. To top it all, the people of the house had left their mattresses on the beds. It was a perfect place for us to stay, and we decided unanimously to stay there for another night. We were in no hurry. No one was waiting for us.

On the following day a messenger came to tell us that we could not stay there longer. "The lines have collapsed behind you, and you have to leave tonight. You must travel night and day to get out of the danger zone. Otherwise you'll be caught up in the front lines."

We did as we were told and kept going, stopping only for short rests when necessary. The nights were light, but no bombers appeared. Midsummer Day was rainy; there were many travelers, and everyone tried to find shelter from the rain, as well as a fenced field or some enclosure for the cattle. We got into a nice house, where there were a lot of other people. A young woman with a boy in her arms came out of a bedroom and said in a tearful voice, "Last week I heard that my husband was killed in the war. Now you refugees come here and trample all the grain fields. At first I tried to stand at the edge of the field, but I couldn't stay there night and day. What shall I do now? The cattle have trampled all the grain. Oh, my fields!"

There was a sergeant in uniform with our group. He rose, shook the woman's hand, introduced himself, and started talking, "My good lady, I beg pardon for all of us who have been forced into this situation. We sympathize with you in your sorrow. I heard the news on the radio, and it isn't good. The Finnish forces have had to retreat continually. If they can't stabilize the front, it will be here in a few days. In that case, it won't matter what condition the fields are in. We are all in this together so that Finland will stay free and so that we can live in peace. You may remember that Marshall Mannerheim said, 'We do not want war. We love peace.' We will leave our homes rather than throw ourselves on the mercy of that Eastern barbarian. Shall we sing our national anthem together?" The sergeant began the song, and everyone joined in. Peace returned to the house.

The following day dawned bright and clear, but we had a feeling that something bad was going to happen. We were traveling a side road with the woods to shelter us if bombers came. A number of them flew over during the day. It was a grassy woods, and we sat on soft hummocks for some hours. The soles of my shoes had worn through, and the shoes were rubbing my toes. I decided to walk barefoot since the shoes were of no help. I showed them to Father and he said: "They're so worn out that they can't be fixed, but put them on the load in case your feet really hurt, and they might still be of some help."

Later in the evening we started off again and after walking for a couple of hours, we found a hay-filled meadow on the shore of a lake. A huge spruce tree grew nearby, and we made our house under it for the night. It was a lovely, peaceful nest.

A couple of soldiers arrived and began to talk of the day's happenings. Elisenvaara had been bombed. A long evacuation train of old people, women, and children had just been loaded. There was no count of the victims yet, but there were at least a couple of hundred. The injured were taken to the Parikkala military hospital. Soldiers on rest leave from the front had to clean up after the bombing.

"I've never seen such a ghastly sight, even at the front. Parts of human bodies littered the whole place," said one soldier.

"Hands and legs were hanging from the branches of trees," said another.

SISU MOTHER

To top it off, there were stories that the raid had resulted from the work of traitors. I couldn't stand to listen further, and asked another soldier who was off to one side, "Is there a better shore nearby? There are only reeds here."

"If you round that bend, there is a good sand beach. You can even swim there. I'll come and show you the way."

I started off after the soldier along a narrow path. We began to talk about my home area and all kinds of things. We sat down on a rock, and I soaked my feet in the water. The soles of my feet were blistered, and it felt good. It would have been lovely to plop into the water and swim, but I had no swimsuit. In a group of girls, I could have gone in my underthings, but not now. The soldier's name was Arvo. He was from Satakunta and was a very pleasant companion. He gave me his address and asked me to write when we reached our destination.

"What destination?" I asked.

"Well, you must know where you're going," he said doubtfully.

"We don't have any set goal. We were just ordered to leave the danger zone as quickly as possible. No one is waiting for us. Probably someone will say, 'Are you here again?'"

"Don't talk nonsense. You can't stay there and get tangled up in the war. Those of us who have seen action in the war can understand your fate. Of course there are all kinds of us."

"And of us, too," I said with a laugh.

A couple of hours flew by in his pleasant company. Arvo took me back to our campground. Varpu gave me a slightly mischievous glance but said nothing. *Look if you like, I was up to nothing wrong*, I thought. Father was never the least bit worried; he trusted me completely. Sometimes he even complained that his daughter always had to be among old people.

One night we bedded down near a railroad. Just at morning milking time, a hospital train stopped near us. Soldiers on crutches came to the door. Others peered from the windows, their heads wrapped in bandages or one eye covered. All were as pale as ghosts; they had probably lain in the hospital for months. I asked if they wanted milk. Naturally they did, and went to get a container. Soon a nurse arrived with a large milk can, into which we could pour the milk. When Varpu had poured it, she said: "That will be five marks." Oh, that damned skinflint—I boiled up inside! We had often been forced to pour milk onto the ground during this trip. Now that tightwad wanted to collect money from those poor soldiers. Fortunately the train started off, so that Varpu did not get her money.

It was a hot day in July. The cows were tired of the everlasting traveling. Our brown Lemmikki especially began to slow down. Father gave a sign to the others to stop and rest for a while. "Lemmikki looks as if she means to calf. She's due this summer," he said. There happened to be a brook nearby with hay growing along the bank. We did not have long to wait before a calf popped out with no great difficulty. There would have been meat a-plenty, but how could we keep it from spoiling in this hot weather? Father drew the calf to the shore of the brook, cut its throat with one stroke of his knife, and shoved it into the water. Soon it was gone. A streak of red swam in the current for a while, and then disappeared.

We were getting out of the danger zone, and we could spend nights in a house. The food we had brought with us from home was beginning to run out. We asked for the use of a separator, put all the cream into the same can, and onto the wagon. When we bedded down in a house that evening, Mari Tahvo went to check the can to see if the cream had already soured. A broad grin spread over face, and she called the rest of us to come and see. "Good lord, there is butter already made here; it churned itself on the wagon! Now we have fresh butter and buttermilk for supper." We had flour with us, and that night we baked bread in the house.

We were somewhere near Parikkala and the cows were grazing along the side of the road. An oldish man came along and started to talk to us, "I rented this field in the spring and paid 300 marks for it. I bought 150 marks worth of oat seed and it was sprouting nicely around Midsummer. Now look at what it's like. Nothing but black mud soon. You're not the first ones. People have been going by for weeks."

"We can't help it. We're like gypsies, but we had to get out from under the war," Tahvo explained.

We got to Punkaharju just at the lushest part of the summer. I had never even imagined seeing this spot so famous for its beauty. Lovely pine woods, and the waters of Pihlaja to the south and Puru to the north. I felt as if I were drinking in a new zeal for life from the beauty of nature. I forgot the cares of everyday and the brutality of war, if only for a moment, until the heavy puffing of an approaching troop train awakened me to reality.

Soon Olavinlinna loomed up in the glow of the morning sun. The massive, nearly five-hundred-year-old fortress looked mysterious and enticing. *If I could only go inside and listen to its tales from all those centuries*, I thought.

Idle dreams. We were approaching the city of Savonlinna. Since we were not the first, the streets had already been marked to show us which way to go. The animals walked cautiously along the old cobblestone streets. There were small shops along them, and since it was summer, their doors were open. And didn't Varpu's long-horned cow go and stick her head into one of them! She stood there and gaped in astonishment. There was an ear-piercing shriek, "Oh, my God, a strange cow is coming in!" But the animal turned calmly back and went on its way. We got through the city without any great mishaps.

We had come so far that we no longer saw any bombers. Travelers thronged the roadsides. We even met people from our village and other acquaintances. Hey, there's Elma, a former school chum of mine! We arranged to meet after milking.

We sat and giggled on the bank of a brook a little apart from the others. A truck stopped and a couple of good-looking soldiers came to chat with us. One of them said: "It's such a nice, clear evening, wouldn't you like to go for a drive to pass the time away?"

Ready for adventure, we piled into the truck. We drove for a long distance on the Kerimäki highway and were already beginning to exchange worried glances when we came to a lovely, wooded heath. One of the boys said: "There are lots of blueberries here; let's go and see if they're ripe. So we set off arm in arm along a little path leading away from the road.

The boys became more and more bold. Soon I was wrestling one of them in the heather with all my strength. A kick in a sensitive place with my bare heel made him cry out in pain, and he let go of me. I leaped up and ran, looking back over my shoulder to see what was happening to Elma. She too was racing towards the same woods as I.

We did not dare go back to the highway since, for all we knew, the boys might be lurking in wait for us there, but we walked so close to the road that we had a clear view of it. Relieved, we saw some houses. We were safe. Fortunately our clothes were whole, thank God! We went back to the highway.

"They were really devils! You wouldn't believe it, to look at them. I never even thought they could be so shameless," said Elma.

"Nothing like this ever happened to me before either. Maybe a little tussle, but no more than that. This was *some* berry picking. We have quite a distance to go. It must be at least twenty kilometers to Kallislahti. It could be daylight before we're there."

We knew how to walk, and it was a bright summer night. A truck came up from behind us and stopped. We froze with fear. There was an older man alone in the truck. He looked trustworthy, and we hopped in. He was going in exactly the same direction as we were. It was a case of good fortune in misfortune, and we got back to our families. Years later when Elma and I got together, we laughed about our adventure on Kerimäki Heath.

We had spent several days near the Kallislahti railway station waiting to board a train. Soldiers were also stationed in the area. On Saturday they began to heat the sauna. Our neighbor Liisa was bold enough to ask, "After you've been to the sauna could the women go? We'll carry in all the water we need."

"You don't have to carry the water. I'll take care of it. I'll tell you when it's empty," said a manly voice.

It was very late when we got permission to go in. Mari, Liisa, Varpu, and I began to undress hastily. The others were already naked, and I was just pulling my dress over my head when a steaming, naked man came out with a small towel on his shoulder. He looked at us and went out without saying a word. The women put their hands over their crotches to cover up, but paid no attention to their breasts, which dangled limply over their bellies. I blushed a furious red, and could not do a thing. I was infinitely ashamed. No man had ever seen or touched my breasts, not to mention other parts. I felt as if something that belonged to me alone had been bared. But at least it was dark night, and there was no light for him to see my face.

The older women went into the sauna first. It was a solid building, all fogged with steam. You could see nothing, but I could hear someone washing up. I slipped into the darkest corner. Sauna had always made me feel good, but now after three weeks—ah, the blissful delight! I would not trade this for all the world's treasure. My poor, blistered, calloused feet. Oh, if the world would end here, nothing could be more beautiful than to drift off into everlasting sleep.

We decided to sleep in the sauna entry room. I got our scant bed clothing from the wagon, and we spread them on the floor. It was so peaceful there. For at least one night we were spared the whining chorus of the mosquitoes.

After a few more days of waiting, we were again on board a train puffing toward the west. Now our destination was Jyväskylä. The journey ordinarily takes only a few hours, but army transport was on the front burner, and refugees had to wait at every station. We jolted along for nearly three days before we reached our destination. From there we walked ten miles along the west shore of Lake Päijänne toward the parish of Muurame. Now we were in Häme.

"Well, now we can see what it's like around here. I've never even seen a person from Häme before. The fields are fertile, and the houses are big. If only the people aren't too high and mighty toward us poor Karelians," Mari Tahvo declared.

Life is exciting, I thought childishly. *During the Winter War we got to see Bothnia and Satakunta. We went on foot through Savo and got to know the placid people there. It's neat that we're in Häme now. Even war has a meaning. The tribes of Finland will get to know and to melt into each other.*

Father and I got the very farthest house, which was named Ruislahti. In the shade of huge trees at the end of a winding road, we found a dark, two-story house. We got a friendly reception. The owner was a widow named Bertha, about forty-five years old, who had a sixteen-year-old daughter. They lived on the second floor, and we, too, got a room there, with a stove. The land was rented to a city couple, who lived on the first floor. I got the impression that they were the kind of city folk who imagined that the land would grow crops even if they were idle.

In the morning Father went to Korpilahti to look for Mother and Aunt Anni. The cows had been brought to the farm and were in the pasture with the farm cattle. I went back to rest. In the afternoon I began to look around. What a great place; the fields sloped gently down to the shore of the lake. Now I could touch the waters of Lake Päijänne, the longest lake in Finland. There was a good sand beach for swimming. I looked around. It was very still and no one was in sight, so I slipped off my clothes and plopped into the water. *We really got a lovely place to live, when I can even go swimming every evening. Just like at home in Pyhäjärvi,* I said to myself enthusiastically.

We were soon at home at Ruislahti. Our room was small, and so Bertha suggested that I sleep in her guest room. Bertha was small, dark, and brown-eyed, and she made us feel at home. It occurred to me that here in Häme, things were not as they were said to be in the song. Why? "The girl from Häme has blond hair, / a blue-eyed maiden she. / Her cheeks are rosy . . ." One couldn't trust anything in this world, even local songs.

Bertha turned out to be a pleasant person with much experience of the world. For example, she spoke openly about love without a trace of embarrassment. "When one person cares for and loves another, there's no controlling her. She's in such a trance that she forgets everything human and important. Her brain stops working and revolves around her loved one." (The version I'd heard was that one's stockings spun on one's feet and one's toenails fell off.) "I was seventeen when I fell in love for the first time," Bertha went on. "He was a lot older than I was. I looked out the window and dreamt when he walked by. I thought that some day I would have him. He had a lot of bad points, but I didn't see them. My parents forbade me to speak to him. But I wanted him, and along came this Kerttu, and he didn't even want to marry me. When my parents found out, my father said, 'You're not going to marry that man even if he asks you,' and so they brought up Kerttu."

Bertha had come to this farm as the housekeeper for a bachelor. She had served here for fifteen years when her waist began to expand. "It wasn't love, but loneliness. The relatives pressured us and we went to the parsonage and got married, and so I became the mistress of the house. The master waited hopefully for an heir to the farm, that is, for a boy, but when it was a girl, he sank into total depression. The child was six months old one day when I came back from shopping. The master had shot himself in the parlor downstairs, and the child had cried herself hoarse. The ambulance and the police took everything away. I've lived on this second floor for years. I always see that awful sight when I open the door of that room," Bertha concluded softly.

Now she was happy because her daughter had inherited one of the richest farms in the parish. And she had still not forgotten the art of love. Often someone came riding a bicycle toward Ruislahti on a Saturday evening. In the morning, he would ride back, whistling.

It took a week before the soles of my feet healed and I was able to buy a pair of wooden shoes, for no others were available. If there were only some kind of work, I could earn a little money. Bertha suggested a furniture factory; there were a lot of girls working there. I went first to the office, and was told to go to the factory section and ask for the foreman. I opened the factory door shyly and stood in the doorway looking around. On every side there were whirling machines, which buzzed and hummed in their separate voices. The air was thick with dust, and more poured out from every machine. I whirled around quickly and closed the door, hoping that no one had seen me and vowing that I would never go into that place. *A person would go crazy, listening to that noise day after day. The air was so polluted it would stick in your throat in a few seconds. But I have to try something to earn my bread.*

On the way home, I stopped in to see Little Antti, who told me that the owner of their farm had just been asking about haymakers. He and I went to speak to the man. "Uh-huh, you can come and try it for a day. We start at seven." The man said little, and looked at me doubtfully.

I was pleased that I would be able to earn a little money, for I needed it.

In the morning I was in the Penttilä yard early, waiting to go to the field. We began to pile the hay onto staves, which Antti set up. With us there were a couple of other women, two prisoners of war, and little thirteen-year-old Esko, who was everyone's errand boy. We were supplied with food by the house, which was good, since food was scarce. In the evening a long table was set with delicious country food. The owner of the farms sat at the head of the table, and the rest of us, the prisoners included, sat around it. After supper, the farm owner gestured me to one side, and I thought he would fire me, but he began to speak in a soft voice. "By God, my girl, you're a hard worker, better than some men. If you like, you can spend the night here, so you won't have to walk so far. Here's something for you as a starter." He pressed five marks into my hand without the others noticing.

The work was hard, but the days passed quickly. But the boy Esko was a pest, especially to me. Perhaps because I was the youngest, he gave me the most trouble. One day my temper boiled over and I seized the boy, put him on his belly across my knees and paddled his rear with all my strength. The boy began to yell at the top of his lungs. "Good, good," laughed the others, clapping their hands.

Esko was ashamed all that afternoon and played no pranks from then on. In the evening the owner again put five marks into my hand and said, "You did a good thing. That's what the boy needed. I would have liked to punish him before this, but what can I do, I'm so old and crippled." He went limping with his cane toward the yard swing.

I went to Keuruu once a week to see if our packed-up goods had arrived yet. Surprise, Saimi was there. She had gotten married in the spring. The goods were kept in a lovely wooden church, built in the 1700s. A lot of time had been dedicated to its beautiful woodcarvings. The ceiling and walls were covered with paintings, some of them depicting the devil and some angels. Now this historic church was full of goods belonging to evacuees.

It was late one Sunday evening and some twenty of us were there. A man came from somewhere and opened the doors of the new church. "It looks as if you don't have a place to spend the night. Sleep here in this church." We stared at each other in astonishment but followed the man into the church. Saimi and I went up close to the altar, stuck our wooden shoes under the red carpet as pillows, and made ready to lie down.

"I'm sure you'll let me lie down between two such pretty girls," an older man came scrambling over to us.

"Go to hell! Shame on you! And don't come here during the night! No one is going to come between us here! There's plenty of room for you elsewhere."

We slept well there on the church floor. We woke up refreshed in the morning, squinting in the bright morning sunshine. All the others had already left. The churchwarden took us up to the bell tower and explained to us what bells were rung on what occasions. What a tremendous view it was! Blue water was sprinkled around in every direction. "That bigger one is Keuruu Lake, which is a part of the famous Keuruu Route," the man explained.

After a few days I went to the Jyväskylä station with the horse to get our stuff, which I had found at Keuruu. A tall man in uniform was walking down the street. I knew him; he was a former schoolmate. "Hey Kauko! What are you doing here?" I couldn't believe my eyes. "I'll give you a ride." He was on leave and was looking for his family. We found a place for the horse among some piles of wood, and sat down on a grassy spot nearby. There was so much to talk about, for we hadn't met in years. I had lunch with me, which we shared, and washed down with a cup of coffee substitute. The horse began to get restless, so it was time to leave. Kauko suddenly seized me in his arms and kissed me hotly. In that moment I forgot the war and the world's tempests. A feeling of happiness took over my heart. We exchanged no vows, no hopes for the future and parted without a word.

A few weeks later I heard that Kauko had fallen to enemy fire. Another of my life's dreams had been shattered. Again there was an open wound in my heart.

The war continued, but the line had been stabilized at the Taipale River. There was a food shortage in Finland, and even the crops in Karelia had to be harvested. Father got permission to go there with his horse. A letter soon came saying that I could go too. I left the next day, taking my bicycle.

I was riding toward my home from the station singing, when I again heard that loathsome drone from somewhere. "Won't those damned hornets even let me go home in peace?" I thought as I went into the woods for shelter. The planes passed over, and I covered the rest of the seven kilometers easily. I was home again.

My father was some kind of group leader and had to report to someone higher up once a week. He wanted me to keep the books, and I spent the days sitting inside and scratching away with a pen. I was certainly not cut out for that work, but I did it dutifully.

There were a lot of soldiers working at the harvest. Often we would gather at some house and dance to the music of a harmonica. I didn't want to have a close relationship with any of them. I had had too much of it. Every time a little flame was kindled, I was robbed of it.

I was home alone as usual when Urho appeared at the door. I was in his arms that instant, in a burning kiss. "I was at a rest area in Riiska, and wanted to come and see what had happened because you didn't write all summer. Why didn't you write?"

I told him what had happened.

Urho wanted to meet my father. When I wondered why, he did not answer my questions but smiled mysteriously. Father was at work in Husus meadow, and we rode there to meet him. Urho introduced himself.

"I'm a friend of Elsie's. We've known each other for two years already. It's been a year since I last saw her."

"So you're a friend of Elsie's? I didn't even know she had any boyfriends. The poor thing has been through a lot this summer."

The two chatted for a while, and suddenly Urho said with a smile, "I'm so taken with that girl. If I come through the war okay, I want to share my life with her. As her father, do you have anything against it?"

I blushed a deep red and felt a surge of anger in my breast. Why hadn't he asked me first? It was my life. Father too was shocked and nonplussed. After thinking for a moment, he said, "It's really not in my power to say anything in the matter. The girl has done whatever she wanted since she was thirteen. Have you asked her? I have nothing against you."

"No, not yet," the boy said shyly.

"Isn't it better to leave it to the future? Now is a time when we live from one day to the next. We're alive today, but we may be cold tomorrow. If the war ends and you get home, you may change your mind. Maybe another childhood sweetheart will seem dearer. Keep in touch. The girl is still so young, not even eighteen."

Sober and silent, we rode back home. We said a warm goodbye, and Urho was gone. After he left, I thought the whole thing through and decided that I wasn't ready for marriage yet. I really knew nothing about him. Was he the son of a landowner or a tenant farmer? If a landowner, I wasn't ready to take on all the responsibility that would entail. I thought of the stories Bertha had told at Ruislahti. Urho's kisses didn't really send me to seventh heaven. If love was really so overpowering, then this wasn't really love.

The armistice began on the Fourth of September. We worked day and night now, since there was no danger from air raids. The harvest had to be gathered from this war zone. Soldiers came daily to help with the harvest. The rumor spread that Karelia was lost again.

On September 19, 1944, peace was proclaimed. For the most part, the same areas were lost as in the Winter War, with a few small changes. Hanko was returned, but Porkkala was lost, with the result that the Russians allowed trains to pass through it, but the windows had to be covered from the outside. For the passengers, it was like traveling through a long tunnel. But anyway the Russians returned it to Finland in 1957.

Father and I packed to leave. He loaded as much as he could on the wagon. I sat over the wheel well, and there was even a bundle tied to the tongue. The order was that we were to cross the future border on our own. I could have gone quickly on a bicycle but had to wait for the horse.

"Hey, Saimi, you're just what I needed. Father has enough company with these horse drivers from home. We can go by ourselves. We're sure to make it out of here," I said, happy to see her.

"I was thinking the same thing and looking for someone to go with me. This is just great. We've always had so much fun together."

Somewhere in Vuoksela we separated from Father. Saimi planned to look for her husband, for soldiers were also traveling somewhere around here. In a couple of days, we found her beloved. We were allowed to spend the night in one house. Saimi and her husband had to show their rings to prove they were married, and they were permitted to sleep on the floor of the *tupa* while I slept in the entryway. We were even served coffee substitute in the morning. The people in the house were also in the throes of packing. Again we drove through Punkaharju from one side to the other, but it did not look as lovely as in the summer. It was a cloudy and rainy day, and the water seen through gaps in the trees was a somber gray. Birches here and there lent a yellow tone to the green pinewoods. We had planned to cycle to Jyväskylä, but the days turned cold and rainy. Ahead of us was the familiar Kallislahti Road sign.

"Let's go and ask at the station. We might even get on a train."

"Yes, let's. We're not going to ride in this kind of weather. The roads are so soft we'd have to push our bikes half the time," said Saimi.

What luck! We got on the next train and were able to take our bikes with us. In a few hours we were already at the Jyväskylä station. Saimi continued her trip to Åhtäri with her husband. It was sad to part, but we promised to stay in touch. What would life bring? My feelings in confusion, I headed for Ruislahti. Father had to drive the whole distance, and it was two weeks before he arrived at Ruislahti.

CHAPTER IV

November 1944. I was a home-helper for a sheriff's family near Ruislahti. Soldiers were being relieved of their war duties, which had lasted for three and a half years. Prisoners of war were being exchanged. Late in the evening, the names of those who had been freed from prison camps were announced. On this day, the last of the names were read off, and the name of our neighbor, Veikko, was not among them. Where could he be? I had heard from a reliable source that he was a prisoner of war.

After a couple of weeks, a man named Jussi from the neighboring village brought news of Veikko. They had been at the same camp. Poor, dirty food and constant dysentery had weakened him fatally. A few days before departure for home, he had died. It was too heavy a blow for his old parents. Their older son, Kauko, had been blown to bits at the start of the war. They had lost their home and both of their sons, without so much as a grave mound as a memorial. Our neighbors, Juho and Liisa, died within a few months. No illness caused their death; their hearts could not endure. Why does war have to be so cruel to so many, I thought.

When I got the job in the sheriff's home, I thought that I would finally have a chance to learn to cook. Although the woman of the house was responsible for preparing the food, I helped her. All through the war, I had driven a horse and worked outdoors. Actually I had never really been interested in cooking.

The people of the house ate in the dining room, and I waited in the kitchen for the signal to bring in more food. I could not eat until they were finished, and the dining room table had been cleared. While waiting, I began to take food from the stove, since it was warm. Once the lady of the house surprised me at it. She looked at me angrily and stormed, "You've been told not to eat, Elsie, that you are not to eat until we are through."

"Forgive me ma'am, but it was getting so late, and I was hungry."

"You'll remember now. You're not to do it again."

Uhuh, uhuh, I thought, my ears red, and feeling rebellious. I was just like a dog in that house. My room was small, like a doghouse. The place was some sort of a big manor, and I gathered that workers there were regarded as beneath consideration. The sheriff, however, was a good-natured man of the people.

Almost every Sunday, the sheriff went out hunting. I wondered how he could do it; he was short, fat, and sixty years old, and he always bagged something: wood and heath grouse and rabbits. Somehow I learned what the story was. Three or four men would set out to hunt. At the edge of the hunting grounds was a house where the sheriff was known, and there he would sit with the master while the younger men were out chasing rabbits.

Of course it was my job to clean the prey, and a couple of times I forgot to save the heart, liver, and gizzard. Once when I was cleaning a bird, the master of the house came to watch. "I came to check that you didn't throw away the delicacies. If you do, I'll throw you in jail." He laughed and walked away. The next day we had roast wood grouse. When I checked after the meal, the delicacies were there, still uneaten. Now it was my turn to feast.

At least once a week, I went in to Ruislahti. There was a severe housing shortage. Anu and Eka lived there in one room. I seldom went to dances, and I didn't know many young people. I had to be at home by ten o'clock. The lady would not give me a key, and I always had to wake her up if I came in late. Before that, I had always been able to come and go as I pleased. My parents trusted me, for I had never gone astray. Now I felt as if I were in a prison.

It was like being in a strange, foreign land. The woman was very suspicious, too. When I cleaned the parlor for the first time and had all the furniture back in place, she came into the room. "You really cleaned this room in a hurry," she said. "Did you dust the window sills?"

"Yes, I did that first," I said humbly.

The woman took a white handkerchief from her pocket and wiped the windowsill, then left the room without a word. I sighed with relief.

The family's middle daughter was getting married on New Year's Day. The bride's sister practiced the wedding march on the piano, often for many hours at a time. I got so tired of the same plinking that I wished I would never again hear a piano play. Preparations for the wedding went on into late hours every night. Even Mother stopped in when passing by to ask, "I came to see what's wrong with you. You haven't been home for a whole week. I missed you, even thought you might be ill."

"I didn't have the time. They're making food for the wedding every night."

"They're treating you like a slave here. Have you had a single Sunday off since you came here?"

"I've been to church a couple of times, but I was there for only about two hours. I'm really tied down here. I never get any days off."

"You could go to that factory. At least you would have Sunday off. And they could at least pay you better wages since you have to work day and night. Do you at least get good food?"

"The food is really good, but it's always cold. I can't start eating until the family is through and the dining room cleaned."

"Good Heavens! Come home if you don't like it here. You don't have to do slave labor anywhere," Mother said angrily.

"Well, I can stand it at least until the spring. I'll decide then what to do. I don't want to go into the factory. The racket there would drive me crazy. I've saved money, and I plan to go to a gardening school toward spring. If I happen to get in, I'll at least be able to work out of doors. I don't know if one can get work in that line."

I didn't get into the school because there were too many applicants, but I was urged to try again the next spring. What was I to do now? I would not continue this slavery for long, and I did not want to go into the factory. I wrote to Saimi asking if there were any job possibilities where she was. An answer soon arrived: "You are sure to find work here. My husband is in a factory, and they hire women too. There is also a shortage of workers in farmhouses. You can live with us if you come."

So that spring I went to Åhtäri. Saimi's living quarters were very cramped, so I took a job at a farm, where I got a large room on the second floor. Food was scarce, especially in the cities, and I felt that at least I would get food here. The elderly couple received me warmly, as if I were their own child. There was also a forty-year-old son in the house, who was a little cross-eyed, but he was a good worker.

The farm was near beautiful Lake Peränne, and in the evening I would run to the lake and swim in its cool waters. The owner of the farm had been in America in his youth and often talked of his experiences. If I had known anyone there, I would have left at once, but there was no one, so that dream faded.

In the spring, I noticed Urho's engagement announcement in the paper. It caused a little pang in my heart. I had to admit that I was disappointed, but I hadn't sent him news of myself since I had seen him at home. So I got what I had wanted.

I got to know the neighbor's young folks and took part in the youth club doings. I also helped in organizing parties. At one the last number was "The

Waltz of Fate." I didn't mean to take part in it, but they ran short of girls and so I joined in.

I saw a pair of good-looking gray eyes gazing deep into mine. Their owner bowed to ask for the next dance, and said shyly, "Are you new here? I haven't seen you before. I live over on the Töysä side. A bunch of us boys sometimes come over here to Peränne."

"I live a couple of kilometers away. I worked with the others arranging this party. We still have all kinds of cleaning up to do."

"Is there anything going on here next Saturday?" he said, sounding interested.

"Of course, and there are guests coming from somewhere."

"Will you come, since you live so near?"

"I think so," I said. He squeezed my hand warmly and left.

The week went by quickly. Now and then those gray eyes popped into my mind. The neighbor girl Eeva and I went to the dance together. I noticed while the program was still going on that the gray-eyed boy was standing in the doorway. Eeva's brother Aarne came to chat with us while we were waiting for the dancing to begin. Aarne asked me for the first dance. In passing I got a gloomy look from the doorway. After the number, Aarne went his way. Gray-eyes came hurrying toward me when the next dance began. He bowed shyly and said, "May I?"

In the whirl of the dance, he began to speak hesitantly, "It looks as if you already have a boyfriend. I came here for nothing. You seem to have plenty of partners to dance with."

"They're my neighbors. I see them every day. My master and their mother are brother and sister. You can see that they're dancing together over there."

I saw a look of relief on his face.

"My name is Saul. I live about seventeen kilometers from here. I came alone, and I'd like to take you home from the dance. Do you mind?"

"Saul—it's a manly name, and it's straight out of the Bible. My name is Elsie, and I'm one of the refugees from Karelia. We've been scattered all over Finland and it looks as if we won't get to go back. I'm a helper at a farmhouse here."

"So you're a Karelian. I couldn't have guessed it from your speech. I was on the Isthmus during the war. It's a pity it all went to the Russians. But you haven't answered my question yet."

"I don't mind at all, but let's leave a little early; otherwise we'll be with a whole gang."

"Let's leave during the next dance."

He was a fast talker once he got started. He said that he had attended a metal-trades school before going into the army. Now he was a driver for a mail and messenger service.

"Metals is a broad field. Just what were you learning there?"

"First of all, anything that has to do with iron, that is, smithing. Plus the maintenance of tractors and agricultural machinery. I'm interested in armament smithing, but you have to have more schooling for that."

"You know, I doubt that we would ever have gotten to know each other except for that Waltz of Fate. I never danced it before in my life. Have you?"

"No, but since all the others bought a ticket, I did too. Maybe it was a good luck waltz for us," he said, looking deep into my eyes.

We met each other every Saturday night. Sometimes we danced, but often we walked along the lakeshore. We were getting to know each other better and better, and often the time seemed too short. Winter was coming, and with it, bad weather. Sometimes he couldn't make it, and then a letter would arrive during the week.

Often my thoughts began to revolve around him even during the day. His kisses were passionate, but they did not send me floating to seventh heaven, as in Bertha's stories. I began to feel she had embellished her stories considerably. There is no such thing as a love that makes one forget the world and all its needs.

We had decided to spend New Year's Eve together, to pour tin together, but where? I could not bring a man home with me, for the lady of the house had forbidden that from the start. Nor did I want to do it. The temptation would have been too great. I was resolved to leave all that for marriage.

I carried extra wood into the barn cookhouse that evening, covered the windows, and we built a fire under the pot. Saul brought the tin and the melting dipper, and we began to pour. His tin took the shape of two people embracing, mine was something like a heart. There in the cookhouse of the barn, he took both my hands in his and whispered into my ear, "Will you be mine for the rest of my life? I've thought this over for a long time. Now I'm sure that we belong to each other, since even the tin shapes tell us it is so. Have you thought much about me?"

"I have. You're in my mind day and night. But I am surprised. I didn't think you took this so seriously. And this I promise you. I will be your wife."

He seized me in his arms and whirled me about the floor, and finally we sank down in a passionate kiss. He touched my breast gently and his hand began to grope below my waist. I started as if from a dream, caught his hand, and drew it higher. He did not resist.

"Take it easy. We're not married yet," I said with a laugh.

"I wasn't really trying. I can tell that you surely haven't gone that far. I would be ready now, since we've given our word; a preacher's permission no longer means anything. If you want to wait until we're married, I'll try to hold out. I feel so good now that you've promised to be mine. I was afraid you were just playing with me. Sometimes you're so wild that I don't know what's going on in your head. That's probably why you're so charming."

"So, I'm wild? I didn't know that," I said with a smile. "But not so wild, at any rate, as to give myself in this barn shed. I've dreamed a lot of my wedding day. I hope I can walk down the aisle by your side wearing a white veil as a mark of purity with a good conscience. I hope and pray it doesn't remain just a dream. I'm nineteen years old now. There has been more sorrow than joy in my life, but I've come through it all. I hope and pray that you understand me."

"For your sake, I'll try my best," Saul said seriously, and then he added: "Our life together will have to wait until summer. I have to find a better job. I work only two days a week, and we can't live on that. I live at home, but Father just made out papers giving the farm to my two brothers. I've never really gotten along with him, and I don't want to be a farmer. I learned automobile repair in the army, I think I can get a job in that line. When I get a job, we'll have to rent a place to live nearby. I don't want to start living at home; there are too many people there."

"I won't be ready for a long time either. I want to get my things ready first. I have flax growing, and the neighbor lady will spin it. You know you can't buy anything anywhere. I want to go home for a little while. I'll try to make something from the linen. We'll need a lot to set up house together. We can get ration points then to buy bedclothes, for example, if there are any in the stores. Now I have nothing to set up housekeeping with," I said shyly.

"I have two quilts that I snitched from the army," Saul said hopefully.

After midnight, we said a warm goodbye and parted. *What will this year of 1946 bring?* I thought, as I went to bed. I couldn't sleep, I was so happy.

Tomorrow is different. It may not be better, but at least it's different.

CHAPTER V

February 1946. I am in the Korpilahti Hospital for Contagious Diseases. I had gone home for a week's vacation with my parents and was stricken by diphtheria. Now I would have to be in the hospital for at least four weeks. I asked the nurse for stationery so that I could write to Saul; otherwise he would think that I had disappeared from his life completely.

"You are allowed to write from here, but the letters must be pressed with a hot iron so that the bacteria won't spread. I hardly think you'll be able to write. You had a fever this morning. When your temperature goes down, I'll bring you some paper."

Mother came to see me, and I asked her to write to the place where I was working and tell them I would no longer be there, and that I would get my things later.

Alli, a girl I knew from Muurame, was a medical assistant at the hospital. She brought me paper and took my letters to mail. I didn't want that old-maid nurse to read my love letters. My roommate was an eight-year-old boy, and the two of us made up all kinds of pastimes. One day I began to see spots before my eyes, and for short spells I could see nothing. I felt as if I were sinking into a deep gulf.

I woke from it almost three hours later. A doctor, two nurses, and my mother were at my bedside. I did not remember where I was, and the doctor began to explain to me, "You've had a heart attack. Diphtheria is such a bad disease that it almost always has consequences. You are young, so I think there will be no permanent damage to your heart. You can thank Esa for getting help so quickly. He heard your breath rattling, and he rang the bell for help immediately. If you had been alone, who knows what might have happened? Your heart had stopped beating completely, and your condition is still critical. We have to move the boy for a few days, and a nurse will be here at all times, and will give you shots every two hours until the danger is past. You are not even to sit up, just rest, and all will be well."

After the doctor had left, Mother moved her chair closer to me and started to speak in a troubled voice, "I was so scared when a neighbor came to tell me—there's no telephone at Ruislahti. I didn't believe you could be so sick until I heard that doctor. He did give us hope. You've always been a good girl, and believed in God. I remember when you and Katri went to teach that Sunday School there in Karelia. Who can tell—maybe all you saw during the war weakened your heart. Can you see—your father, sister, and Esa are in back of that window? They let only me come in, you're so weak. They made me put this kind of coat on, and I have to wash my hands with soap when I leave. Just be good and do what the doctor says, and you're sure to get well."

I grew stronger day by day. Esa came back to the room for the last few days of his stay. When his parents came to get him, they asked me to come and see them when I got out. His mother was particularly insistent, "Esa has been a different boy, Elsie, since you became his roommate. I even stopped worrying when I saw that he no longer cried out of homesickness."

"Be sure to remember to come," Esa called out as he waved from the door.

Perhaps the heart problem lengthened my stay at the hospital. The bacteria were always present in the tests; otherwise I felt strong. Now I had a little, blond-headed boy named Kari for company. He was a year old, was running a high fever and kept up a constant soft whimpering. His mother was with him the first night caring for him, but in the morning she said: "I can't stay here longer. I'll lose my job. Kari has no father; his grandma usually takes care of him. Will you see to it that they take good care of him?"

The day went by somehow, but in the evening the boy would not stay lying down. The nurse, a nervous old maid, tied the boy to the bed and left him there screaming, turned out the light, and closed the door. I could not stand the sound for long. I took the boy into my own bed, and the crying stopped immediately. When Kari was sound asleep, I lifted him carefully back into his own bed, and even redid the ties so that the nurse would not discover my deceit."

When the nurse came in the morning, the boy began to cry immediately. She changed his diapers and began to take his temperature. Kari kicked and screamed in panic. "Let me hold him in my lap. See if that helps," I said to the nurse. Soon the boy was laughing at me. I managed to take his temperature and feed him with no trouble at all. From then on it was my job. After a while, the nurse said, somewhat abashed: "You must have had a lot of experience with children, since Kari always reaches out for you when I come into the room."

"I like children, but I haven't had any experience with them. I'm the youngest in our family. But I do hope to have children when I get married. Now I don't know if I can even think about it, with my heart acting up, and I doubt if my boyfriend will even have me when I'm so sick. And there seems to be no end to these bacteria."

"You're sure to get better. The doctor says your heart is stronger. And the bacteria will end some day," the nurse laughed.

In the room next to mine was a thirty-year-old man named Jukka. He came often to chat with me during the day to pass away the time. He was concerned about my heart and afraid of the aftereffects of diphtheria. The older one was, the more dangerous the diseases he might get. He gave me his home address and asked me to write how things were going with me. I wrote to him for a long time, and then it happened—a stroke left his legs paralyzed. He recovered from the stroke, but it was eight months before he was able to walk by himself.

> It was such good fortune that I met you there in the hospital. I was in despair, lying in bed for months, not knowing if I would ever walk again. Your letters gave me faith and the courage to live. I hope your future husband will honor and esteem you. You deserve it. I feel as if I don't dare ever think of marriage after such a grave illness. To tell the truth, I've never been seriously in love. There aren't many girls in the world like you, Elsie. I dreamt of you there in the hospital, but I've tried to shake those dreams from my mind. I have to concentrate all my energies on the possibility of finding work. I'm in the electrical line, but I can't go on with it, at least not outside in the cold. I will still look forward to your letters, even though you are getting married. These aren't any kind of love letters, so there is no need for your future husband to be jealous.

That was how Jukka ended his letter. I did not answer it.

At the end of April, we were busy moving to Kihniö. There we got half of an old farm to replace the property we had lost. There were no buildings on it. A truck drove our belongings to the Jyväskylä station. Mother had even kept a few hens, which were in a chaff box with an old quilt thrown over it. Just as the hens were being loaded, the wind blew the quilt off and the box tipped over. The frightened hens began to fly around the tracks and under the coaches. There was nothing we coud do but start chasing them, Janne, Father, Samppa, and I. Just when we had them surrounded, one would hop over us. Again and again. "Chick, chick, chick, come here now," Janne called out. "Come here, come here," Father called, and he did catch one of them. That scared the others into flight. Mother had stopped in at a store, and now came out wondering and panic-stricken: "Good Lord, what's happened now? Here chick, chick, chick, come to Mama." The hens calmed down, and Mother caught them one by one. One of them was still flying around in a panic, and hearing Mother's voice, flew blindly toward her. In its fright, it dropped an egg with the shell still unformed into her lap. "Of all the things to happen! There's no way to get this clean with nothing but cold water. How can I go on the train with other people with this on," Mother prattled to herself, trying to wash the front of her skirt. "I'm going to have to ride the cattle car with you. I would have to wait for you at the Kihniö station anyway."

The farm was pretty much out of the way. We were in a great rush with the spring planting facing us. There was only one small room for rent in the old farmhouse. I slept in the *tupa*. Letters from Saul arrived, but there was no chance for us to meet.

One day Lasse, the brother of the man who owned the house, came to visit. He was very good looking, a happy-go-lucky scamp. He talked of everything under the sun, and then said, "Come to a wedding in the church village. You'll get moldy here out in the woods. You can come as my guest. There'll be eating, drinking, and dancing."

"I can't say. Let me think about it. How far is it? I do have a bicycle, though."

"If we meet at the church, it will be ten kilometers. But that's nothing when the days are so light. We live past the church village, but the wedding is a couple of kilometers in the other direction. You will come, won't you?" he begged. "I'm not going to the church for the wedding, but then in the evening I'll go straight to the house where the wedding party is being held. Let's meet at six, then, at Lahtinen's store. Be sure to come. 'Bye now."

The weather was nice as I rode toward the church village feeling confused. I wasn't married yet, and what harm was there in going to a dance? My heart had mended so well that there was no sign of illness when I left the hospital.

When I met Lasse, his brother, and a few other boys, I realized immediately that I was with the wrong crowd. I pondered over the easiest way to escape from them. They had already been drinking along the way to raise their courage.

They were just eating when we reached the wedding house, and we joined them. We circled the table with our plates, and each one found a place wherever he could. I stayed with the boys, since I did not know anyone else. One of them came to me with a glass in his hand.

"There plenty of wedding punch over there in the big bowl, and you can scoop up all you want with a dipper."

"Here, let me taste," he took a glass and sipped it. Then he let it circulate among the others and handed it to me.

"Taste it, girl," he said. "It's good."

"It is," I said, trying not to make a face as I drew it away from my lips.

"Take a glass and let's go and get some from the kitchen."

"You boys go on ahead. I'll be right there," I said.

The boys began to crowd toward the kitchen. There were a lot of people in the place. I turned suddenly toward the open door and ran out to the yard. Luckily my bicycle was on top of the pile. I went quickly to the road and around a corner so that no one could follow me. I rode the three kilometers to the church as if my life depended on it. There I checked to see that no one was following. I had been right in thinking that booze was much sweeter to them than any girl. "Of all the things to get mixed up in. I was a fool to come. Why didn't I turn around right at the church? It's good that I got out of it so easily." But another voice said: "Lasse was so nice when we met, but now he was so different. He even offered that booze to me. Fie, of all the muck people drink. My mouth still tastes nauseating! Luckily no one knows where I am. I'll tell the lady of the house that I was out looking at the landscape around here."

Saul and I arranged to meet one Sunday. There were about ninety kilometers separating us. I packed a lunch bag of sandwiches and a thermos of coffee. I had biked about twenty-five kilometers and was walking the bike up a long hill. He was coming, I could see him far off. In a stretch of woods Saul tossed his bicycle and mine into a ditch. He snatched me in his arms and whirled me around breathlessly. Finally he managed to utter, between kisses: "You came! You came! I thought you had taken another road! Let me look at you. You haven't changed a bit since we parted four months ago."

"Still the same refugee girl. You started early, since you've come so far. I left at nine, as we agreed."

"I sneaked off early so you wouldn't have to come as far. I thought that maybe you weren't in good condition yet. You have a new outfit too. A white blouse and a blue skirt—the colors of Finland's flag. My Finland girl."

Sisu Mother

The lake gleamed blue through gaps in the trees. We found a path that led to the lake. We walked, arms around each other's necks and sang:

*A little trail leads through the woods
under aged linden trees.
On summer nights it was my path
to happiness and heart's ease.*

We sat on a green, mossy hillock, hugging and kissing endlessly. There was so much to talk about. Occasionally we snacked on the lunch. The coffee substitute tasted like some divine miracle beverage. The summer day passed too quickly. Pentecost was in two weeks, and we decided to become engaged then.

The place where my family lived was about a kilometer away from our fields. The only building on our land was an old threshing barn.

"Listen Mother, I found a neat little room in the loft of that threshing barn. It has clean walls and a smooth floor. We could fix up the inside. The cows would be close by in the morning, and all our supplies for building the house are near there. What if I move there to sleep?"

"In the barn loft—aren't you afraid of ghosts?" said Mother. "They always say that threshing barns are haunted. (The superstition arose from the fact that bodies were washed and prepared for burial in these buildings.) But it would be good if someone were near to watch the building supplies. Have you talked to Father about it?" she asked.

"Not yet, because I just got the idea today. I'll go there this evening to brush away the cobwebs and wash the floor with water to get all the dust out. We can take the bed there tomorrow."

Mother kept on wondering and shaking her head doubtfully.

I talked it over with Father, and he pondered, "It would be good, all right, if someone were there. The times are so bad. You might even take care of the cows, but aren't you afraid to be there alone?"

"The girl is sure to come running home when old Kaisa comes drifting along at night. Someone saw Kaisa haunting the place. She lay there dead in the loft for more than a week. Devil take it, I wouldn't even go walking there in the middle of the night," said Väinö, the owner of the house.

"What if Samppa came with you. Then it would be safer," Mother suggested.

"I wouldn't go into that loft if you paid me," snapped the boy.

"I don't believe in any ghosts," I said defiantly.

The next day Samppa and I moved my bed into the frightful threshing barn loft. I even found an old chair for the place.

"You didn't know you would be honored in this way, you battered old chair. You'll now be the queen's throne in this beautiful, festive hall," I laughed, in a good mood as I washed the chair. In the evening I headed, bravely laughing, to my bed. Väinö shook his head. "I warned you, you fool," he called after me.

The summer evening was light when I reached my home. The fresh smell of the pinewoods wafted toward me, mingled with the grainy smell of the threshing barn. I could not believe the odor had been preserved for so long; the threshing barn had not been used for years for threshing in the old-fashioned way. The smoke from fires for drying the grain had not penetrated the loft to blacken the walls. "The chair looks like an orphan, I have to get some kind of table to keep it company," I said to myself. Going down the stepladder, I fetched two wooden boxes and put one atop the other. Then I dragged them up and put a clean towel over them. They went well with the chair.

I went down again, found a bottle somewhere, which I washed and filled anew. All I needed now was some flowers. Wild rosemary was just beginning to bloom. I broke off a few sprigs, and sniffed their overpowering fragrance. "There won't be too much of an odor here, since there is a large opening into the straw shed in the back wall. Now my room is homey. I'll drag the ladder up inside, just in case, so that no uninvited guests can come in. I hope I'll be left in peace here, although the story will soon spread in the village that a silly girl is sleeping in a threshing barn."

Contented with my achievements, I went to bed. I enjoyed the fresh air, but sleep would not come to my eyes. I had probably dozed off, when I awoke to the sound of scraping. I started, and froze with tension, I opened my eyes slowly. On the roof I saw pale stripes flickering back and forth. Now I remembered where I was and Väinö's warning. *That doesn't look like any ghost,* I thought. The flickering and scratching continued in the same way. It dawned on me that there had to be some natural explanation. There had to be a moon, since it was so light. The light fell in stripes through some kind of opening. A wind had begun to blow, and nearby tree branches were causing the scraping. Satisfied, I turned onto the other side and slept sweetly. In the morning I awakened to a huge bird concert. Swallows must surely have had a nest in the straw barn, for the sound from there was constant. Now one was sitting on the edge of the opening in the wall. "Good morning, did you come to greet your new neighbor? I won't disturb you; there's room for us all," I said.

The bird chirped a small trill and flew away. What a beautiful morning in the fresh air, and I had my own home. I was the happiest girl in the world.

After milking, I of course went home. They all stared at me wide-eyed, perhaps wondering that I was still alive.

"How did the night go, did you see anything frightening?" Mother was the first to ask.

It sounded as if she had been very worried about me.

"Nothing at all, I slept like a log. The birds woke me up a little too early in the morning, though."

"Thank God, I started to think about what that man said last night and if anything was happening to you. It's so strange to sleep in a threshing barn."

"There's nothing to be afraid of there. I've done no one any wrong, and even if they haunt the place, there are good ghosts, too."

It was a few days till Pentecost. Saul and I had planned that he would come on Friday night. I decided to test myself and spend the night here with him. My thoughts were in a confused whirl. He would be here in two nights. What would he think of this room? Perhaps he would be afraid like all the others.

It was hard to get to sleep, but at last I did. I had a strange dream: I had arranged to meet Saul in a city somewhere, and when I arrived, I saw him in the distance, drunk, and fighting in a gang of men. I withdrew behind the corner of a building and watched what was happening. The men went on fighting, with Saul as the chief cause of mischief. Someone's mouth was already running blood. The police came and took Saul away, and the others disappeared too. After that I was in a room somewhere. Our wedding was supposed to be held there, and we were waiting for the groom. I alone knew that he would not come, for the police had taken him away. His relatives were there, his sisters and brothers whom I had never seen before. His brother Masa looked so good and peaceful that he must surely be good-natured. Why hadn't I fallen in love with him instead of Saul, for whom I was waiting in despair? At that point I woke up.

The dream remained so vividly in my mind that I could not get back to sleep, although it was the middle of the night. My thoughts were in a crazy whirl. I felt my future to be uncertain; after all I knew very little about him. I had never met his family. What would I do when he came? The dream was some kind of warning. The horrible dream I had had at home in Karelia had come true. If I only knew where I might find a fortuneteller, I would have gone to ask for advice. I was so alone now; there was no one I could talk to. Not even Mother. She wouldn't understand.

I got up in the morning tired and downcast. Even the concert of the birds could not cheer me up. The dream kept coming to mind for the entire day. One part of me said: "Don't believe in such things. Has he ever deceived you? Don't you remember last summer? He came every time he promised to, and he never smelled of liquor. He said he had even quit smoking during the war. He must have a lot of determination if he could just go ahead and do that. Not everyone could."

Friday morning I told the family that we planned to become engaged on Saturday. Father thought for a long time and then said in a troubled voice, "I don't know him at all, but if you've arranged it, then I have nothing against it. But don't leave yet because we need you to work at home. If you could be here this summer until we finish the house, then we could have the wedding in the fall."

"We haven't talked about getting married yet. There's no hurry. I still have to make some kind of trousseau," I said.

"Oh dear, bringing a sweetheart into a place like this," Mother put in.

"Don't worry, Mother, the place doesn't matter. He loves me; at least I think so. If he doesn't then he can leave. He has asked me to share his life with him. Make enough coffee substitute in the morning so that you can serve him too. I told him he would have to ask Father in the Karelian way."

On Friday evening I went to meet him in the appointed place. I hardly recognized him. He was wearing a new suit, and was overjoyed to see me. Noticing my melancholy, he said, "What's the matter, darling? Are you having second thoughts? I've been dreaming of this day every night."

"I'm tired today. I guess I must be too tense. This is a serious step we're planning to take. On New Year's Eve, we made a vow to share our lives. I've thought the matter over a lot. Are you sure you will love me in bad times too? I'm a little bit afraid; I don't know much about keeping a house, and all our food will be rationed."

"I don't have a house to take care of. You know that. There'll be just the two of us. There's no cow to milk and no pig to make headcheese from. I hope you'll have the best days of your life."

We arrived at the threshing barn, and I explained the situation.

"This is a nice room. Have you seen any ghosts?" he asked.

"Everyone tried to scare me with stories about them. I've been here two weeks already, and I love it. In the morning the birds wake me up with a concert. You know I love music. Often it's a little too early, but then I have time to think about everything under the sun."

We did not really sleep at all. He did not demand more than gentle caresses and long, hot kisses. I could tell that he would have been ready to go farther, but he was a man and kept his word.

As we dressed in the morning, Saul said with a mischievous gleam in his eye:

"Not every boy sets out on his engagement trip from the loft of a threshing barn."

"I doubt if any do," I said.

Down below, we washed our faces in a nearby brook. Everything went well with my parents and now there lay ahead of us a twenty-kilometer ride to the station on our bicycles, then a trip by train to Pori, the nearest city. He wanted to buy a wedding ring too, although we had not talked about it. I had no money to buy him a ring, for I had not earned anything for half a year. I had saved a little money, but it had disappeared little by little. Some of it I had loaned to Father, but I didn't want to ask him to give it back. He had too many money worries while trying to build a new home. Saul seemed to understand that.

There was a wedding at the neighbors on Pentecost Sunday. Mother urged us to go, since they had been kind enough to ask us, even though we had just come to the neighborhood. The couple had been married during the day, and guests had been invited for the evening.

We arrived so late that they were already dancing. The bride's white veil swirled in the dancing. It occurred to me that her waist seemed a little tight, but she seemed unconcerned by that fact. If I were in her condition, I could not have worn the white veil, and I hoped that my dream of a white veil would be realized.

After a few dances a neighbor boy, Jouni, whom I knew, came to ask me to dance. We had a lot to talk about.

"Is that one of your relatives visiting? The one you're dancing with?" he asked me.

"Well, how shall I put it? He's my sweetheart; we got engaged yesterday. We've known each other for a year now."

The boy looked surprised. After the dance, he came to congratulate us, and began talking to Saul. "We young folks thought we would have some new blood at our small farm doings when Elsie and Samppa moved here to Jokiperä. So you're going to snatch the girl out from under our noses?"

Saul was taken aback and could not answer. When Jouni had left, Saul looked at me sharply.

"It looks as if you've already found some boyfriends here. He was very friendly. I thought you were faithful to me."

"My good man, don't even think there's anything between us! Our lands border on his, and we asked for government aid to drain the swamp there. I had to go to the church village once with Jouni when neither Father nor Samppa had time. There had to be one from each family to sign a paper. We both rode our own bicycles, and it was in the middle of the day. Since then Jouni has stopped a couple of times at the building to see how things are going. He promised to come and help when he doesn't have to work in the fields."

Saul seemed to be pacified. *Why had he made an issue of it? I thought. He's jealous, but that's common when one is deeply in love. Or doesn't he trust me? And why?* From then on, talking did not come easily to us, and we left after a couple of dances.

In the morning he seemed his former self. It was Pentecost Monday and he left in the evening to bicycle home, since the next day was a workday, promising to come again on Saturday.

In two weeks sad news arrived. Saul's father had died. I still did not know any of his relatives, but I was asked to come and be with the family a few days early to help with the funeral preparations. I rode my bicycle to the house where I had worked in Peränne and was received with open arms. I still had some things there. In the evening, the lady of the house thrust a clean sheet under my arm.

"You can go to your former room; no one is living there. We couldn't get anyone to come when you left, so our son Heikki came home, and we turned over the whole farm to him. We would still have kept it if you had stayed with us."

"I would have stayed, but I got sick and had a heart attack to boot. The doctor warned me that I shouldn't strain myself. I've woven the linen thread you gave me into cloth, since I wasn't able to do anything else. Then we moved to Kihniö, and there was plenty of work to do there."

"Well, when are the wedding bells going to ring?"

"Not for a while yet. The family needs me at home, since we're building a house. Maybe late in the fall, when the house is finished."

"Poor dear Elsie, you don't even have time to get married. Here's a little money as a wedding gift for you. I might forget it in the morning. I'm getting old and I forget things, no matter how important they are."

"Thank you, thank you so much! I'll buy something with it to remind me of you for the rest of my life. Good night."

"Good night, my girl," called the lady as she went down the steps.

In the morning I drove to the Åhtäri church village to say hello to my friend Saimi. She already had a baby a few months old.

"Are you ready for this?" asked Saimi, changing the baby's diaper.

"I don't know if I could handle such a little one," I said.

"Well, this is what it comes to, there's no escaping it. Mother will take you, darling," Saimi cooed to the baby.

In the evening Saul came to meet me, and we rode to his home. Heart beating rapidly, I greeted his brothers and sisters under the birch trees in the yard outside the house. I felt a prickling in every cell of my body as their eyes surveyed me. To my amazement, I recognized one of the brothers as someone I has seen in the dream. His name was the same too—Masa. Cold shivers ran down my back, and I could see the dream clearly before my eyes. I felt stupid and clumsy, my thoughts contradictory and far removed from reality, but I regained my composure to some extent when we went into the dark *tupa* to meet Saul's mother.

She made me feel at home by speaking to me as her child. She was not old, but arthritis had bent her over, and her hands were misshapen. She had given birth to and raised nine children. I liked her at first sight. She spoke softly and calmly. Saul had always spoken respectfully of her, but he had criticized his father. Now, of course, I heard only good of him, since he rested in the coffin.

The oldest daughter, Alli, was directing the funeral preparations. She was the mistress of a large farm a few kilometers away. She had a two-year-old boy, and I thought another child might come any minute. *How can a person stretch so much*, I thought in horror. One of the brothers was newly married, and his wife's belly was about two months behind Alli's. *It looks as if additions to our family are guaranteed*, I thought. I guessed that they were looking at me to see if there were any reason for our getting married quickly. There were two younger sisters, with whom I was soon acquainted. Another sister, Taimi, arrived from Savo with her husband. She, too, was quite visibly pregnant.

On Sunday morning the house was decked out for the event. Alli and Taimi could not go to the church; they would stay and prepare the food. The summer was at its most beautiful; it was only a week till Midsummer. The lilacs were just blooming, spreading their lovely fragrance around the yard. Large old weeping birches shaded the house, which lay on the slope of a hill. From the windows, one could see a deep blue pond, its surface mirror calm. It was a romantic landscape. Leaving the house, one descended into a hollow, where an old wooden bridge crossed a stream. Then another steep climb before one reached the road. Although this was already part of South Ostrobothnia, there were no open, burned-over fields here. The landscape was more like that of central Finland. Steep rocky hills and crags, with deep valleys between them. There were fields here and there on the gentler slopes. Bread had not been wrung easily from these lands. People must have cleared the land and built their houses when they were young, and brought up large families on the side. No wonder they sank into early graves. Now the house looked old, its red ocher paint faded almost completely.

The funeral was at ten o'clock, and we all went on a truck, which Saul drove. In the evening, all the people of the neighborhood gathered at the large house. They all knew each other—I was the only stranger, but they were all very friendly to me. In the early evening, Alli began to feel bad. Her husband had driven over with a horse, and they set off hastily for home. At night Taimi took sick, and one of the brothers went to the neighbor's house to call up a midwife. She was not at home, but a physician arrived in his own automobile. The birth was difficult, but the result was a healthy girl. The infant's father was there to witness the birth, but he fainted at the sight of blood.

In the morning we heard that the midwife had been at Alli's house, and twins had been born there, a boy and a girl. It was remarkable! One of the family had died, and three were born in his place!

I stayed at Saul's home for a few more days. On a warm summer day, we decided to go rowing on Liesjärvi. We took along worms and fishing rods. It was a bicycle ride of a few kilometers to get there. We got a boat from a relative's house.

The sun was being prodigal with its rays, but nevertheless we got a plentiful haul of big perch and even roach. Suddenly a wind and a dark cloud arose. The heat had been a harbinger of it, and now the thunder began to roar. "The shore is too far, but that island is closer. How can the weather change so quickly. It's starting to rain already." Saul scarcely had time to get the words out as he began rowing into a head wind with all his might. We reached a bed of reeds, which beat against us. It was shallow enough now, so we leaped into the water and dragged the boat the rest of the way to land. Taking the fish with us, we went down a path to look for shelter from the rain. We found a little lean-to where fishermen had apparently spent the night. The shower ended as quickly as it had begun. We fried the fish over a campfire. They did taste good.

"This turned out to be a real expedition. It's a good thing it rained; otherwise we would never have come here," I said, hungrily chewing on the fish. They are so good when they're fresh from the coals."

"Yaah, it's nice here, and we're in no hurry. Let's find a good place to swim. It's too shallow and full of reeds here."

We changed into our bathing suits behind a bush and followed a path along the shore. It was too shallow there; perhaps it would be deeper on the other shore. In the midst of everything, we began to hug each other passionately, leaning into a tree. "I haven't had a single kiss today," said Saul, and began to caress me hotly. I could say nothing but enjoyed his embrace to the full. My back scraped against the rough bark of the tree, and I felt it prick through my bathing suit. Tearing myself free from his arms, I ran toward the lake, with Saul in pursuit, shouting: "Hey, don't do that!"

I was already in the water. He stood on the shore and shouted, half-mocking, "What are you afraid of? You're like Aino of the North, running away from her suitor! I'm not as old and bearded as Väinämöinen!"

"No, no you're not, but still you're from the Kalevala. And do you know that my other name is Vellamo? I ran into the water to seek protection from Ahti."

"Shit, that Ahti is a lot hornier than I am," he said laughing, and began to wade after me.

"Ha, ha, you came after me anyway. You didn't dare leave me here alone, in case someone should snatch me from under the water," I teased.

He looked at me sharply, but said nothing. But soon everything was forgotten in the blue waves. We fished on the way home.

"You have good luck fishing," I said, as he pulled a large perch into the boat. "I don't even get a nibble."

"Even the fish know that you were mean to me on the island. Why did you run away? Don't you feel like it at all? It would have been so romantic there. We belong to each other. At least tell me that you feel like it sometimes—or is there something wrong with you?" Saul grumbled unhappily.

"I do have feelings, and sometimes passionate ones, but my brain always wins out. Luckily the water was close enough to cool them off. We've managed to hold out this far, so I hope we can till the end," I said.

"When will that big day come? We should decide that too. I put in an application to be a driver for the Co-op store, but I won't hear from them for a few weeks. It will be hard to find a place to live. I'll try to find a job somewhere that has a place to live along with it. I don't have to work here."

"We do need a place to live. Father says that if I can stay at home until the house is finished, they'll have a small wedding for us. It will probably take until the end of October. We have to keep waiting for building supplies," I explained.

"I guess there's nothing to do but wait. I may be able to come for a week's vacation during the summer to help with the building. We can be together for at least that time," Saul said hopefully.

The summer passed quickly and the evenings grew darker. The worst thing was going to the loft of the threshing barn in the dark. I had only a flashlight to light my way. I had just gotten to bed one night when I heard someone's voice. I raised my head and plainly heard these words, "Elsie, Elsie, are you there?" It was our neighbor Erma's voice.

"I am. I just came. What's the matter?"

"Come to our house as quickly as you can. When Emppu gets drunk, he beats me, and it scares the children. He won't do anything if there is a visitor in the house."

"Does he have a weapon? If he does, I won't come. Then it's better to call the police."

"He doesn't. He punches me with his fists. I'm going now. I went out to get water, and ran over here at the same time. Just don't tell him that I asked you to come," cried the woman as she ran away.

In a short time, I knocked at their door, my heart pounding in fear.

"Who's there? Come in," I heard a man bellow.

"Good evening. It gets dark so early that I don't feel sleepy yet. I thought I'd come here and knit on a stocking while chatting with a neighbor."

"Yaah, eight o'clock is early to go to bed. Now you have a good life. It will be different when you get married. Then you'd better keep out of the way with a wet brat when your old man is in a bad mood. That's what the life of a poor man's wife is like," Emppu ranted.

"Well, if that's what it's like, there's still time for me to change my mind. But things aren't the same with everyone."

"It's been that way since the beginning of time, and it's not going to change. You're no better than anyone else," Emppu declared positively.

"No, I'm no better than other women," I conceded. I was seething within. *No man will beat me more than once,* I thought. *I'll walk out even if I have a wet child on my arm if a man were so vicious as to beat me.*

Emppu began to tire of his own blabbering and went into his bedroom.

"He's gone to bed now, but stay a little while until we're sure he's asleep. Things went very well now. Would you like me to make some tea? I know you don't care for the coffee substitute so late in the evening."

"Well, I'm not in any hurry. And I don't think I'll fall asleep after all this. I'll admit I was awfully afraid when I came."

"Everything went well. Emppu has always liked you. I was afraid he would hit me and then I would have to go to bed with him. We've been married five years and have three children. The first was on the way when we got married. He's careful when he's sober. Every one of our children was started when he was drunk. Raija is a year old now. I might easily get pregnant."

'Oh my God! Aren't they born defective if they're conceived when drunk?" I asked, horrified.

"Kaarina is five years old, and she's a sweet girl. She's crazy about you, but I can't let her go to bother you all the time. I don't know about the boy; he died at the age of two. He had some stomach problem from the start, the doctor said. It was hard on Emppu and me. He was pig-drunk for two weeks."

"Isn't there some way for a woman to keep from getting pregnant?" I asked. "I don't know anything about these women's things."

"I can't give you any advice, and every person is different, but I saw that a paper was selling a book *Pregnant Again after Three Children*. What if the two of us order it together?" the woman said.

We wrote out the order, and I took the letter with me to mail. Emppu did not wake up again, and I groped my way to bed in the dark. Thinking of what Emppu had said and the way he carried on, I could not get to sleep. If one was in love, why should he be so nasty and beat a person? There had never been any fights in our home. I couldn't even remember my parents ever arguing. No, Emppu was just bad natured. I had heard that a person showed his true nature when tipsy. I had never seen Saul drunk. Where could one get a bottle of whiskey—that too was rationed. With these thoughts in mind, I fell asleep.

The wedding of a relative was being held in Muurame, and I went there. Saul came to meet me in Jyväskylä. There was still time before the train's departure, and we went to a park and started to hug each other there. Two nursing sisters were walking through the park as if on some kind of inspection tour. They stopped, and one of them said in a very official-sounding tone of voice, "What are you doing here? You can't make love here."

We stood up, and Saul began to explain doubtfully, "We're engaged and we're waiting for a train. We didn't know that you're not allowed to sit here. I didn't see a sign prohibiting it."

"Excuse us. In that case, you can stay."

"Do people really make love here in the park. It looks as if they were driving them away. I've heard that in the city there are women who are willing to lie with men in the bushes," Saul said. We started walking toward the station.

I got off the train at Keuruu and stopped in to see my aunt's family. Her husband was away, and she was delighted to see me. "Oh, if you could only stay and help me for a few days so I could get this laundry done. Arja takes up so much of my time," she said.

While she did the wash, I took care of the lively, year-old girl, and cleaned the house, which needed a cleaning badly. "Do you remember in Tyrvää, when they took the twins to the hospital? They would have been five years old now if they had lived. It was their good fortune to pass away. Life is nothing great when you start from scratch. It may be better for you since your man has a trade. I hope you won't have a lot of children," my aunt warned me. I did not have the nerve to start asking her for advice. Soon I heard the sound of snoring from her bed. I could not sleep. If only I had the courage to speak to Saul about these matters before we got married. Or did I dare get married at all?

The next morning I started out for home. Mother wanted an Angora cat, and my aunt had a whole brood of them. With the cat-box in hand, I walked singing toward the station, which was a couple of kilometers away. I was sitting on the train with the box in my lap when the conductor eyed it suspiciously. First there was the sound of scratching and then a miserable "Meeow."

"Is there a cat in that?" He pointed to the box.

"There is, but it's just a little one. A tiny kitten."

"It can't stay in a passenger coach. Why didn't you tell them when you bought the ticket," growled the conductor. "We can't put it into the baggage coach now. Go into the corridor for the rest of the trip."

"Thank you, I will," I said humbly, and left.

It was twenty kilometers from the station to Jokiperä. I started walking toward home, hoping a vehicle would come along so I could thumb a ride. If I got to the church village on time, I could get a bus there. A couple of logging trucks roared toward the station, but not a single soul came in the direction I was headed.

It was a brisk autumn day. Cat-box in hand, I marched along the road. When I reached the church village, the bus had left. There was nothing to do but trudge the last ten kilometers on foot. I began to dream. If I were rich, I would buy a car. I was sure I would learn to drive easily. Then I would give a ride to anyone who needed it. I would speed this distance in no time at all. Now pacing it off on foot took two hours, even though I tried to walk with long, rapid strides, breaking into a run on downhills. I could feel my belly growling. My aunt had made a lunch for me, but it had been left on the kitchen table. The food would have tasted good now when I was walking. There was a bright, gurgling brook. I left the kitten at the roadside, lay down beside the brook, and drank the cool water thirstily from my palms. It would do no harm to wash most of the dust from my face, so I splashed the water over it. I was just drying my face in the sun when a truck roared by. It was traveling so fast that it sent the cat-box spinning from the roadside. My eyes opened wide when I saw it splash into the middle of the brook. The poor kitten leaped inside the box and set it spinning like a mill wheel in the current.

And the yowls the kitten let out! I would not have believed that so small an animal could emit such loud and ugly sounds from its throat. Finally I was able to fish the box out onto dry land. A suspicious looking, brown fluid ran from one corner of the box. The smell also told me what the kitten had done in its panic.

I had a paper bag with me, which had a change of clothes in it—after all, I had been to a wedding. I groped through it, thinking that all the clothing would go into the wash anyway. I decided to give the cat a cold bath: "Don't kick and scratch so much, darling. I'll wash you and you can go and lie on the warm clothing in that paper bag. Let me dry you, and you can lie on that party dress like a crown princess," I chatted to the cat. It did calm down when it got to lie down, and was soon purring contentedly.

Finally I reached home when the sun was casting its last rays. Wearily I dumped the box on the floor in front of Mother.

"Oh, how sweet and pretty it is," said Mother, taking the kitten carefully into her lap. "Did she stay in that bag so nicely during the whole trip?" I told her the whole story.

"That kitten must really be hungry. I left Keuruu at nine," I said wearily. Mother went at once to get it some milk.

"Here, kitty. Here kitty, kitty, kitty."

One of the farmers in the neighborhood had hurt his back just at the busiest time of the grain harvest. His wife was going around asking for volunteers. Of course we promised to go and help our neighbors. As she left, the woman said, "I'll prepare a good supper for you, and we can dance after that. There's plenty of room and a smooth floor in the drying barn."

Neighbor Emppu had cut the grain and bound it into sheaves with his machine, and the rest of us were following up on his work. We finished the work in good time, and after eating, we went home to clean up for the dance.

Emppu's wife had asked my mother to stay with her children, so Emppu, his wife, Samppa, and I walked together to the dance. It was a walk of about a kilometer, and the music could already be heard when we got there. We joined in the dancing, with Samppa as my partner. Emppu came to get me for the next dance, and I could smell the whiskey on his breath. After a few dances, Emppu went out with some other men. Soon Erma came over and began to pull me outside with a look of panic on her face.

"Have you seen Emppu inside? I was talking to the lady of the house on the porch, and I don't know where he disappeared to."

"I don't think I've seen him since he went outside with some men," I said, peering around.

Erma went out to look. Our neighbor Jouni came to ask me to dance. We were both good at doing the polka. During a pause between songs, I saw Erma in the doorway looking around. When the number ended, I hurried over to her.

"What happened? You look all white," I said anxiously.

"Come with me. Let's go home. You can hear about it there," Erma mumbled.

"Did you find Emppu?" I asked, when we reached the main road.

"I found him," wailed Erma, and began to weep uncontrollably.

"Don't. Try to calm down now." I put my arm around her shoulders, which were still shaking with sobs. Gradually she calmed down. We walked in silence, the sand grating under our feet.

"There was a girl there from Mustikkakorpi, and a number of men were hanging around her. Emppu was with them. You can guess what they're doing. It cut me to the heart, and I almost fainted. All the devils that are born into this world! That slut! It's too bad you had to leave the dance early, but I was afraid to go alone. I thought I might even have a heart attack," she said, pleading for pardon.

"It wasn't at all early. I don't have to stay till the end. I don't even dare tell Saul about this—he's so jealous. This is a terrible world! I've heard and I believe that they do just about anything in the cities, but here in Jokiperä? It makes me want to throw up," I said in disgust.

"I couldn't agree more. My stomach turns over and there's a bitter taste in my mouth all the time."

"What will you do? Do you think Emppu will dare to show his face tomorrow? He was a little drunk when he asked me to dance."

"Probably the farm owner offered drinks to the men who came to work, and there is someone who makes bootleg liquor too," Erma went on.

"What about other women? Have there been others before?"

"I've suspected it sometimes, but now I know. I really have a rotten husband. We get along well when he's sober, but he's worse than the devil when he's drunk."

"Do you think he'll be angry tonight when he comes home?"

"I shouldn't think so. I think he'll leave me alone."

"Marriage is supposed to be a calm harbor, but yours seems to be a pretty stormy one. I'm supposed to tie the knot, but I'm terribly afraid. I don't know him too well."

"He seems to be different. They aren't all the same," Erma began to console me. "I knew Emppu well, he was from a neighboring village. I knew he was kind of wild, but I found that attractive. I was a lively chick myself, he wasn't the first one for me. And I can't get a divorce. How could I live with two children? I know he won't pay for their support. I'll forget this in time. I'll try for the sake of the children."

We were already at Erma's home. The children were already asleep, and Mother was able to leave for home.

"Come home with me, too," she asked. "I haven't been out in the dark for a long time."

"Yes, I have the time, I'll just go and get my flashlight from the building," I said, and ran to the corner of the house to pick it up.

"Tell me the truth. Have you seen any ghosts when you've been sleeping in the threshing barn all summer," Mother whispered to me as we passed the building.

"I haven't seen or heard anything, but it would be good if I could move out now when it's so dark and rainy in the fall."

"What happened to Emppu, since he didn't come home with you?"

"He fell in with a bunch of men who were drinking. He really does work hard. He cut all the grain with a horse," I said.

"Remember, don't go there no matter how Erma begs you to. You never know what a man might do when he's drunk. Let them lick their wounds by themselves, the way dogs do. I've never seen anything like it before. It's not bad if a man takes a drink once in a while to ease his nerves. But why they should raise such a row I can never understand," Mother rattled on.

We were already at the door. We said goodnight, and I retraced my steps to my roost. I did not feel tired, although it was already late. Too many things had happened that day to occupy my mind.

Saul had a new job as a mechanic with a large bus line in Jalasjärvi, some thirty kilometers away. He was promised lodging by Christmas. Our house was almost finished too. We were already living in it, but finishing work was still being done. Plans were under way for a small wedding.

Everything was rationed, and we could not buy clothing from anywhere. I stopped in at Jyväskylä, where I was able to rent a white wedding gown. Anu still had her veil in storage, and promised to lend it to me. They would bring it when they came for the wedding. The church was so far away that it was better to have the pastor come to the house. In other words, we did not have a vehicle to drive to the church. There was only one truck in the neighborhood, and we used that to fetch the pastor from the church. Saul arrived the evening before and brought the bridal bouquet of white chrysanthemums. The pastor was already waiting, book in hand, when we walked into the *tupa*. Saul walked on my left and switched to my right before the pastor. Just as the pastor began to speak of the significance of marriage, I had an urge to sneeze. In panic, I buried my face in the bouquet of flowers, since there was no handkerchief available. As I sniffed the flowers my eyes began to sting and my nose itched more than ever. Fortunately my aunt noticed and secretly flicked a handkerchief to me. Finally the time came for me to say, "I do," and I almost stammered it.

During the congratulations, my eyes watered, and I suddenly had to sniffle. People thought I was overcome with emotion. When it was over, I went into the hallway and said to the nearest people:

"Take these flowers somewhere or throw them out in the snow. Their smell stung my eyes and made me cry through the entire wedding."

"Don't do that," said Valma. She sniffed at the flowers. "They do have a strong smell. Atchoo!" She opened the door and tossed the bouquet out into the snow. "And I thought you were crying because you were so happy. I believe now that it was the flowers," she said, wiping her eyes.

The food had been served and the tables stacked for dancing. A five-row button accordion had just set the tempo. We had earlier arranged that the accordionist would play the wedding waltz. I would have wanted it to be "The Vagabond's Waltz," for that suited me as a poor wanderer on this earth. But Saul would have none of it. He recommended "The Waltz of Yesteryear." I didn't want that, for I had no past, only a future. We decided on the beautiful "Wildflower Waltz." For I was a child of nature who loved heather and wild rosemary.

The waltz began. He bowed manfully, and I smiled happily. I had always loved the waltz. *This is our own waltz*, I thought. He held me gently against his breast, our cheeks touched, and I felt an electric shock in every cell of my body. A prayer rose from my heart: *The Lord bless us and shelter us. The Lord make His face to shine upon us and be merciful to us. The Lord turn his face to us and give us peace everlasting.*

I awoke as if from a dream when I heard the musician sing: "I am forgiven; I seem to have found the road to Paradise again. . . . The trees are greening in the woods, Sunday wedding bells are ringing. . . . Knowingly we smile at each other. . . . Only we know. . . . It was the flowers that caused our wedding."

Now everyone began to dance, and naturally the bride was sought out. It was, after all, a family party, and many of my relatives had not even seen me since my childhood. Finally the groom got a chance to dance with me, and he said a little sourly, "You could refuse to dance with the others. This is too much. I never get a chance."

"Try to understand. I can't refuse. They are my friends and relatives. You have to be a little quicker when the music begins," I said with a laugh. "After today we can be together day and night. When can we get to move into our own place?"

"In two weeks, just in time for Christmas. I'll go to work that Tuesday and come back on Saturday. I'll get a truck from the place I work and come for you with it."

Erma had told me earlier that if we had a lot of overnight visitors, we could use their guest room. So we decided to spend our wedding night there.

We left in the middle of the last waltz and walked hand in hand through the falling snow towards our neighbor's.

My future's so bright I gotta wear shades.

Life is not what you want, but what you get.
Stick a geranium in your hat and be happy.

Quotes from The Best of Barbara Johnson, by Barbara Johnson, Inspirational Press: New York, 1996.

CHAPTER VI

The truck roared along the snowy road on a dark December night. We were on our way to our first shared home. Snow had drifted across the road thickly in places, but the tires plowed through it. The truck stopped.

"I'll check to see if we can drive any closer to the building," said Saul.

I looked around curiously to see whatever I could through the frosted window. There was a large main building with a light in only one window and an outside lamp turned toward the yard. In a smaller building in the yard there was light in one window. Was that where we were going?

"I can't drive any closer. We'll have to carry our things from here. The lady has warmed the room, since she knew we were coming. A retired couple owns this place. I bought metal bed frames, and they're already here. They gave us a table and a couple of chairs."

I shook our landlady's hand, and she began to chat in a friendly way, "Welcome. This is a humble place, but you can look for a better one when you get a start. The housing shortage is so severe. You can manage to live here as long as there are only two of you. Aren't you newlyweds?" she asked.

"Yes. Only a couple of weeks," I said softly.

"I'll leave now. If you need anything, just come and ask," said the woman, wrapping her sweater around her.

"Good night, and sleep well in your new place."

"Good night, and thanks for helping us get a start," I said.

Saul had to take the truck back to where he worked. He had a bicycle there. While he was gone, I unpacked the indispensable things and made the bed. It was already late. He was back quickly, even though the place he took the truck was a kilometer away.

"Are you hungry?" I asked. "I brought bread and butter if you want to snack."

"I'm not hungry. This is where I want you, darling." He clutched me around the waist and took me to the bed.

Now we had to cope with the realities of everyday life. Almost all food was rationed, and even then we could not always get it. I had saved several days' ration so that I could buy a half-liter of milk. I had to go to the dairy cooperative in the morning, and it was still dark. The weather was rather mild. I left with the kick sled. There was a steep slope down from the main road to the dairy, which was on a riverbank. It was very slippery, and I slid down it with the sled, my feet sliding on the ice, and almost went through the window of the dairy.

Leaving I tried to climb up along one side of the road. Just when I was halfway up, someone came sliding down crosswise with a sled and knocked me into a heap. An old woman got up, complaining about her head. My elbow hurt a little, but the glass jar containing many days ration of milk was broken and the milk spilled on the ground. A milkman with his horse smiled as we rose and straightened up our clothing and asked, "Did anything more serious happen? Are there any broken bones? Grab hold of the corner of the sleigh, and I'll take you to the main road. No one can get up that slippery place."

"Let the milk go," said the old woman. "I'm going home now, since I can get a ride. The boys can come and get the sleigh. It's all twisted and will have to be straightened out before you can get anywhere with it. It really is skull-splitting slippery," she lamented.

Saul came home for lunch every day, which was pleasant. I told him of the morning's adventure when I went to get the milk and showed him the elbow, which I had bandaged because it bled.

"That was a stupid thing to happen. It's not so slippery out that a person can't stand up."

I looked at him oddly. Why was he talking like that? This shouldn't have caused a quarrel between us. I complained bitterly about the loss of the milk. He left for work without saying a word.

Why was he so cross? It was almost as if he were accusing me of something. I was glad to have come out of it with only a scare. I could have been badly hurt. Was he having problems at work, was something wrong there? I would try to forget this when he came home at night. I waited tensely for his arrival, and went out to the hallway to kiss him as usual. Everything seemed to be well, and I sighed in relief.

It was Christmas Eve, and I was waiting for him to come home. His work was supposed to end at two, and it was already nearly three. He had promised to bring a Christmas tree when he came. The only trimmings would be cotton batting and two candles. Dinner was ready: a small roast, potatoes, and oatmeal porridge with a berry sauce. I could see no one from the window; all the food would go stale.

Sisu Mother

The woman of the house stopped in on her way to warm the sauna to wish me a good Christmas. I told her about my worries; it was nearly six o'clock.

"He doesn't drink, does he? He doesn't look that way," the woman said.

"I wouldn't want to believe that, but everything comes to mind waiting like this. I don't know. This is just our second week of living together. I've never seen him drunk."

"It's just so strange that he's so late on Christmas Eve," said the woman.

"Time for sauna," I heard her voice in the hallway.

She could not resist peeking in, towel over her head.

"Hasn't he come yet?" she whispered.

"He hasn't," I said, almost in tears.

"I thought so, when I didn't see his bicycle at home. If only something hasn't happened. We have a phone if you want to call the place where he works? They'll know there if he's left for home."

"No, I won't call. They can let us know if something has happened. I'll wait a little while before I go to the sauna."

"There's lots of steam there. I warmed it enough so that it would last for everyone. Good night," said the woman and went into the house.

It was approaching nine when I heard a stamping in the hallway. Heart pounding, I peered through the door. Saul was stamping the snow from his shoes, holding a small Christmas tree in his hand.

"Good Lord, what kept you so long? I was about to cry," I said.

"And I've been thinking about you," he said. "The truck broke down near Laihia and had to be taken to Vaasa. There was nothing to bring me back from there until now. Do you see? I brought you a Christmas tree from Laihia. I went to warm up in a farmhouse, and they gave me coffee and Christmas treats. They laughed and said they were not as stingy as the world says they are. (There are any number of jokes about the stinginess of people from Laihia.) They even let me get this fir tree from their woods."

"I think it's best to sauna first. It's been almost an hour since the landlady told us to go. The food must have dried up. I've been keeping it warm for nearly half a day."

It was already late by the time we had eaten and decorated the tree. I had a couple of small packages for him. He was happy to get them and said timidly, "I have nothing for you, since I didn't know what to buy."

"I didn't expect anything since there is nothing to buy in the stores," I said.

Was I still so childish? A small sense of disappointment pervaded my mind. We had just gotten married, and it was Christmas, a time when people should at least think of those dear to them. It was hard for me to get to sleep; many confusing thoughts kept coming to mind. It even occurred to me that we had not known each other well enough before getting married. That evening I prayed in my heart for our marriage.

Early in the morning we went to church about a kilometer away. There I found true Christmas peace in my heart.

On New Year's Eve, after melting the tin, we decided to go to church, where a service was being held at midnight. I had never attended such a midnight event, and it seemed as if a guardian angel's spirit had descended on the people. All worries and griefs were forgotten, at least for the moment. We walked hand in hand along the snowy road in the bitter cold, wishing for all good fortune in the year of 1947.

From day to day I discovered how weak my cooking skills were, especially when the meat and vegetables I had gotten from Mother began to run out. The ration portions were so worthlessly tiny and not always available. Every morning I was literally in fear over what I could put on the table for supper. Days began to seem long, although I did handwork. I was in strange surroundings, and I didn't know anyone.

We lived on the outskirts of a church village, from which a road led into the woods. Farmers often drove by with their horses, but the road was not open for vehicles in the winter. One cold morning I went along the woods road with my kick sled. Someone must live there, since there was a road. After I had kicked along for a while, the woods opened up into fields with houses here and there. I guided my sled into the yard of the first house and knocked timidly at the door.

"Just walk in, you don't have to knock," said a firm voice.

I stepped over the high threshold, but my eyes, blinded by the bright sun, could see nothing at first. Soon they began to make out a dark *tupa*, in which the housewife was just taking coffee bread out of the oven. It was an old log house, and the graying wall timbers made it even more colorless.

"Good day," I finally managed to utter. "It's cold out there."

"Hello. Yes, it's kind of cold. How far have you come?"

"From the church village. I came out sledding, since it's such a nice day. Since the rations are so small, I thought maybe I could buy a little more milk and maybe even some meat. You have to be talented to come up with something to put on the table every day," I said.

"Well, sit down now," said the woman. "Excuse me for not asking you sooner. Have you lived in these parts for long?"

"We just moved in at Christmas. My husband works for the bus lines."

"Oh, I see. Is he one of the drivers? They say they keep adding buses all the time, and they drive everywhere, even to Vaasa."

"There are over ten already. My husband is one of the mechanics who maintain and overhaul the buses."

"Well, it's plain they won't run if you don't keep them up. You must be a very young couple. You look like such a child."

"We've been married just about a month."

I watched as the woman took bread from the oven. If only I had the nerve to ask her for advice. As she went by she felt the side of a coffeepot.

"There's still a couple of cups of substitute left over from the morning if you'd like to join me. I'll see then what I might be able to give you."

"I'm in no hurry. The drink will taste good after being out in the air. Thanks a lot. Listen, ma'am," I said shyly, "will you tell me how you get your bread so nice and smooth. And it tastes better too, it has such a good, sour taste. I'm such a beginner that I don't know all the tricks to make it come out right."

"There are no special tricks about it. I was born in this house; it's my childhood home. Since I was an only child, Mother taught me all about running a house. You probably don't have the sour starter to begin with."

"No, I always wash the kneading trough after every use. That must be all wrong."

"Yeah, you must never wash it," the woman said. "Listen, my good child, I'll give you some of the starter from this dough." She scraped up some dough from the bottom of the trough and put it into a bag. "Then when you are going to bake, put this soaking for many hours on the day before." She went on to give me all the instructions for baking the bread.

"Oh, if I only had a daughter. I wanted one so badly, but we were not granted any children," she said in sad, trembling voice. She patted me on the back when I left.

I was able to buy milk and meat from her, and, as I left, she even asked if I wanted to buy a loaf of bread. We agreed that I would come once a week, whenever there was anything I could get. "If the man of the house is home," she whispered to me, "don't say anything about the meat. He doesn't let us sell meat to strangers."

Happily I rode the kick sled home. She certainly was a nice woman. Now I had a friend. And she charged only the regular price for what I bought. She was a good-hearted woman.

Singing happily, I prepared dinner. There was even fresh bread.

"Now my wife is in a good mood. We even have honest-to-goodness bread," said Saul happily. "You've baked a real loaf. I'll put it on the bread pole to dry out."

"I went on a jaunt to the neighboring farms, and I was able to buy a little extra."

"Don't they cost a fortune on the black market? We don't have the money to squander on such things," he stormed, and looked at me grimly. "And you bought that bread, too. Some wife I have, who can't even bake her own bread."

"These cost no more than at the store," I said. "You just can't get along on the card rations. Often there's nothing in the store even if you have the coupons. Till now we've had the extras I brought from home, but they're gone. You don't seem to care for the round loaf, but I'll learn to bake the flat northern ring loaves. Our life is just beginning."

"Yaah, you have to learn. We're not going to start buying ready-baked bread. We already spend too much money on living. I just don't understand where all that money goes," he said, and went out angrily.

He liked the food well enough, but he expected to get it for nothing. He had never handled his own expenses before this. His mother had, of course, prepared the food, and he knew nothing about expenditures. My morning good humor was gone. It was hard to understand that man. I decided to buy an account book, which of course would be considered a waste of money. But I would not give in—since we had started on this journey, we would have to travel in harmony. I would record every purchase and its price and show him what had been squandered if he mentioned squandering.

I was so upset that I could not even knit. I went to the woodshed and began to chop wood so hard that the walls rang. Our landlady heard, and came to peer in through the door.

"It's you banging away in here. I thought your husband was home already. It must be dark every night when he comes."

"It is. A couple of nights he worked overtime until eight o'clock. I thought I would help him a little," I said, breathless.

"I tell you Elsie, don't start chopping wood. If you learn to, he won't want to do it. Men learn such things so easily. It becomes a habit," she said, and left.

"That may be," I said to myself. "But I have to work out my anger on something. I took him for my husband, and I have no one to blame but myself. I should have heeded the warning of my dream. We'll see what happens when he comes home. I'll pretend nothing happened today."

Saul brought the mail with him when he came home. I could tell from his face that something out of the ordinary had happened and waited for him to tell me the news. He folded the letter and put it back in the envelope.

"It's sad news," he said, his voice soft and thick. "Mother died last Monday. The letter was from my sister."

"That is sad," I said, and began to rub his shoulders. "Did the letter give any details? Was she more ill than usual? Her arthritis was so bad."

"There wasn't anything more. She just died in her sleep. She had a bad heart too. She was only fifty-five."

"So young? I thought she was a lot older. But then she had all those children. Weren't there nine of you?"

"There were, and Father ordered her to work in the fields too when things were rushed. And she had to take care of the cows in the evening. She never had any outside help. That's why she grew old before her time and took sick. There were the eight of us, and then Jouko came along seven years later. Everyone called him "Extra-Boy." He's sixteen now. He's good in school."

"It's all so sad. When is the funeral?"

"Sunday after next. We'll go a day or two early."

Saul suggested that we make a funeral wreath ourselves. There were plenty of fir branches in the woods, and I bought paper flowers and ribbons from the only florist in the village. We would tie them only when we got there so that it would be easier to carry them on the train.

We were sitting together on the train with nobody near us. He slid his arm around my waist and suddenly pulled me toward him.

"Ouch!" I cried out, and jumped to my feet.

"What's the matter?" he said, releasing his grasp.

"I felt a little hard spot on my left side yesterday, almost like the start of a swelling. It hurt more and more, I could feel it throbbing. It's in a place where I can't see it."

It was late in the evening when we arrived at our destination. We went up to the second floor to sleep. As I was undressing, the side felt sore.

"Look at that side now. It's as tender as the pupil of an eye."

"It's big, and it does look swollen. There's a broad red space, and it's even worse in the center."

"Where the devil did that come from, on top of everything else?"

"Old men say that a man gets them when he starts having sex."

"Then you should get them and not me," I said unhappily. "Actually I wouldn't wish them on anyone. They hurt."

All the family was together again for the mother's funeral. We rode in a truck to the church village, Saul driving, with me sitting between him and a neighbor. Every time Saul turned the wheel, he jabbed me in the side with his elbow. I clenched my teeth to keep from crying out. On the way back it felt as if something burst in my side, and I felt better. My clothes were getting damp. *Lucky I'm wearing a black dress,* I thought in distress.

When we got home, I ran quickly upstairs. Pus had soaked through my clothing all the way to the coat lining. I changed my underthings and wiped off my dress. It was a funeral, and I had to have a dark dress. Luckily I had a long, dark-blue sweater that reached below the waist. No one noticed anything out of the ordinary.

On the way home, I put my arms around his waist, gazed into his eyes, and said, "I've missed you. There was always such a rush that I couldn't even get to talk to you."

"Well, it's over now and we can be together again. Do you know what I heard?"

"Well, what?" I said quickly, bursting with curiosity.

"One of the village women told my sister that you're pregnant. Is that so, and why haven't you told me?"

"I don't know if I am, but I've been wondering about it. And how would those women know? Maybe because I had that sweater on and you couldn't see my waistline. They must have thought I was hiding something."

"Some of those old women have an eye for such things, and they know. It shouldn't have come so early," he said quickly.

"I don't know, because I haven't felt anything unusual. Some women have all kinds of signs: they feel ill and they faint and all that."

After a month I began to believe that the old women really did know. We talked about it one evening, and I decided to go to the doctor, who was a near neighbor of ours.

"It's true, I have to believe it now," I said to myself on the way home from the doctor. On the one hand, I was glad of it, although we had not planned an addition to the family. We would see what Saul had to say.

"How did it go?"

I nodded, smiling.

"Oh, hell. Did it hit home right off?" he said, annoyed.

"Is it such a bad thing that it makes you angry? Aren't men supposed to take precautions?" I said timidly.

"Well, we can't do anything about it now. Next time we'll have to be more careful. You seem to be quick to sprout. We can at least finish this since it's already started," he looked at me with a laugh.

"Yes, yes, we will." I threw my arms around his neck and we fell onto the bed.

It was April. The snow had already melted in spots. The horse road to my hideout was still hard and icy in the morning. I enjoyed these weekly jaunts on the kick sled to visit my new friend. Saul said no more about squandering money after I showed him the account book; he sometimes thanked me for the delicious food. There was something about him that I didn't like, but I couldn't say just what. Sometimes he sank so deep in thought that he seemed actually to wake up when I started talking to him. After those periods of thought he was cold, almost like another person. Was he trying to start a quarrel with the harsh words he sometimes used? He had not, however, said anything bad about the child. He seemed to have enjoyed listening against my belly to the faint heartbeats. What kind of father would he be? He was a hard worker, often working evenings. Of course we would need money with another in the family, perhaps we could save a little toward a house of our own. *Yes, and the only furniture we have is a bed; it's all we need now.* I laughed at my own thoughts.

Toward spring Saul came home and started talking enthusiastically.

"We're getting a better place to live. The owner of the house opposite the place where I work says someone is moving out. There is a room and kitchen upstairs. I'll be able to come home even during the day."

"That's great. Did they say when we can move in?"

"In the middle or at the end of June. We have to get some furniture. I'll start making a table in the woodshed. There's a carpenter's bench in it; I think the owner will let me use it if I ask. I'll stop at the sawmill to buy the boards on Saturday."

"I have the material ready for making cloth if I only had a loom. I could make a bedspread, just a simple one. I can't do anything more complicated because I haven't gone to school."

"There are stores closer to the new place, so you won't have to walk as far now that you're getting so round."

"I don't know of any way we'll be able to get the extra milk. At least, I won't be able to walk that far. Meat is easier to get, but we should have extra milk."

"I can go there once a week on the bicycle. The food situation seems to be getting better. And we'll get a third food card when the baby is born. At first the baby won't need more than his mother's milk," he said with a laugh.

"I should think not," I said in confusion. "This world is a wonderful place."

"What a really nice place," I said, delighted at the move.

"And it's so close to work," Saul said, pleased. "I'll ask for a truck from work on Saturday and go and buy furniture from Teuva. You can get it cheaper from the factory."

"Can I come with you?" I asked.

"No, it's better if you stay home. Women are supposed to bring the furniture with them when they marry," he muttered to himself but loud enough to be heard.

"Where would I have gotten furniture? You knew that I was poor; I never tried to hide it," I said dejectedly.

After he left, my mind was as gloomy as a thundercloud. Why did he say such things? I had brought more into our common home than he had. He had had only the two quilts stolen from the army and no house into which furniture could have been brought. I had not wanted to associate with the rich for the simple reason that I felt myself so poor and worthless, and didn't want to be the target of their jibes. I had seen enough examples of it. And now to be subjected to this! Were all men so nasty? A person never knows what she is letting herself in for. I should have believed the dream I had before getting engaged. I remembered my Aunt Anni's words: "A poor person has to be flexible and pliant, like a withe to bind a fence." What were withes now? Oh yes, they had been used to make a double-pole fence in the days before there were nails, or when nails were too costly.

This was the "worse" from the marriage vow, and I had promised to love then too. He was nice most of the time, but what the devil got into him at times? He didn't drink, I knew that. I could only guess what he would be like when he came back from Teuva.

When he did, the morning's slate was wiped clean. He seemed proud of his purchases, even humming as he carried chairs in. Amazingly, he was a completely different person. How could he be so changeable? But why mope —all was well again.

The summer passed quickly. I tried to take good care of myself for the sake of the little one. I felt strong, except for one time when I began to feel dizzy in a line at the store. Was it from the pregnancy or was it a reminder of the heart attack? But that was a year and a half ago. I believed that my heart was in good condition.

I no longer knew what to wear—everything was too tight. The woman at the Knuuttila store whispered to me, "We got in a little bit of cloth. Come in the back way and you can take your pick. You know how scarce fabrics are. We only give them to customers under the counter. Don't say a word to anyone."

"Of course not. I'll sew it myself. Oh, thank you so much for thinking of me when I have nothing that fits me! I'll take the one with the red flowers; it's so bright."

I went home contented. The woman also promised to let me know when I could get fabric for sheets; I still had not used my bridal coupons.

In the evening I happily showed the material to Saul. I would start sewing the next day and was already planning the pattern in my head.

"Why did you get such a bright color? I suppose you want to show off your big belly to everyone," he said bitingly.

"How can you say that? I don't think it's anything to be ashamed of. I've been embarrassed by my skirts' being so tight. I think this is nice."

"Can't you at least speak better! You're not in Karelia anymore. Sometimes I'm ashamed of the way you talk."

"Yeah, yeah, and the way you talk—is that supposed to be proper Finnish?" I said angrily, mocking his northern dialect. "From now on I'll try to talk so that my master won't need to be ashamed of me. But what's eating you now to put you into that kind of mood?"

I heard no answer. He put on his cap and went out. After a short time he came back, hugged me warmly, and everything was the same again. Was that supposed to be an apology? He was two people—one good and one bad. I had to learn to live with them. I sometimes noticed that he seemed to enjoy it when tears came to my eyes. It was a devil's trick—making another person suffer.

In a couple of days I went to the store in my new dress. To my surprise I saw many others wearing a dress of the same material, or of another which had been available. No one said a word, lips merely curved in a slight smile. The woman from downstairs had also gotten fabric of the other color. "Aili seems to have new duds, too," Saul mused. "Probably got the cloth from under the same counter as you. It's really an ugly color."

There you have it, I thought. I would have been scolded if I had taken the other color, too. Sometimes it seemed that everything I did was wrong. Let him say what he liked—I vowed not to take it seriously from now on, as long as I felt in my heart that I had done right and tried my best.

It was a Saturday. After a restless night, I felt as if the time had come. Saul said as he left, "I'll go to the phone booth at the store to call. I won't call from work. They don't have to know everything that happens to us."

What a start for a father. What was wrong with the man? He isn't ready for fatherhood yet. Good Lord, what might come of this yet! Oh Heavenly Father, I prayed. *Have mercy on me. Let everything turn out well in our life. You alone can do it. Give me the strength to bear all adversities.*

Before six o'clock that evening, after a day of pain, a girl was born. "It's good that she was born at this time, we can all have a day of rest on Sunday," said the midwife. "Look at her now, father, isn't she a husky girl, really a record weight, almost five kilos. Her skin is as clear and white as a two-month-old's. Thank God everything went well, since she is a firstborn. Remember, young man, be a good father and help take care of her."

We got a housekeeper for a week so that we could get through the most difficult time. Saul had appeared proud and happy after the birth of the child. In the evening, the housekeeper went to stop in at home, and Saul came to sit down beside the bed. I smiled with the happiness of a mother.

"Now we have a third, who is from both of us. Do you see what slim little fingers and nails she has? Everything is so pretty. We had a good turning lathe since the product is so good," I said happily.

"She's pretty, but she's not mine," he mumbled.

I was struck dumb and couldn't believe my ears. Finally I managed to say, "What? What did you say?"

"I just said that she's not mine." His voice was faint.

I burst into an uncontrollable fit of weeping. Finally when I grew a little calmer, I said in a voice mingled with weeping, "You're crazy! You imagine things! Now I understand those spells of sulking. Man, you need a psychiatrist. I could see a long time ago that you were jealous, but I thought it was because you cared so much for me. Now I understand that it's an illness, a miserable illness. I'm so unhappy." I started to weep again.

"Stop bawling like that. I didn't mean anything by it."

He came over to the bed and patted me gently on the shoulders.

"If you didn't mean anything by it, then why did you say such crazy things? They make no sense at all," I sobbed.

He tried in every way to soothe me. Now, I thought, the better "I" was in control. How could he stand it when good and bad were always struggling within him? Did he really believe those devilish notions? He had to get rid of them. I vowed to show him every minute that I loved him so that he would not have time to conjure up such fiendish ideas.

In the morning everything was well again. Saul helped me with all the chores and popped in often to look at the baby. I too tried to forget what had happened yesterday, although it stung me to the heart.

He watched while I nursed the baby and mused aloud, "A child's food—there it is. Nature really has arranged everything. A human being is really a complicated machine, wonderfully planned to the very last detail. She's so sweet and peaceful. Have you heard her voice yet?"

"She did whimper a little very early this morning. I brought her in here and fed her, and she went to sleep again. People say that if the mother is calm, the baby will be too," I said.

"Well, you haven't been nervous, at least not yet. Didn't Hilja wake up? You shouldn't lift the baby yet, and she's so heavy too."

"That girl doesn't hear a thing. She snores so loudly that I couldn't even get to sleep."

"You should wake her up. That's what she's here for. You should rest so you'll recover sooner. Yesterday took a lot out of you. It's no fun, although men always make jokes about it to each other. I wouldn't believe it myself if I hadn't seen it."

On Monday when Saul came home, there was no sign of lunch. He came over to me and said impatiently, "What's that girl been up to? She's just starting to prepare the food. Did you tell her I was coming at twelve?"

"Of course I did, and reminded her that she had to prepare the food, but she seems to be very slow."

Sisu Mother

"She'll never get anything ready. I'll make up a sandwich and go. I have to be back on time."

The same thing happened the next day. I began to make lunch—a man couldn't go without eating well for many days. I was a beginner when it came to cooking, but Hilja didn't know the first thing about it.

"Let me make that sauce," I said. "You set the table, he'll be here soon."

"I guess he didn't like it yesterday when the food wasn't ready. I don't know why it was late. I tried to hurry."

"He's used to having the food ready, and he has to be back at work on the dot. Otherwise he's not particular about food. He just couldn't afford to be; these ration allotments are nothing to rave about."

In the evening Saul and I talked over the situation. I said, "It's better if Hilja goes somewhere else. I can get along here if you carry the water up and take things out. There isn't even a drain here. Nothing will come of her cooking. She's in the wrong profession. I don't know how she can manage in a farmhouse where there are cattle too."

"It's no wonder she's an old maid. She's so ugly too that no one could care for her. She must be about forty."

"Well, uglier women have gotten men," I said. "She seems to have a screw loose, or maybe she's lost one completely."

"You said it," he laughed. "I guessed that you took care of things today, since everything was on time. Well, what is she doing here, anyway? I'll help you bathe the baby in the evening. You be careful not to lift anything and remember to rest."

"Hilja can bake the coffeebread tomorrow, since it's almost all gone. I can do the rest of the work," I said firmly.

Everything went according to plan. Even the coffeebread turned out well.

"Listen, Hilja," Saul began calmly. "It looks as if we can get along without help, so you can go home this evening. You must have other places where your help is needed."

"I was supposed to be here the whole week. If I leave now I won't get paid," said Hilja, annoyed.

"But you draw a monthly salary from the county and you get an apartment, too. We pay only a part of your wages," said Saul.

"Yes, but if I don't work enough days, they cut my pay."

"Everyone is responsible for making his own living, and you are responsible for yours. This is your last day here," said Saul sharply.

Hilja filled her bag and left, looking at me appealingly.

"Maybe I'll stop in on Monday and see how things are going."

"Whatever you like. There's a nurse nearby if there is an emergency. Thanks for making the coffeebread," I said.

Visitors were coming for the christening. What would people from a large and prosperous home think of our small, inadequate dwelling, I thought unhappily. They were, however, his relatives, so why should I be ashamed. If only I could make something good from the skimpy foods we had. The guests would sleep in our room and we on the kitchen floor.

In the morning Saul and the godparents went to the church, where the baby was baptized. Just after they left, Aili, who lived on the lower floor, sent for a midwife. That ended any desire to celebrate, at least for me. Three weeks ago I had been in the same situation. Cold shivers coursed through my skin when I heard Aili crying out downstairs. They already had a boy. *Oh, if only she doesn't have to suffer for a long time,* I thought anxiously and prayed for her. Her husband did not even dare stay with her but walked the streets uneasily. Everything went more quickly than expected, and they got the girl they hoped for.

A few weeks later, we were on the lower floor for the christening. Later, the owner of the house, who also was a bus driver for the firm, arrived. He had a room there, but I had never seen him. After I was introduced, he sat next to me, in the only empty seat. After exchanging words with everyone there, he looked at the baby in my lap and said, "Hi, we haven't met before, even though you've lived here for several months. I'll have to start visiting more often, since we have such lovely ladies living here."

"You'll be welcome. A landlord can always visit in his own house." I noticed a look of gloom and suffering come over Saul's face, but I continued chatting with the landlord.

"What do you have to say when you've gotten two more girls in the house within three weeks?"

"Girls are nice. I like big girls, but the little ones are so cute. And they soon grow up," said the landlord. Saul rose suddenly and went out into the hallway. I heard him run up the steps. Everyone looked at me.

"What happened to him?" they said, with one voice.

"I don't know. I'll have to go and see. Goodbye, and thanks for a nice evening."

Heart pounding, I went up carrying the baby. Now what was happening? The devil was in control again. Saul was pacing the floor of the kitchen, a dark look on his face and hands clenched behind his back. He gave me such a murderous look I thought he would attack me. Stuttering with fear, I managed to say, "Why did you leave so suddenly? Everyone looked at you so strangely. You didn't even thank the hostess but rushed off like a madman."

"I couldn't stand watching you flirt with Tom any longer. Aren't you at all ashamed, even when I was there? Going and sitting next to him and everything."

"Listen, where are your eyes? Tom was the last to come in. I was sitting on the sofa, and that was the only place left. I don't see anything wrong in saying a few words to the owner of the house. I'm used to talking to people, be they men or women."

"You could have gotten up from the sofa, but since you like other men, you stayed there so he could tickle you. I know Tom will start hanging around here now that he's found a new customer. He has them everywhere. Damn it to hell. Everything has gone to pieces! I can't stand to go anywhere with you after this. It's the devil to have to start getting a divorce right away, and there's that baby too."

His railing went on and on. When he finally paused a moment, I said, "You're absolutely crazy. Come down to earth with your imagination for a minute, or is the devil leading you to hell again? In that case, come up," I said, with a flicker of a smile at the corners of my mouth. "You've spewed out so much rubbish, I don't know where to start. Oh, that tickling of Tom's—he sat so far from me that our sides weren't even touching. And you surely must have seen that his hands were crossed over his knees the whole time. If you don't remember, shall we go and ask Topi and Aili? And what was that you said about mattresses?"

"That's what they call women every man can have," he said cuttingly.

"Listen, my man, and listen carefully! You know very well I'm not one of those women!" I shouted, red with rage. "I never have been and never will be! I'm ready to divorce you tomorrow. I won't put up with this hell for one single day. You accuse me of things I've never even thought of doing. You know very well that I was pure when we were married. How could I have changed into something like that?"

"Well, they say some do when they once get a taste of it," he said, dragging out his words.

"You've given me all I want of that. It never occurred to me that I should get more. If I ever felt like it, I would go to you. Do you understand? I love you. I don't love anyone else. That's why I married you and gave you everything a woman can give. I can't even imagine going to bed with another man. I doubt that I would, even if we were divorced or you died or we were separated in some other way. Believe me now, you stupid blockhead or whatever I should call you."

It all seemed to be changing into a comedy, and I started to laugh aloud, although my heart was weeping.

Saul stared at me wide-eyed at first, but gradually a smile began to tug at the corners of his mouth. Nothing more was said of the matter that evening. We went to bed as usual, as if there had been no quarrel.

Saul began to snore as though everything were settled. How could he relax so soon? I would lie awake many nights and think about what I could do. I did not believe the matter would end here. It was morning before I fell asleep, weeping softly.

Life went on rather nicely. We never said a word about the matter. Then an unusual crime occurred in an out-of-the-way corner of the parish. There were banner headlines in the paper but not all the details. One of our acquaintances was a policeman named Kannikko. He stopped to visit one evening and began to talk about the subject of the day, "We shouldn't talk about these details, but they will be made public in court anyway. We found this man hanged in a hay barn. We thought it was a suicide. When we took him down, I saw that blood had run from his mouth and dried at its corners. An autopsy was ordered, since there was something suspicious about it. The couple had been separated for a time. They had a seventeen-year-old son who lived with the mother. A neighbor told us the mother had a lover. The woman planned to kill the man so she could get the house for her new lover. The man was now living in his childhood home, and did not visit his wife. One day she came and asked him to come back home. The man did not want to go. As she was leaving, she stood in the doorway and opened her coat buttons. She had nothing on underneath. The poor man got excited and went back home with her. It isn't known whether she killed him by herself or if her lover helped her. The boy admitted that he had helped his mother hang the body so that it would look like a suicide. He had been sternly warned not to say anything, but when he was arrested, he confessed everything," Kannikko concluded his account.

"There are all kinds of women," said Saul, giving me a nasty, doubting look that startled me.

"It looks as if women are sometimes crueler and more deceptive than men," said Kannikko, completely unaware. "A few months ago they found an abandoned newborn boy. Following some clues, we went to investigate the matter the next morning. We knocked on a door and a young woman came to answer. She said, 'No, I don't know of anyone here who was expecting a child.' At that moment we saw that milk dripping from her breasts was soaking through her blouse. But she would not admit that the child was hers. She was given a couple of years behind stone walls."

When the visitor had left, Saul began to talk heatedly, "There now, you see how devilish women are. I'll soon have to fear for my life."

"Come back to earth, dear. There aren't many women like the one in Kannikko's story. Maybe not even one in a million."

"There are so. Every other woman is looking for more from somewhere else. I know all about it," he said emphatically.

"You have some imagination. I, at least, don't know of anyone in the nearby neighborhood," I said unconcernedly. "Give me an example."

"At least I know that everyone goes to bed with the taxi driver's wife. I don't remember any others right off."

"I've heard that, too. But she's the only one in the church village. Her husband loves money and as long as his wife earns it, he doesn't care how."

"There, you see how treacherous and crooked the world is."

"You know it all so well, it sounds as if you've been fishing in that pond too," I said jokingly.

"I haven't been there," he said, looking foolish. "I hear them talking about it so much."

"Of course I don't believe that you've been there. You've been home every evening. I was just teasing you because you said everyone had been there. I don't believe that any of our friends have strayed there."

"You just don't know how they go at it in the great world," he said. "They know no limits."

"Well, I don't believe everything I hear. I'm a country girl and will always be one. I'm a very simple person. I believe in God, and I obey His holy commandments. At least I will never break the sixth and tenth commandments.

I think you know that I'm not ready to walk off with anyone. Think what crazy ideas you are brooding over. I hope and pray that your imaginings will end with this; I don't want to hear any more of this in the future."

Saul looked very downcast but said nothing.
CHAPTER VII

Early in the spring of 1951 the stork arrived again, and we got a little girl. It was a considerable disappointment for Saul, but otherwise things had been going rather nicely for a long time. We were planning to move to his home area, since he suffered from gastritis, or thought he did. We did move during the summer and lived at first in his childhood home, where the *tupa* was empty.

He rested for that summer and then bought a circular saw, which he moved from place to place, wherever there was work. This took up most of his time. He had two men working for him, and I kept the books. We bought a piece of land on which there was a half-built house.

In between times, he began to work on building the house so that we could live under our own roof. We were able to move in by Christmas, although the house was only half finished. At first we had only two small rooms. The new year of 1953 had begun, and we were again awaiting a child. We did not have the money to get electricity installed, and so we began the year with oil lamps and candles for lighting.

He tired of the business with the circular saw and sold it. Now money was so tight that he went back to work at his old job in Jalasjärvi. He left on Sunday evening and came back late on Friday. I was afraid of how things would go. I hoped and prayed that his wretched delusions were a thing of the past.

To top it all, the bigger children had caught the whooping cough. Pipi, who was two, could hardly sleep at all. I would light a candle whenever she got a coughing spell, take her in my lap, and slap her back to bring up the phlegm. Sometimes I counted the number of burned matches in the morning. The average number was fifteen. I was continually tired, and I worried about how the little one would develop in these circumstances. If only the children would be better by the time the baby arrived so that it would not catch the cough. The day the baby was due was approaching. I was afraid it would come during the week. We had no telephone and no nearby neighbors. It was surely by the Almighty's direction that it came on Sunday. There were a couple of automobiles in the neighborhood, and we had already arranged for one. Saul rode off on his bicycle, and soon Arttu Kaisla came driving up. He asked quickly, "Is there a rush—will we make it to the hospital?"

"We will get there. I'm always slow," I said painfully.

"As you know, we have seven. Sometimes we've had to hurry. That's why I got this car, since once the midwife didn't make it, and I had to take care of everything myself. I took her to the hospital for the last two. We can't have them born at home when there are so many around. Now my wife has told me: 'Stop!'"

We were already at the door of the hospital. "Give me a call then, and I'll let Saul know," said Arttu. He waved a hand and left.

On Sunday March 1st in 1953 a third girl was born. I was so disappointed that I wept. A nurse tried to console me, "Don't start crying now. She is an exceptionally fair and pretty child. Even her eyebrows are white. She'll grow up to be a golden-haired beauty. She's so well developed too, weighs almost five kilos, when babies are usually about three or four kilos." She went on to say: "There are seven of us girls in the family, and every one of us has found a place in this world. We're scattered all over Finland, but we all gather at home for Christmas. We, too, may have been a disappointment to our parents at one time."

"I'm just afraid how my husband will take this. He was so sure it would be a boy this time."

"He can't be such a fool as to start blaming his wife. It depends on the man, and they haven't found any way to deal with it yet. Who knows—maybe in ten years they will be able to determine sex. Medicine is always advancing."

That same night there was a snowstorm. Even in the hospital the power was out, and the nurses brought candles into the rooms. I thanked God I had gotten there before the storm. What would have happened if the automobile had gotten stuck in the snow with twenty-five kilometers to go? I believed that I had a guardian angel.

There were four new mothers in the room, and one of them had a radio. It said on the news that Stalin had died on the second of March. The nurse entered the room and said, "Too bad he didn't die long ago. We Finns wouldn't have had to suffer so much during the war."

"How can you speak so ill of Stalin?" said one of the women.

"Well, what good did Stalin ever do us?" said the nurse angrily.

"Stalin didn't start the war, the Finns did."

"Stalin would have taken all of Finland if we hadn't resisted him. Would it be better if we were all slaves of the Russians?" said the nurse.

"Maybe we would. There's nothing great about a worker's lot here," said the woman, and turned over in her bed.

The nurse left the room, giving me a slight smile and a significant look. Later in the hallway she whispered to me, "It's too bad that I opened my mouth in there. I didn't know there were communists here too. If only it doesn't get to the politruks. Those Russian security men are all over the place."

"I don't think anything will come of that kind of small talk. I would certainly never say anything good about Stalin."

The doctor made his morning rounds and asked everyone how they were feeling. The same woman, who was usually silent now spoke up, "Listen, doctor. I know that the usual stay is five days, but since we have so much work at home, couldn't I stay longer and get a good rest?"

The doctor looked at her and replied, with a slight twinkle in his eye, "You can, of course, stay; we even have room now, but usually women are in a hurry to get home and start on another one."

The woman pulled the covers over her head angrily. The rest of us could not suppress chortles of laughter no matter how hard we tried. The woman did not stay in the hospital any longer than the rest of us.

Arttu came to get me with the car. Saul could not come, since he had to stay home with the children. My thoughts were in a whirl again. What kind of reception would I get from him since his moods were so changeable?

Saul came out to the car to greet the new arrival. Everything was in order in the house, and there was coffee ready. This was one of those rare occasions which warmed my heart for a long time. *Now the "good I" has the upper hand,* I thought. If only that would always be the case. We could live as in the fairy tales, "happily ever after." Could it be true that some people were always happy? It was hard to tell by surface appearances. Most people conducted their affairs behind closed doors. Our acquaintances thought we were a very happy couple with pretty and obedient children. They knew nothing of the struggle and the nightmare that hovered over us. I prayed in my heart, *Oh, God, sweep away the dark cloud that hangs over our home.*

The summer went by pleasantly; the children grew and developed. Saul worked at temporary jobs. We managed somehow, and I did not complain if money was scarce. In his spare time, he worked on building a sauna, and that too was completed. Now we did not have to depend on a neighbor for that convenience.

Late in the fall, I discovered that I was again pregnant. The youngest was only eight months old. How would I dare to tell him about it? I had to approach the subject very carefully.

"Listen dear, I have a little something to tell you," I said timidly. "Our efforts haven't been successful. I'm with child again."

"Darn it. Don't tell me! Did it strike home again? Are you sure?"

"It does look that way," I said.

"Well, goldarnit! Do you know when yet?"

"Of course I've figured it out. At the end of July."

"The only thing for me to do is to go back to work at Jalasjärvi. I'll save money so I can stay at home next summer. There's no question of moving back there. We'll see how much we clear on the sale of the woods. Maybe I could get started on my own workshop next summer, the way we planned."

It was January, and his back was so bad that he couldn't go to work. I started for the church village on my bicycle, a distance of fifteen kilometers. I had to get an ointment for his back and go to the doctor's for a check-up at the same time, which was free for expectant mothers. It was good that Saul was at home; there was no need to have a neighbor baby sit. And I didn't want to tell anyone about the new arrival until it became obvious.

The weather kept getting colder and colder, and I peered at a thermometer in a window. It read twenty-three below. The winter sun was just setting in a clear sky, and that meant a further drop in temperature. *It's so cold, and I still have fifteen kilometers to pedal home*, I thought fearfully. The first five kilometers went quickly, but the rest of the way was along a forest road. It was getting dark already. I stopped often to rub my cheeks and the tip of my nose. My legs from the top of my socks to my underpants might as well have been bare—my skirt did little to shield them. My coattails flapped to either side as I rode and did not cover my knees. At last I arrived home. Saul was very worried, "Where have you been so long? It's all dark already."

"I came as fast as I could, but I had to stop to rub my cheeks and nose now and then. It's so cold out there."

"It's not cold enough to freeze anything," he said.

"Let's look and see," I said, taking off my outer garments.

"My God, your thighs are all white! Wait, I'll get some snow," he said.

"I was able to rub my cheeks with one hand, but I couldn't rub those places," I said.

"It's good you made it home and didn't freeze along the way. Wasn't there anyone coming this way?"

"Not a blessed soul the whole way. If Arttu had come along, I would have asked him for a ride."

"He would have given you a ride without asking. The frozen places are beginning to turn red. They'll turn out all right. It's a wonder you didn't freeze stiff out there. It's twenty-six below now," he said, coming back into the house with a flashlight. "I didn't notice because I spent the whole day inside."

My thighs were touchy and blue for a long time, but eventually even their color returned to normal.

It was already the middle of May in 1954. Saul had planned to stay at home all summer. I was outside one Sunday afternoon when a neighbor lady rode a bicycle into the yard.

"Hey, I'm on the way to see Laina! Do you want to come along? Your husband is at home already, isn't he?"

"He is. I'll go and ask him if he has to go anywhere."

"I just thought that since you've spent the whole winter in the house it would be refreshing for you to go and visit people too."

"Well, Laina keeps on asking, but you know I don't have much chance to go visiting."

"Hey, could you stay home with the children if I go visiting with Ilmi," I said gaily as I entered the *tupa*. "She's going to the Hakala's and is waiting outside."

"Well, so you have to go hopping around visiting now?"

I could tell by the tone of his voice that the devil was now in control.

"Yaah, you have to go and show off that big belly of yours," he said, with an ugly gleam in his eyes. Tears ran from my eyes, and for a moment I could think of nothing. Trying to wipe away the tears, I went to the door and shook my head to Ilmi. She said nothing, but looked oddly at my reddened eyes.

I was still riding my bicycle to get the milk. It was a hot July day, and I was sweating twice as much as other people. When I was returning with the milk, the front wheel of the bicycle jounced into a pit in the road, which was only a rutted wagon trail. It jarred me so that I felt it all through my back. I began to have pains at night and could not get to sleep.

It got worse during the day. It felt like birth pangs, but there were still nearly three weeks to go.

"Don't go to far away, I don't know what this is. It hurts here and there," I said. Perspiration caused by the pain was dripping down my back. "This is something unusual. It's different from the way a birth starts. I hurt myself somehow when I was getting the milk yesterday evening."

"Do you still feel the small movements?" he said anxiously.

"Yes, I don't think the child was hurt at all."

I waited for two days, but the pain kept increasing. The next day I felt as if I were on fire. The pain did not let up even for a moment. Saul went to get Arttu and his automobile again.

Arttu drove like mad when he saw the pain I was in. I got into a doctor's hands immediately. "Everything is going well. The birth process has begun. We don't have a single room empty, but there is a bed in that bathroom and we'll put you in there."

The pain began to let up as I waited. From time to time, it pierced my left side. The delivery room was open and I was moved into it. There the pains ceased entirely. After a while a nurse came in to look at me and listened to my belly. "Everything is okay; the little heart is beating strongly. I see by the doctor's notes that the birth began during the day, but I don't even think it's close. They're bringing someone else in here; I'll move you into that empty room. I'll stop in every time I go by to see how you're doing. You can still walk; here let me take you under the arms."

I lay there feeling no pain of any kind, even rose and walked around to see if movement would bring on the birth. There was no way I would go home from here. I hadn't slept for many nights, and had had all that pain, and now there was no sign that the birth was starting. I jumped as much as I was able, and tried to make all kinds of movements. I might even have tried a couple of somersaults. I really had to get things started.

I had just sat down again when the nurse peered anxiously into the room.

"I heard the strangest thumping in here and thought you had fallen out of the bed. Have the pains started?"

"Not at all, not even a pinch. I've been exercising. Maybe that will get it started," I said.

"You really have to spend the night here. We'll see about it tomorrow after the doctor makes his rounds. Ring the bell if you need help. Good night." The nurse left.

I could not sleep, although I was tired. I was so frustrated that I cried. I tried to exercise and do all kinds of stunts, but nothing happened. In the morning the doctor sent me home to wait.

Downcast, I went to look for a bus going in my direction. I knew that there was no transportation for the last ten kilometers, unless someone from the neighborhood happened to be shopping. I had only money enough for the bus, and would have to pay for a taxi at home.

The taxi arrived in our yard. All the children were at the window, with their father above them, everyone wide-eyed with astonishment. Saul paid the fare, and we went in. Our bright four-year-old said, "Didn't you bring the baby home, Mother? Father said you went to get it. Did you leave it in the car?"

"It wasn't there yet. I'll go again," I said dejectedly, looking in shame at Saul. "Go out and play. There's a ball and a doll."

"Well, what happened?" he said crossly.

"Nothing, as you can see." I explained it all to him from A to Z.

"You didn't know what the pain was then, and all the money went to waste for the taxi and everything."

"You yourself saw yesterday the pain I was in. I tried my best, but here we are. I'm afraid of giving birth now. I feel as if I'd been beaten, and every place hurts."

"Is that so," he repeated a couple of times. "Go and rest. You look so tired. I'll take care of the children."

He left the room quietly. I stretched out on the bed and fell into a deep, restful sleep.

Two weeks went by quietly, and I did not ride the bicycle again. Early on a Sunday evening I began to feel that the time was at hand. I refused to panic. I would not leave too early even if it were to come in the automobile.

It was already ten o'clock at night when I said we needed a car quickly. Would Arttu still be awake?

"Are you sure now? Let me check. I'll start out walking when the pains begin."

They were coming at five-minute intervals.

"Let's go right now so you'll get there on time," I said hurriedly.

Everything went well. I was in the hospital for an hour when a boy was born into the world. This was the easiest of all the births. Perhaps I had already suffered the pains on that first occasion. The boy was a placid and fat little chunk. At first we called him old man.

Saul himself came to get us with Arttu's car. We drove in silence for almost the whole trip, and then he broke the silence.

"Now we have a boy. This is the last one. We have four now."

"That's okay with me. Here's my hand on it—agreed?" I extended my hand to him, laughing. He gripped it strongly, and we both laughed aloud. I had not seen him look so happy in years.

I can handle any crisis. I am a mother.

CHAPTER VIII

It was a few days before Christmas in 1954. Our oldest was seven and already a schoolgirl. The boy was a round, chubby five-month-old. The children were healthy and took up my time during the day. I was doing the Christmas baking late at night. This was already the second night.

Saul had been working at his former job for a week, and I was waiting for him to come home that evening. He had done all the gift shopping for the children. I could not go anywhere during the day, and the stores were far away.

There was a small knock at the door, and I guessed who it was. I rushed to the hallway, my hands full of flour. Just to be sure, I peeped out the window.

"Hi, it's wonderful that you've come!" The door was left open, and he seized me in a warm embrace.

"Oh, the week is so long! I miss you every evening. Now I'm home for the whole Christmas holiday. What would you do if I carried you right into the bed," he said, smiling.

"Don't be silly, darling. I've got Christmas tarts in the oven, and I'm getting others ready. Be patient for a little while."

Later we wrapped the packages, but it was hard to hide them for lack of space. We had only the two rooms.

Finally the long-awaited Santa Claus arrived with his packages. The children played games and sang for him with their troll hats on their heads. The littlest sister was the most fun. She bounced around like a balloon with her little thumbs up: "Tip-top-tip-top!" The little house was a really noisy place when everyone got their packages, each child crying out in delight as she opened hers. I felt the spirit of Christmas settle into the house, filling every nook and cranny. I had never gone to bed so completely happy.

Around mid-April, Saul began to come home unexpectedly in the middle of the week, saying there was no work to do, so he had come home. I began to sense that something strange was going on again. He said very little and was deep in thought. He did very little at home, not even helping me even though the water had to be carried in. I did not ask him anything, but waited for him to explain his worries.

One evening when the children had gone to bed, I sat doing handwork and listening to the radio. Going through the hallway to the food pantry, I glanced out the window, which had no curtain, and saw someone walking on the road. I could not make out a face, but I could tell by the walk that it was Saul. What was it now? He had left for work yesterday morning and was not supposed to return until Friday. Now it was Tuesday, and he was walking along the road. Something was badly wrong.

Gradually it grew clear to me. He was watching out there to see if anyone was coming to visit me. Oh, the poor man! Now the devil had taken him over completely. Let him watch—he would see that no one was coming here nights. Had he still not escaped those delusions? We had four children; I took good care of him and loved him as much as ever. I had hoped that he was free of the illness. I did not mind if he was sometimes nasty, but these groundless accusations I could not stand. "Oh God, have mercy on me and the little children. Let him see things as they really are. Clear his mind of those senseless thoughts," I prayed aloud.

I guessed that he was staying with his brother nights, or rather days, watching this house nights and sleeping there during the day. The next day when Tytti was in school and the sledding was good, I went there with the little ones.

We were received there in the usual friendly way. I mentioned something about Saul's coming home on Friday and saw by my brother-in-law's face that what I suspected was true. He changed the subject. Were they really all against me? I did not want to ask any questions. I regretted that I had never spoken of Saul's obsessions, but I had not wanted to bother people with my own problems. They will come to realize that I am innocent, I thought, as I sledded home with my flock.

I woke up that night to a furious pounding on the outside door. Frightened, I sprang out of bed and wrapped a sweater around my shoulders. The hammering was so heavy I thought the door would cave in. I peered out from behind the curtain to make sure, although I was certain it was him.

"Why didn't you come to open the door right away?" he said, running into the bedroom flashlight in hand, then into the unfinished part of the house where there were only a few planks across the floor joists. I stood in the hallway astonished, watching his search. He ran back into the bedroom where there was a trap door to the basement. He opened it, rushed down the ladder, and flashed his light into every corner. Without a word he went to the outside door, which I had already locked. I peered out of the kitchen window to see where he was going now. I saw him checking with the flashlight the tracks on the path leading to the house, which was flanked on either side by high snow banks.

"He managed to slip away this time," he said as he came in.

"I don't understand what's going on. Who are you looking for? Who got away?" I said almost hollowly.

"Your lover was here, but when you took so long to open the door he slipped out through some opening."

"Has the devil got into you again? You have a key—why didn't you open the door with that? I came as soon as I woke up, and that didn't take many seconds. If you had told me you were coming, I would have stood waiting in the hallway if it took all night."

"He was here. I've been watching all night. I'll find his tracks in the snow in the morning. I couldn't see them on the road now," he said, half to himself.

"May I ask who was here then? I haven't seen anyone."

"Don't pretend to be stupid! You're one of those who gets all the men on your side. Jaska used to be a good friend of mine, but now he won't even talk to me."

"So that's the way it is? It's nice to know who was here. As I recall, Jaska hasn't been here since the time he brought the mail once. Do you remember how many months ago that was? He sat there, and you talked to him. I was nursing the baby in the other room. When I came in, he had already left. I haven't even seen Jaska since then, not here or elsewhere."

Saul went to the other room. He came back in a few minutes straightening a leather belt in his hand, his frightful-looking eyes wandering like those of a madman. *I will not flee*, I thought, *even if he kills me*.

"You have to confess now," he said harshly. He came nearer, raising the belt in one hand to strike. Cold shivers ran down my spine. In spite of my fear, I managed to keep my voice steady as I answered without a quiver, "Even if you beat me to death on the spot, I have nothing to hide or anything to confess. Keep in mind that if you hit me once, I'm walking out of this house for the last time. I will never be able to forgive that. I'll go even if I have to beg food for my children. I will not leave them here for you to whip."

I waited in terror for the belt to fall. I could feel his panting breath on my neck. Slowly the hand holding the belt descended, and he walked into the other room without saying a word.

I sat in a down in a chair, frozen with fear. What would happen now? From the bedroom I could hear the breathing of the children. One of them sounded as if she had a blocked nose. What was he doing in there, since there was no sound? Thank God he had no gun, but who could know in his deranged state of mind? How many weeks had he been spying on me without going to work? There was a father for you! It might be best to get a divorce. But what would I do then with a flock of kids? I would not give them up, nor leave them to be brought up by an insane father. Nor did I want to go back home, where they had enough trouble starting afresh in their advanced years. Saul had not allowed me to visit home more than twice since I had left. Mother and Father had not even seen our last two children. At first I used to write, but now he had forbidden that too. He always spoke of my relatives scornfully and offensively. But my life could not be worse if I were to get a divorce. I was a prisoner in my own home; I couldn't even sleep for being in constant fear. How long would my nerves hold out? He would never get better, would only grow crazier. My thoughts were in total confusion. I did not know what time he had come home, but now the clock already showed three.

I crept to see what he was doing in the other room. He had plumped down in a sitting position on the bed and was sound asleep with all his clothes on. Nature had done its work; there was no danger now. The poor man. I could not even pity him after suffering so much on his account. I didn't even begin to think about what might happen in the morning.

I could not even think of going to bed after a night like that. I began to light a fire in the stove and make a good pot of coffee. And Poju was an early riser; it was best to see that there was food ready for him.

I breathed in the aroma of strong coffee. Sitting at the kitchen table sipping it, I gazed out the window with unseeing eyes. The night's happening seemed like a distant nightmare. If he were not asleep on that bed as proof, I would have believed it all to be a bad dream.

I heard Poju rustling as if he were already awake and hurried in to get him so that he would not awaken the others.

"Hey there, Poju, eat so that you'll grow up to be a good, strong man. The toy truck is waiting there. Just eat your belly full," I said softly to the boy.

"Is it Friday already, since Daddy is home? Why is he lying on the bed like that?" Pipi asked curiously.

"Shh, shh. Let's be quiet so we don't wake up the others," I warned her. "How is Daddy sleeping. Show Mother," I added with a smile.

"Like this, his hands are like this," the girl settled her hands behind her neck and turned her small, round feet inward. "Daddy's feet are like this, and he doesn't have any covers on."

At that moment her daddy came into the room, a sullen look on his face and matted hair sticking up in every direction. Without a word, not even seeing the children, he went to the coffeepot and felt its side. Finding it warm, he got a cup and poured the steaming brew into it. Cup in hand, he went into the hallway. I heard the door to the empty room open. Then I heard a rustling from the hallway and thought that he must be opening the outside door. I listened tensely to every sound, on guard against any possibility. Now I was determined to fight for my children, if necessary. I was like a lioness protecting her young.

"Mother, come and look at what Daddy is doing, wading in the snow." Pipi was concerned. I went to see. Sure enough, he was out in the snow sometimes reaching above his knees. He was looking for the tracks of last night's escapee. Poor man, a wretch among wretches.

"I don't know what he's looking for. Maybe he lost something," I said.

Pipi came into the kitchen boots in hand and sweater under her arm. She began putting on her boots, and now she stood there with them on the wrong feet trying to find the sleeve of her sweater.

"I'm going to help Daddy, but I can't find my mittens. Will you help me, Mommy?"

"Oh, my little pumpkin. It's still so cold outside. You'll sink right up to your neck in the snow. Daddy will come in soon. Don't worry about him. He'll be all right," I said casually.

The girl forgot her worries immediately and began to play on the floor. Poju was a happy child; all he needed was food and a couple of trucks. Little sister was up now too, and Tytti was getting her school bag ready.

"Who's chopping wood in the woodshed?" she asked.

"Daddy came home last night, and we didn't have any chopped wood left." He hadn't done that work for ages. I usually did it during the day when Poju was asleep and Pipi and little sister were playing outdoors. I remembered our first landlady's warning: Never start doing that work . . .

I had done my best to make a success of our marriage, and this is what it had come to. Everything was a mess, and there were four small children, I thought hopelessly. Two small rooms for a roof over our heads and a husband who was crazy.

After Tytti had left, Saul came in with an armload of wood. He went out again when he saw that there was room for more in the wood box. The children did not run into his arms as they usually did. Little sister looked at him, but turned her back and went on playing. Saul looked for something to eat, and saw that there was some porridge left. I handed him a plate without saying a word and set a milk pitcher on the table. I went into the bedroom myself; it was Poju's naptime.

"If you're going to be home, I'll start the wash. It's so hard to do it alone now when Poju is sleeping so little."

"Just go ahead. I'll take care of the children." His voice was soft and timid.

It was approaching evening. All signs indicated that he had forgotten everything. In the evening, he said he was going to his brother's. I was so sick of him that I thought, "Let him go wherever he likes." I felt freer when he was out of sight. I could listen to a fun radio program; perhaps it would make me forget this nightmare. It would be all the same to me if he ceased to exist. I would be lucky if he died. Then I could go and ask for aid from the county. If we separated, he would not pay a cent of child support. An idiot like that, who didn't even think they were his. He would be sure to weasel out of paying even a red cent.

Now I had begun to think totally stupid things, wishing death on another person. He had the same right to live as I, even with his delusions, if only I could get out of his snare. I could not visualize my life from now on. It had come to a dead stop.

Saul came home in a surprisingly short time. It was as if the evening's happenings and his disturbed state of mind had been completely wiped away.

"My brother and his wife urged me to go to Sanni from Lapua."

"To Sanni? Isn't she a nature healer," I asked, puzzled. "Are you beginning to believe that you have delusions?" I added.

"Stop talking about delusions. That's not why we're going there. They say she will know if you are guilty," he said hotly.

"Good, good. Let's just go then, and you'll get over your suffering," I said.

"We have to take her two clear bottles of liquor, White Horse. My brother has ordered it. He has a liquor card. It will take a few days to come in the mail."

"I'll ask Aira Korpi, if I happen to see her at the mail box. I'll tell her we're going to go shopping in Seinäjoki. Maybe she can come to stay with the children for a day."

We sat in the train on the way to Lapua. The landscape flashed by. There were spots of bare ground in the fields, but in other places the snow still lay deep. Saul seemed quite calm.

"This will settle the matter once and for all. You must be really scared," he said self-confidently.

"Not at all. I feel as if I'm going to be freed of a nightmare. Remember now, you have to believe Sanni, since she knows," I said emphatically.

After several hours of waiting, we got in. He gave the bottles of liquor to Sanni, and even added, "We have four children, and I don't believe they're all mine."

"Let's take a look, we'll soon see," said Sanni, and fussed at a cupboard with her back toward us. We heard a match scratch at least a couple of times. She poured liquid from one bottle to another, then turned to say, "Young man, you are wrong. Your wife hasn't ever even thought of other men. Ask her forgiveness nicely for all the groundless accusations you've tormented her with. I'll prepare a nerve medicine for you, and remember to come again in a week. Delusions are hard to cure, but I've had success with almost all cases. Remember to honor your wife; she deserves it."

I felt my cheeks flush as soon as Sanni began to speak. I saw Saul staring pale-faced at the wall. I took his hand and squeezed it. He looked me soberly in the eye.

"This medicine is ready now. You can take it here already. Two tablespoons morning and evening. There now, here's a spoon. God bless you and your little children," Sanni bade us a warm goodbye.

Outside he took my hand and said with a sigh and the trace of a smile on his face, "Well, now it's done and we know the truth."

"And the burden is lifted from my shoulders," I said happily.

Sitting on the train on the way back, I felt as if all the problems between us had melted away. I saw that he was again the happy man who had attracted me. "Oh, if this goodness would last, and the old devil had died forever."

We had left our bicycles at a relative's house and they asked us, "Where have you been? You look like a honeymoon couple."

"That's where we've been," we said, looking at each other with a laugh.

In the evening after the children were in bed, we decided to go and tell his brother's family the good news. It was only a short ride to the old home, as the children called it. They could already tell from our expressions that the trip had resulted in good news. Naturally we told them everything. Saul even added, "That Sanni is quite a witch. I really believe in her. She pulled a strange trick on me. When we came home and started to change clothes, I noticed that my underwear were inside out. I'm sure they were on the right way earlier. I would have noticed it during the day."

"There, you see. She wanted to show you so that you would believe she spoke the truth. An inside-out coat is a sign of good luck," said his brother. We all burst out laughing.

"Good night," we shouted as we started for home. The long and eventful day was ending.

On Monday Saul again went to work for the week. I never did ask how long he had been away from work spying on me. Everything now seemed forgotten, at least I hoped so. Nevertheless a fear crept into my heart. He should not have gone there alone for a week. I waited prayerfully on Friday night. I prayed that he was cured, as Sanni had hoped, although she had not definitely promised he would be.

On his way, Saul was supposed to stop at Sanni's to pick up the medicine. The knock at the door was earlier than usual. I rushed to open it. I saw from his look that the devil was in control again. There was no caress, and I asked in panic, "What's got into you? Why are you looking like that?"

"Nothing. I was a fool to believe that old woman. She doesn't know anything; she just thinks she's a witch. Next time I'll take her a broom. She can find a black cat herself. I was stupid to believe something like that. Damn it to hell, this world is slippery and treacherous."

He went on and on in that way. I tried to stay cool, but tears were running from my heart and there was a heavy lump in my breast. I remembered how full my heart was on the way to Lapua when all was well and all our troubles had seemed to melt away. When he had finished cursing, I saw him calm down. I myself began to feel easier and asked him timidly, "Did you go to Lapua at all?"

"No, I left work early and bought a bottle in Seinäjoki to take to Sanni. I was waiting for the Lapua train when I began to realize how stupid I was to believe in such a witch woman. Women are all alike. They pat each other on the back and praise each other. She praised you to the skies. How does she know what you're like? She wasn't there to hold your legs."

I had reached some kind of state of self-confidence, and the matter had begun to amuse me in a way. I was used to this now, so I said, "Listen, my man. I've lost who knows how many weeks on these delusions of yours. If I suspected that you had another, I would soon find out."

"Well, since you won't admit it, how can I find out?"

"I can't admit it, since I'm not guilty. You see, there are two sides to the matter. Am I betraying you or am I not? If I had been spying on you for weeks, I would surely have seen something. Have you ever seen anyone or anything suspicious?"

"Not for certain."

"Then there you are. It's all in your mind. If you had seen anything, you could have brought your brother to witness it, and you would have had separate confirmation. But it is impossible for you to see since there is nothing to see. Sanni told you that I had never been with anyone."

"Yes, because you have such an honest face. I don't believe a word that Sanni says."

"You were the one who wanted to go there. I had never heard that she was a wise woman, just that she was a nature healer," I said.

"I've heard stories for years in the village of all the marvelous things she's done. A man from Härmä lost his storeroom keys and couldn't find them even though they hunted all over for them. Someone told him to go to Sanni. He went there to try just for spite. Sanni said, 'Is there a fence to the right of these storerooms?'

"'Yes, yes there is.'

"'The keys are on the ground near the second pole. Someone stuck them there for a second when coming from the storeroom, and they fell to the ground.'

"The man did not really believe her, but thanked her and went home. He found the keys where Sanni had said they were. She does know something, but she didn't know in our case," Saul concluded.

"But you would have believed her if she had been on your side?" I said.

"Yes, yes, of course."

"Oh, you poor man," I said, and laughed loudly. "Don't you see how muddled your thinking is? Of course, you don't believe that you suffer from delusions?"

"I don't believe that witch-wife," he said.

"I'll ask you one more thing—do your brother and his wife believe you when you tell them your delusions?" I asked, looking at him searchingly.

"They don't. My brother said he would throw me out. But they didn't refuse me when I asked to spend nights there."

"Then you don't even believe your own brother? You always have a devil on your back."

"I usually believe him, but not in this case," he said testily.

"Why do you think your brother is on my side?" I said.

"He doesn't know you so well."

"You'd think he would. We lived in the same house for almost two years," I snorted.

"You didn't try it with anyone then. I was at home all the time."

"I was afraid when you left for the whole week that the devil would take over, and that's just what happened."

"Yes, since you always do it when I'm not at home. You can't trust yourself."

"We're in the same vicious circle." My head was spinning. No matter how I tried, I could make no sense of it.

"You need to find a job where I'll be in sight every second. But we haven't got the money to start our own business."

"What if we move to a city? I would try to get a job close by," he said hopefully.

"Do you think you would get rid of those crazy ideas?" I said.

"Yes, when I'm at home every night you won't have the chance."

"Is that so?" I snorted, shaking my head. Nevertheless I said, "It's hard to get a place to live with such a large family if it doesn't go with the job."

I was completely downcast again, but one might as well try. His disease would never be cured; some said it would get worse with age. It was best to keep the family together as long as I could. The children would soon grow up, and then it would be easier to leave him. My love for him was completely gone, but of course I would have to go to bed with him. I woke up when I heard him say, "I have an aunt near Helsinki. What if I go there to ask about a job? I can stay with my aunt overnight so I won't have to pay for a hotel."

"Why not? It sounds like a good idea. When do you plan to leave?"

"If I work at the job I have for a week, I can use that money for expenses. We have money in the bank for moving. And we can rent some kind of shack for the winter to see how things go there. If it looks as if we'll stay, we can come back, sell this place, and buy another there."

Sisu Mother

To judge by his letter, there was a lot of work to be had in Helsinki, but it was difficult to get housing for a large family. He promised to come home on the weekend to get more clothing.

He was happy and lively when he arrived home, full of plans for all of us to move to Helsinki. "If only he can find a place to live before the wind shifts," I prayed in my heart.

During the week a letter arrived, which read in part: "I have a little bit of news about a place to live. It's on the Espoo side, and there is good bus service. The landlady would like to meet you. Could you get someone to stay at home and come on Sunday? Write at once so that I can come to meet you. Always yours, Saul."

I got someone to stay with the children and pedaled off to the station at four in the morning. The sun was glimmering in back of the treetops when I arrived at the station after ten kilometers of bicycling. I enjoyed the fresh morning. It was easy to distinguish the odors of different flowers and shrubs in the morning dew. Someone had just mowed hay the evening before, and its fragrance dominated the area. If only a person's life could be so calm and peaceful. Would that be happiness? Perhaps a person had to have misfortunes. These happy moments were like roses in life's garden. Some had fewer of them, as did I. At this point it looked as if they all had withered. Perhaps thorns and briars were my lot. I awoke from my meditations as the train came gliding into the station.

The landscape flashed by quickly. Lovely mirror-calm lakes, beautiful white-trunked birch woods. Oh, how attractive—a red-painted house with white trim, with a sauna right on the shore. Birches around it, and a pair of red rose bushes under the window. Whoever lived there, I hoped their life was as happy and balanced as their home seemed to be.

Absorbed in thought as I was, the five-hour train trip was soon over. I said hardly anything to my fellow passengers. Perhaps I had been thoughtful from birth, or perhaps circumstances were making me so. I recalled that Saul had sometimes warned me against talking too much. I had observed that a person's nature changes with her life; perhaps circumstances sweep people along with them.

The buildings were getting thicker and thicker; this was indeed a wilderness of stone. I certainly didn't want to live in barracks of that sort. Only a little stretch of sandy yard for the children to play in. I could not imagine Poju's taking his first step in such surroundings, among the garbage bins. It didn't look as if I would like the city, but circumstances would force me to adapt, even to being a "fence withe," as Aunt Anni used to say.

There he stood, waiting for me. He seemed free and happy this time.

"It's good that you came," he said, pressing my hand warmly.

"I came since I was asked. Why did the lady want to see me?"

"I don't know, but don't worry, you'll pass the test. Let's have something to eat in the station. You must be hungry; at least I am. I was so excited that I left two hours early."

"What were you excited about?"

"I missed you. It's been two weeks already. You wouldn't believe how lonely one gets here, even though people are buzzing all around you," he continued. "We have to be in Pasila at two. The lady sells ice cream there and leaves for home then, so we can go with her to see the place. They've promised it only until the spring; I told them we'd buy our own place then."

"We'll worry about that later. It's too soon to bother our heads about it now."

"This is nerve-racking," I said as we got off the train at Pasila.

"Be quiet. She's over at that booth. Let's go over and talk to her; we'll see if you pass the test," he said, brushing my hand. We chatted and bought ice cream; the lady still had to work for a few minutes. We walked off to one side.

"Good, good. I could see that she likes you."

"I noticed it too. If only she doesn't have a temper. People of her kind tend to."

"Don't ever let her hear you say that," Saul warned me.

"Of course, not. I can certainly get along with her for one winter. I can't promise anything longer," I said with a laugh.

We were on our way to Helsinki, to a new landscape and a new life. The children looked out curiously at the landscape gliding by. I could read the expressions on many people's faces—"What a gang of kids. Stupid people, to have so many kids."

Each one of them is important to society, I thought proudly.

An older man started to talk to us. "Are you on a vacation with your whole family? Where are you going?"

"We're leaving the country for good. I have a job in Helsinki, and we found an apartment in Espoo," Saul explained.

"So that's it. There are so few good job opportunities in the country. Your family looks well cared for. There are better opportunities for schooling in the city too. What kind of work do you do?"

"I'm an automobile mechanic, and there are jobs in that trade."

"It's a good trade. There are more and more automobiles, and you can get gas now too. Good luck to your family in your new home."

Poju was already a year old, and at home he could perform certain important functions with another's help, but the trip was so scary that he could not manage as usual. When we reached the Helsinki station, he began to leak as he stood there. His shoes and stockings were soaked, and there was a big puddle on the street. I stripped him below the waist, including his shoes and stockings, and wrapped him in a towel. We were in a hurry to catch a bus, and I had just enough time to change his clothes up to the stockings, but he had no extra shoes. We made it to our destination without any greater disasters.

Life and people were the same here on the outskirts of Helsinki as in the North. This was a district of private houses, with a marshy and wooded swamp behind it. Sometimes a squirrel would come to the bird feeder, which delighted the children. In the winter rumors of a great strike began to circulate.

"When is it supposed to start? Will you have to be on strike then, too?" I asked.

"I suppose so. Everything is supposed to stop on the first of March. Kekkonen will become the president then. I can't get to work when the buses aren't running."

The general strike began on March 1, 1956. Saul was working in a small private repair shop. A couple of cars drove to the city in the morning, and he went to work for the first two weeks. The windows of the shop were covered so that the lights could not be seen on the street. Finally the owner of the shop said, "It's best to stop working now. Windows have been smashed in many places, and people have been hurt. It looks as if there's going to be a real all-out riot."

The next week Saul went to a doctor for something wrong with his stomach. I had the feeling that it was imaginary, as it had been a couple of years before. It was just as well, I thought. I would be left in peace now that his illness had taken another form.

He was still leaving early every morning to catch the car to the city. One day there was a sharp knock at the door. I started—what was it now? The rent had been paid on time.

"Good morning. What's new? Is your husband still going to work since he leaves every morning?" the landlady asked, looking sternly at me.

"No, he started going to a doctor for checkups now that there's time."

"I thought he might be going to work, and we wouldn't want any capitalists living here," she said heatedly. "To the doctor. That's too bad." Her voice was milder. "What's wrong with him?"

"He complains about his stomach. They check him with machines every day. This may be the last day. We'll see then how big the bill is. I've been worried about it already."

"That's not good, when you have such a big family too," she said sympathetically. "We'll see who buckles in this strike. It's the end of the third week already, and food is getting scarce in the stores. We don't get milk anymore. You must get it. I saw you coming home from the store."

"Yaah, I get a little milk for the children. They say only for those under two. I fudged a little and got milk for two. You can have a little to go with coffee so that you won't have to drink it black. There are no more potatoes left at Elanto, and the freight trucks are not driving. Saul got a kilo from the city yesterday. They're enough for one day."

"Listen, I'll bring you some potatoes, but keep your mouth shut. Our brother-in-law went home with his car to get some. Just let me know when you need some," the woman said and went her way busily.

She was back shortly with a bag of potatoes and some packets of herring in a bowl. They had been given to the strikers at a fish-packing plant. They had not been canned when the strike began, so they would have spoiled.

"What do the potatoes cost? I'm so glad to get them. We'll get by now, when we have potatoes and herring," I said with a laugh.

"Nothing. We're all in the same boat. If your husband is at home tomorrow, he can go to the factory to get more. Have you heard the story of the old couple who were waiting for a streetcar, which did not come, of course, since the strike was on. Finally the old man said: 'Oh for the good old days of Paasikivi, when the street cars were still running.' We'll see if Kekkonen succeeds in anything. He's a good athlete; let's see if he can lead a country. They say he's on good terms with the Russians."

The general strike lasted all of March, that is, during the first month of Kekkonen's presidency. In the city, there was a shortage of everything. Many people already had cars, but they could get no gas. Only doctors and ambulances were allowed to drive. We were not in distress, for we had potatoes and herring.

There was no clear result from Saul's medical testing. I guessed it to be another delusion in a different form. When the strike ended, everyone went eagerly to work. I don't remember who won it. It united us with the people in the house.

We had found a little summer cottage at Korso. It had a lovely lot, and during the summer, we began to make it suitable for winter living. We were able to move in at the end of May, and were now sitting on a train on the way north to sell our other place. We needed money to pay for the new cottage. The children were now a year older, and no one wet his pants on the trip.

Acquaintances dropped in to find out the news, and we were invited to come and visit. When we were alone, Ilmi asked, "How have things been going? Has he had any more freaky spells?"

"Not of the same kind, but he imagined he was sick last winter. They took all kinds of tests, but found nothing wrong."

"It's miserable to put up with something like that. It'll wear you out before your time."

"It's my lot in this life. I try to live with it, although sometimes it seems hopeless," I said softly.

"If things get too tough, get in touch with us. Maybe we can help in some way."

"Thanks. It's nice to know that one has friends. I can't resort to my own relatives because Saul hasn't let me get in touch with them for years," I said, with a catch in my voice.

"That's terrible. He probably thinks they will lure you away from him. It really is sad to be a slave to someone that way. I don't envy you, Elsie. Not many could endure it. You're a gutsy person."

"I try my best because of the children. I hope that I can hold out until they are grown up. I have no other future."

We sold our house and were packing to leave when someone brought us the evening paper. I noticed an unusual news item in it. My wartime friend, Urho, had been killed in an accident. His wife and daughter survived to mourn him. I felt a nasty throb in my heart when I recalled the past. I had been too childish to marry when he had asked for my hand. Would I have been happy with him? It was all in the past, and now it had suddenly risen to the surface. In any case, I would now be a widow at thirty. Perhaps we would not have had as many children. I loved children and would not have favored having only one.

I tried to shake Urho from my mind, but I could not. Over and over, he kept appearing in my imagination. I remembered him in his army uniform with the corporal's insignia on his engineers' uniform. Twelve years had passed since we had last met, but my eyes still saw him as a young man. And I was no longer the girl of seventeen I had been when he last saw me. "Oh, you dreamer, he's dead and gone forever." I hadn't remembered him for years, and now this had had to happen in such an awful way. If Saul knew my thoughts now, he would have good reason to accuse me. This memory must remain here. I would not take him to Helsinki with me even in my thoughts.

This is a very beautiful place and all our own. I should be happy and thankful here when everything is going so well, I thought on a translucent fall morning as I weeded the strawberry patch. "I don't like the color of that cottage though, it looks as if it were painted with tar." Saul's cousin Sirkka visited us often. Her husband was a foreman in a paint factory. Once when she was visiting, I started saying to her, "Saul works on fixing this shack every weekend, but some day I'm going to paint it. I hate that black paint."

"What color do you want? Tepa will bring you the paint. They throw a lot of it away."

"Something light, it doesn't matter at all. That black makes me feel so gloomy. Will we have to pay for it?"

"It won't cost anything. We'll bring it on Saturday, if it's okay."

The painting was not as easy as I imagined. I set the children to playing in the sand pile, and just as I was mounting the ladder, they needed Mother for some reason or other. Little sister had hurt her finger, Poju had to pee. For three weeks I worked with a paint scraper and a brush before I got the first coat on. The second coat went on rather quickly: "It really does look nice in its cream-colored paint. It's a house now, not a cabin." For once I had accomplished something visible.

That same summer the Olympic Games were held in Australia. Pekka Tiilikainen broadcast the athletic events on the radio, and he also described the country. He mentioned that Australia welcomed immigrants and also helped them with their travel and with job possibilities, as well as giving them free English lessons. Saul became enthusiastic and began talking about it.

"We should go there; the family wouldn't cost us much there. We would never have to chop wood. It's a summer country. All you need to wear is a fig leaf."

"Maybe we could manage otherwise, but what about the language? You're well over thirty, and you've had no basic schooling. It doesn't just stick to your clothing," I said doubtfully.

"It will be easy to learn when you hear it every day," he laughed.

All that winter he kept talking about Australia. I did not encourage him at all. Little by little he began to seek information about the possibilities. I continued to object. One evening he said to me decisively, "I've thought this through, and I'm going to Australia alone since you don't seem to be willing."

"Well, you must know that you just can't leave your family here. They no longer make American widows the way they used to. A man can't go alone unless his wife signs a permission form," I said confidently.

"Don't tell me there is such a law," he said.

"Don't you remember when Kurkinen tried to go to Sweden a year or two ago, but couldn't because his wife would not give her permission. A man has to take care of his family since he's brought them into the world."

"Damn it to hell. A person really gets himself into things. Love costs him plenty when it ties him up completely."

The matter was left at that for the time being.

After a few weeks it came up again without warning.

"What if I go first and you can follow when I get a start? What do you think of that?"

"That sounds very uncertain. I've read the papers there on the table. They promise to take care of the family until they have a home of their own and the husband has a job. If your Australian fever is so hot, then we'll all go. All together or not at all," I said decisively.

He said no more at the time. I had already reached a decision during the day, although it was repugnant to me. Perhaps in a couple of years when the children were in school, I could go to work. Nowadays there was constant grumbling about money. I could not understand why the man could not comprehend that expenses increased as the children grew bigger. Every time I needed money for food, I literally had to beg for it. If clothing was needed, I had to give a thorough explanation of why. We would see to what extremes his stinginess might still go. I still had to laugh at something which had taken place a couple of years before. His cap wore through at the crown, and he said, "Do you have any thread like this? This needs patching."

"Patching—a cap?" I looked at him in amazement, unable to find words. "Patch a cap?" I repeated.

"Well, why can't it be patched?" he said scornfully.

"And you could stand to walk around in a patched cap? That tops everything. There has to be some limit to your miserliness. I'm not going to start patching that thing. Patch it yourself if you want to."

When he came home the next day, he had a new cap. I praised it as handsome, and it indeed was. He must have realized himself that he had gone too far.

There were many matters to take care of before all our papers were in order. We had to book a ship six months in advance. At last we learned that a ship was leaving Germany for Australia on December fifteenth. We thought we could get all our papers, medical examinations, inoculations and whatever else ready by that time.

We got a buyer for our cottage quite soon. While we were making our preparations for the voyage, the children contracted the measles, first Tytti in school and then the three others at the same time. I had just been to the dentist that day. I don't know what kind of a butcher he was, but the tooth he was extracting did not want to come out. The doctor gave me another shot in the gums. Soon things went dark, and when I woke up the tooth was gone. I rested on the sofa for half an hour before I dared start pedaling the five-kilometer distance home.

I had gotten the grandmother from next door to stay with the children while I was at the dentist. When I got home, the cheeks of all three were flushed with fever. I tried to give them aspirin, but it didn't help much and I had to stay up all night with three sick children, constantly spitting blood from my mouth. "It's strange that the hole left by that tooth won't stop bleeding," I thought.

I was very tired in the morning when Saul left for work, and I tried to rest at every chance, even if only for a few minutes. In the afternoon the children began to calm down. When Tytti came home from school, I told her I was going to the neighbors, since my gum was still bleeding.

I got the doctor on the phone. "Yes, what is it, ma'am? Oh, the tooth is still bleeding. Try to lie down, it will stop. Oh, you haven't rested. I told you to lie down. It isn't my fault if you don't follow the rules. Oh, so your children are ill. Get someone to take care of them. It isn't my business." And he slammed down the receiver.

He could have been a little more polite, I thought as I walked home. Yes, just lie down a few minutes. I had not been able to lie down for as much as half an hour with the feverish children.

But we all got through it alive. I sewed clothing for the children, often until midnight. Even the children's dolls got pretty sleeping bags. At the last moment, the two of us went shopping.

One day Saul took me to a jeweler's shop. I wondered what on earth for and what it meant.

"I'll buy you a watch, and you can pick out some kind of adornment, since you have none. I've never even remembered your birthday, but better late than never," he said.

I looked at him in wonder. Could this be true. I pinched myself. He had not said a word about our wedding anniversary, although it had been only a few days before. Once in a fit of temper he had called it the most accursed day in his life. Now for the first time in fifteen years he was buying me a gift. During all those years I had remembered him on his birthday with a gift, no matter how small. As I chose the gift, my thoughts were on something completely different. "Oh, if only the 'good I' were always in control!"

I chose a brooch with a blue turquoise in the center. The jeweler said it was the Sagittarius birthstone. I also got a wristwatch, which I really needed. With light hearts, we sat in the taxi on the way home.

I had been used to moving my entire life, but now I felt somewhat sad at abandoning my home so completely. The entire possessions of six people were packed into two suitcases, along with a sewing machine.

This house and home in Korso had been the happiest place for us during all the years of our marriage. Why had we, of our own volition, destroyed that happiness? Perhaps happy days were meant to come rarely to us. These scant two years were among the few roses on the path of our life.

When you have lost all hope, pray more whole-heartedly.

CHAPTER IX

Hopeful Voyagers . . . Destination faraway Australia.
Helsingin Sanomat February 12, 1957.

Express train to ship in Turku leaves Helsinki station at 14:55

There was a rush at the station before departure: saying goodbye, hurrying to the train, bidding bon voyage. Some fortunate ones were on their way to spend a winter vacation abroad. But that day, there sat in Coach Number 317 a group of people whose expression bore no trace of vacation-time relaxation. They tried to smile, but the smiles were forced. They were on their way to a home in new country—Australia.

Around noon they had arrived by train from Lappeenranta, some of them having come there from different parts of Finland. A two-hour layover in Helsinki, then on to Turku, Stockholm, Copenhagen, Bremerhaven—from where the S.S. *Skaubryn* would leave the following Saturday for a long ocean voyage, reaching Sidney on January 28th.

On the train leaving Helsinki were twenty-two people, most of them parents with their children, and one solitary bachelor, a glass worker. All of them are young and able to work, and there is not a man among them without a trade. All of them have reserved their coach in advance, and their large, chock-full suitcases tell of a long journey ahead.

"We are not afraid. The Australian government has promised to take care of us until the men find jobs," they all declare. But nevertheless there are looks of concern and uncertainty on many faces as they set out for their new land. The only ones who seem totally carefree are the children: enthusiastic and on the verge of excitement, they sit in their seats, but the talk does not flow freely. It is so exciting to go to Australia, the land of the kangaroo.

"We have to go and find work elsewhere, since there isn't enough in Finland to go around," says Valtola, a carpenter, whose wife and three children are leaving with him. They give the impression of being young, energetic, and goal-oriented, people who trust in the future. The children—two girls and a boy, little Ossi—are nicely and warmly dressed.

"We've heard that in Australia carpenters are put to work, even right off the boat," Valtola continues. "So there ought to be enough work there. If I don't get work at once, we can stay at an immigration camp until I can get a job and a place to live."

"We sold our house and goods. . . . This trip will cost a lot . . . the tickets for two adults and three children cost so much that we had to sell the house and goods to get enough money together."

From time to time, the boy Ossi burst out crying bitterly. It was not because of the tension and travel fever surrounding him, but rather because his sisters would not give him enough room on the seat.

"Of course it's sad to be leaving those near to us here in Finland," Mrs. Valtola says.

Sulo Tarjavaara from Lappeenranta, also a carpenter, has five boys with him. His large family—his pleasant-looking, thirty-three-year-old wife and all five boys—sat around him. The boys were dressed in blue and gazed eagerly out of the train window. The oldest was thirteen and the youngest, a kid of two-and-a-half, sat in his mother's lap with a toy car in his hand, happily oblivious of the long journey facing them.

"I, too, have heard that a carpenter can get all the work he needs," says Sulo Tarjavaara. "And I've also heard that food is thirty to thirty-five percent cheaper than in Finland, and the wages double or triple ours. And the local taxes are about six percent for a large family like this."

Naturally they would miss many dear ones in Finland: Sulo Tarjavaara's mother and two sisters are staying there. Mrs. Tarjavaara explained that she had a sister who planned to come to Australia the next spring.

"It was hard to leave our home town," she said. "But we won't miss this Helsinki at all. On the contrary, we'll be glad when the train leaves it."

The Tarjavaaras had decided to leave the previous June. In the hurry of travel preparations they had not had time to start learning English, ". . . but we'll get by somehow." Those who had been mulling over the journey for a longer time had been pounding English words into their heads in order to cope with at least the worst initial problems in their new country.

Also among those leaving was cabinet-maker Tauno Sarvilahti with his wife, Esther, and their twelve-year-old daughter. Finding work was also the biggest reason for this couple's travel.

"And once you're traveling to find work, why not make it a long trip," the couple felt. The longing for distant places was one reason for traveling, and the pair had become particularly interested in Australia during the Olympics, when Pekka Tiilikainen interviewed Finns who were living there.

Tradesmen—Mrs. X sat in the next compartment with her husband, three daughters, and a son.

"I don't want our names in the paper," she said. "Why bother? It isn't pleasant to leave, but since we've made up our minds, we're going."

The father was an automobile repairman and a metal worker. He did have plenty of work in Finland. The family, which lives in Korso, was making its first voyage abroad. The girls sit with serious faces, clutching their dolls to their breasts.

"Friends and neighbors smiled at first when they heard of our plans," Mrs. X related. "But then they saw, to their wonder, that the trip turned out to be true."

In January or February, the next group of emigrants leave for Australia. In the coming half-year, it is estimated that some eighty emigrants will be heading for this distant land.

On December 11, 1957, we had walked to the bus stop, the bigger girls carrying their dolls. Saul led the three-and-a-half-year-old boy by the hand and I led Little-Sisko. There was some twenty centimeters of snow on the ground, and the temperature was about twenty below, centigrade. Nobody said a word. I looked back for the last time at our cream-colored home. I wanted to run back and stay there, to huddle in some corner of the empty home—thinking of nothing. *No, wake up, girl,* I thought. *At least I'll get to see the world. There is no hope of going back. There is a long, uncertain fate ahead of you. You made your bed, so lie in it.*

Sirkku had come to the Helsinki station to see us off. The children had been wearing boots, and there we changed them to summer shoes. Sirkku took the boots to deposit in the Salvation Army Christmas kettles. I was so tired from being awake for many nights getting the children's clothes ready for the journey that I could not tie the children's shoelaces. My hands would simply no longer obey me. Sirkku looked at me in wonder and said: "You're no longer a mother if you can't do that."

"I'm so tired, I'm going to sleep right here," I said, and collapsed onto the bench. A few minutes nap revived me for a little while.

I was completely recovered by the time we boarded the train. Finally we were on our way, I thought, sighing with relief. There was an interviewer from the *Helsinki Sanomat* on the train. They had heard that over a hundred people were leaving Turku for Australia. Most of the people in our coach were making that same journey.

A travel guide joined us in Turku. We ate a quick supper and boarded the boat. It was actually true now; we were leaving our beloved homeland

and the shores of Finland—perhaps forever. I was downcast, but even more, I was tired.

We were already in the harbor of Stockholm when I woke up. Some family was peering out of the cabin opposite ours, looking happy. I looked at my watch, and the woman said: "Do you know that you have to turn your watch back an hour?"

"How come?" I said.

"Swedish time is an hour behind ours," she said.

"Well, of course I have to do it then," I said, and turned my watch back. Just to be sure, I went on deck and saw by the clock in a tall tower that it was eight o'clock.

The travel guide got us to the railroad station in automobiles. In the restaurant there we got acquainted with the Rantala family, who were from Vaasa. There were five girls in the family, the oldest ten years, and the youngest ten months old. The parents both spoke Swedish, and they helped us to order breakfast.

To pass the time, the men began to check the boat tickets, and they discovered that our cabins were right next to each other's. That was the beginning of our long acquaintanceship. In addition, two of the children had the same names.

It was a long day, for the train to Copenhagen did not leave until the evening.

Only three narrow berths had been reserved for us on the train, but there were six of us. Sleeping was anything but restful, but I was dozing off somehow when a loud clamor arose in the passageway. In its narrow confines, a half-naked man and woman were hopping about. The woman was pulling the man's hair, and they were reviling each other for all they were worth. I did not understand the words, but to judge by their expressions, they were not nice. There was a sudden silence when they realized that people were peering out from every door, and they quickly slipped into their own cubbyhole.

After I had dozed off for a brief spell, there was a loud command from the corridor and a knock at the compartment door. The order was repeated mechanically, and we assumed that it was time to get up, for the train came to a stop too. The train was apparently running late, for we were literally thrown off it. Men came and carried our suitcases out, and I walked with the boy in my arms and his shoes in my hands, since I had not had time to put them on. We had arrived in Copenhagen early in the morning.

There in the waiting room of the station, we saw for the first time all the Finns who were traveling to Australia. Most of them were large families, the largest a Tampere house-painter's family with seven children. Some younger families were with us, with a couple of children, and even a few bachelors. There were 125 of us altogether. The guide was Joni, who had lived in Australia. He had his new bride with him. They were not a young couple, but a recently married one.

After a light breakfast, we boarded the train again. Denmark would surely have been a lovely country if the weather had been nicer. But a heavy, wet snow was falling. We could see flashes of colorful country houses through the trees. Only around the houses, which were generally of brick, were there trees growing. Every piece of land was cultivated, even the tiniest.

Now what was coming up? There was only sea ahead of us, and no sign of a railroad. The train was pushed back and forth alternately. Saul went out to see just what was happening. It felt, however, as if we were moving slowly. "Can you guess where we are?" he told me when he returned. "The whole train is on a ferry. The train has been split into sections, that's what all the shoving was about. We're going from one island to another. The weather is really rotten, but otherwise it would be nice to go out and take a look. If you want to go anyway, I'll stay here with the children."

The sea was stormy, even though it did little to rock the heavy ferry. The ship was a sturdy one and must have seen many a wind and storm. People did indeed come up on deck to view the wonder. It occurred to me how little we knew of even such a nearby land as Denmark. I had imagined that we Scandinavians had very much the same kind of country and living conditions.

Along with other Finns, I went to buy something for a snack for the children. It was already midday, and the children were getting restless. When I returned, Saul said, "I saw you put the new brooch on your blouse this morning. It isn't there now." I began to grope for it frantically, but it was gone.

"Oh dear, it must have fallen, and it was such a nice one." Cold shivers ran down my spine, and in I went running headlong up the same flight of stairs I had taken before. But dozens of people had used them, and someone was sure to have found it.

It was expensive, but I was sadder because of the sentiment attached to it. It was the only gift Saul had ever bought me, and now it was gone. We never mentioned it again.

Now we were already in Germany, and the evening was growing darker. We arrived in Hamburg, where lights were shining as far as the eye could see.

The train seemed to be traveling through the air, and some wiser soul knew that it was an elevated railway. After a brief stop, the lights of Hamburg receded, and we were on the way to Bremen, where we would spend the night.

Compared to the previous night, we were in luxurious surroundings. Two spacious rooms and four wide beds in an elegant hotel. After supper everyone was ready to go to bed.

After a good night's sleep, we were in high spirits again. We decided that the whole family would go and see the city. The other Finns had the same idea: we could hear our native tongue on all sides. The children were delighted by the gorgeous Christmas window displays. There were many southern fruits for sale, which were not available in Finland at this time of the year. We met the Lepistö family on the streets of Bremen, a plump pair, short in stature, with two extraordinarily lively children. Lepistö had studied English and German at home. His speaking ability was pretty limited, but it was better than nothing. They were both from Karelia, and their home dialect had stayed with them.

Lepistö's boy was four years old, and they had him on a leash. The girl, age six, was everywhere, like quicksilver. In the hotel, I once managed to snatch her out of the wrong elevator. Her mother vowed to put her on a leash if she could buy one somewhere. No matter where we went, we could hear their voices.

In the evening, we went on to Bremerhaven by train, from where the long boat trip to Australia finally began. We soon realized that we were boarding a refugee ship. It was full of East Germans, as well as Hungarians. It was only the year before that the Communists had taken over Hungary. Also aboard were a few Norwegian families and at least one family from Denmark with many children.

Places for every family had been reserved in the dining room. We got as table companions the family from Lappeenranta with the five children. The ship was of Norwegian ownership, but the main language was German. The waiters were either Italian or Greek. They spoke their own language, which we did not understand. In fact, we understood nothing but our own sweet-sounding Finnish. With regard to the waiters, they were dark-complected, middle-aged men with prominent noses, and they were very courteous.

The food was good, and after eating we went for a stroll on deck. The boat had just left the harbor. Far away in the fog loomed the lights on the shore of England.

We went down to our own cabin, which was four decks below the surface of the water. Of course there were no windows. This, then, would be our home for the next four weeks. The Rantalas' cabin was directly opposite ours. It looked as if all the large families were here on this bottom deck.

At night the wind began to blow. The Bay of Biscay is known for its storms. Nothing bothered our family, although I heard that some people had become seasick. It was sunny in the morning, but quite chilly, so it wasn't really pleasant on deck.

Soon the shore of Portugal came into view. On the rocky strand was a huge white building that reminded one of a castle. Everyone took pictures of it. It was a pity no one knew its name. In the evening we reached the Straits of Gibraltar. The ship traveled closer to the African shore. It was an entirely abandoned desert of sand, with here and there a clay hut. The evening grew darker and gloomy clouds appeared on the horizon. We heard that a storm was approaching.

As the evening grew darker, the ship began to roll more and more. The mess boys ran into every cabin carrying pills. The children began to turn pale. I gave them the medication, but all of them began to feel ill. Saul went up on deck to see what it actually was like. He came down quickly and began to throw up. I had taken a pill earlier and did not feel at all ill. Soon the children quieted down, and I was able to stretch out on the bed. But much to our chagrin, there were only five beds, and there were six of us. I always lay down the last wherever there seemed to be the most room.

In the morning, no one was in a hurry to get up. The storm had subsided a little, but the boat still rocked quite threateningly at times. I even felt rather strong.

"What do you say if I go to breakfast and bring you back something to eat?" I said to Saul.

"That's a good idea. I can't get up. I feel so dizzy. It will be good if I can stagger to the end of that hallway. I threw up at least five times last night," Saul complained.

In the large dining room, where there were usually a couple of hundred people, there were now only six brave souls who had dared go out. The ship's cook knew from experience what was needed on a morning like this. Every morning there were fresh, warm rolls, and so there were now as well. The coffee was indeed refreshing. Plates were heaped with boiled eggs. I tried to ask with gestures if I could take some to my family, and I was able to get a small basket of eggs to take with me. I had to vow with hand over my heart that I would bring the salt shaker back. Then the cook and I both laughed, and I could see that he trusted me.

From then on the family began to revive, and we tried to go to lunch together. Others, too, were beginning to recover, and about half the families were in the dining room. We heard that the longer one was on board ship, the more accustomed he became to the rolling. This was a Mediterranean storm, and it lasted three days. On the third day, no one seemed to be seasick any longer, although the ship was still rolling slightly, and there was no land in sight. Soon we arrived in Port Said, where the Suez Canal begins.

In Port Said, we were allowed to get off the ship, although within a narrowly restricted area. There were many troubles in Suez at the time. Some clashes had occurred just the day before. Just as we were descending the gangplank, there was a large crowd of dark-skinned people below, and we heard loud shouts: "Devils . . . Satans . . . devils . . . Satans."

We were terrified. What was this all about? Did they speak the same language as we did? I didn't know if we dared go there at all, among these people with the ragged turbans on their heads.

"Finns have been here with the United Nations troops and have done their duty. They've also taught them Finnish," explained our guide, Joni.

It felt good to have the ground under our feet, but otherwise the experience was sickening. How could it be that those people still looked like those in our old illustrated Bible? Hadn't they come up in life at all? Almost two thousand years had passed and they still looked the same. Had their development stopped there? How could it be possible in modern times? As I was thinking these thoughts, the line stopped. Joni, the guide, went to see what the problem was. Soon he began to explain: "You've all heard about the Suez Canal clashes, and now they have peaked. We will not be allowed outside of the port area. It's best to go back to the ship, but if you want to feel the ground underfoot, you can walk around this enclosed area. In an hour, the ship will be moved over there to wait for its turn to get into the canal."

I looked at the angry faces on the other side of the enclosure and thought it a good thing that we were restricted to this area. I would not have wanted to take the children out onto those dirty streets. In addition, there were the shouted curses in Finnish. Saul was against our going the whole time, and seemed to be actually afraid of those bearded men.

Sisu Mother

When the people had returned to the ship, it began to glide forward, and then dropped anchor. The weather had become completely summery, although it was December. The ship's crew had changed from dark clothing into pure white. We began to hunt up summer clothing.

In the morning we woke up to a disquieting clamor and shouting. Saul went to find out what was up. Soon he returned, full of bustle and stir.

"Now we're all going on deck. The weather is warm and summery, and there's a lot to see. Come on, Poju, I'll help you to dress. Bring your shoes here, and I'll put them on."

There was an overpowering hum of talk on deck, and we were fascinated by what we saw when we looked over the rail. There were dozens of boats below, selling all kinds of junk. Multicolored shirts, all sorts of carvings of elephants and other animals. Most of the sellers were black, with a few whites among them. Someone knew that the carvings were of a black wood that was peculiar to this area. In any case, a good deal of work had been done in smoothing them out. A bag on the end of a rope would be flung up on deck, and hand gestures would be used to indicate the desired purchase and the price. Money would be placed in the bag, and sent on down. That was how they fished for their sales.

We had no Egyptian money, nor did Saul want to exchange for it. He had a wrist watch, which kept time very erratically, and that he exchanged for two shirts. I would like to have bought the carving of a black elephant, but the money was in my husband's pocket, and I knew it would not be easy to pry it loose from there. And under no circumstances did I want to expel his "good I," which had been in control during the entire voyage.

In the morning the ship began to glide smoothly through the Suez Canal toward the south. The canal was narrow; only one ship at a time could pass through it. On both sides there was only sand: hills and mounds shaped by the wind. A beautiful, undisturbed smoothness. It grew hot. There on the east was the Sinai Desert. Little wonder that the children of Israel tired of waiting in that heat. I don't remember how long Moses lingered on the mountain, while the people waited in that parching wilderness of sand. It was God's great miracle that they remained alive. They must have needed a great deal of bread and manna.

Sisu Mother

It was a great departure from our usual Christmas Eve, but nevertheless the date was December 24, 1957. The seamen decorated a Christmas tree on the upper deck for a Christmas party in the afternoon.

A few men were painting the ship white wherever there were rust spots. The ship was going so smoothly that only the furrow it left behind told us that we were moving ahead.

Ahead of us we saw something green. As we approached, we realized it was our first sight of palm trees. We wondered if this was what they called an oasis, for it was so lush. In the shade of the palm trees were a few barrack-like buildings. Soldiers with rifles stood on guard. "What is there to guard out in this desert?" I wondered. "Perhaps this canal is the cause of the clashes."

At this point the canal was wider, so it must have been where ships passed one another. One ship was already waiting to head north for the Mediterranean. Another ship could be seen approaching from the south. We waited until it passed, and then it was our turn to get back into the canal and continue our journey.

The Mediterranean Sea, the Red Sea, and the Indian Ocean are on the same level, so that no locks are necessary in the Suez Canal. It is different with the Panama Canal, for the oceans it joins are at different levels.

The Suez Canal was built during the years 1859 and 1969. It is the world's longest canal. It is 120 meters wide at the surface of the water and the shipping channel is forty meters wide. Its depth there is twelve meters. It is an event in our lives' history that we happened to be there in this southern land on Christmas Eve.

Of course we were all there on the upper deck for the party, since we had been invited. A large Christmas tree, beautifully decorated stood in the middle of the deck. The servants went around offering something to everyone, a stronger treat for the men, and candy and cookies for the children. The orchestra played Christmas songs, the melodies of which sounded familiar to us, but the tempo was so rapid that they sounded a little strange. Finns were accustomed to slow, devout music. Tommila, who led us in morning devotionals on the ship, gave the Finnish version of the notes to the orchestra. Soon we could hear, "Angels we have heard on high . . ." Everyone joined in, singing eagerly. It was really something; they had become aware of our hopes. It filled our minds with the spirit of Christmas.

"Hey, there comes Santa Claus," the children shouted. He wasn't exactly the same as the one at home. There we had been visited by a graybeard Santa with a sheepskin coat turned inside out. The one here was much more handsome. He wore a red coat and had a snow-white beard, and of course he had a red, pointed cap on his head. "How did he get here when there's no snow?" the little children wondered. White-clad shipboys helped Santa Claus distribute the gifts so that everyone got something. The time came to say goodbye to Santa Claus and go down to our own cabin and open the packages.

"Hey, there's a package on my bed too," shouted Tytti.

"And on mine. Santa has been here, too," said Pia excitedly.

"We have been such good children," announced Little-Sisko, spreading her little hands wide.

The children had their own Santa's helpers' hats with them, and now they played Santa and his helpers, while jingling their sleigh bells. I was pleased that the children had gotten into the spirit of Christmas in spite of the circumstances. I gave them permission to wear their bell caps when we went to supper.

The waiters jingled the children's bells every time they went by. There was also a beautifully decorated Christmas tree in the dining room, which made it feel really like Christmas. Outside on deck it was sweaty hot, even after the sun had set.

On Christmas Day we were on the Red Sea. The Biblical history we had read in school was now as real as real. One shore loomed in the distance, and the other shore was no longer visible. The wind raised gentle waves on the surface of the sea. On deck, it felt like a mildly warm sauna. In our cabin it was appropriately cool.

The Christmas dinner was delicious. A country woman like me did not even know all the dishes that were served. The main dish was turkey. And now what was happening?

All the lights went out, except for those on the tree. The waiters were carrying cakes on the center of which a flame was burning. One was brought to every table. The waiter asked Poju to blow out the flame. Wonder of wonders, there was ice cream inside the cake. In any case, it was delicious.

We were approaching the Straits of Bab el Mandeb, where the Red Sea joins the Indian Ocean. The eastern coast of Yemen loomed in the distance. On the opposite side, the shore of Ethiopia was quite close, and so we were able to follow the everyday life of the people there. On the shore, at the very edge of the water, was a tall column, which resembled a human being. A few dried-up looking palm trees, with clay huts beneath them. Black people with some kind of rag around their loins walking near the huts. Their upper bodies, those of the women as well, were bare. Someone was carrying a child in her arms; other children were playing naked in the sand. Such was life in the warmer lands. At least one did not have to worry about clothing.

A kind of column of stone had been erected, and from it ran a fence of dried bamboo. It marked the border between Ethiopia and French Somalia. There were no gates or guards. It was the narrowest part of the straits, and we could also see some columns. There lay the border between Yemen and Aden.

The ship was now in the Indian Ocean, which glimmered hotly in the sunlight. We were in the Gulf of Aden, and the ship was following the coast of Africa. Here we had the opportunity to get acquainted with the engine room and with the ship's steering system under the captain's guidance.

It was a thrill for Poju when the captain picked him up and let him take the rudder and steer the huge ship. And everyone in turn got to take the binoculars and look at the bottom of the sea. It was literally teeming with fish, big and little. "Hey, why is that bottom so near?" I gestured to the closest seaman to come and look. He came, but suddenly he rushed off. We were about to run aground on a reef. During all these demonstrations no one was actually aware of where we were going. The ship came to a sudden stop and headed back to the regular channel. We survived with only a scare.

It was New Year's Eve on the Indian Ocean. What would the year 1958 bring with it? That was a big question mark for many. We were not even able to melt tin to tell our fortunes. A New Year's reception party was being held on deck, but we decided to stay in our cabin with the children. It was surprising how sleepy we grew here on this ship. We did nothing, worried about nothing, but in the evening we were sleepy. It was probably an effect of the hot, humid weather.

Early in the morning when the children were asleep, we decided to go for a walk on the deck. We noticed at once that something unusual was afoot on the rear deck. We did not understand what was being said, but one of the men crossed himself in the Catholic manner, and we heard a splash, just as if something had been thrown into the sea. Two men carried off a stretcher, which was loosely covered by a white cloth. The other men went soberly off about their business. Someone must surely have died and found his final resting place there in those waves. Then it was true that the dead were not kept on a ship.

During the day, we heard the whole story. A German who was drunk had fallen down a stairwell during the night and died. That was the end of his celebration and his New Year's dreams. The man was traveling alone, and no one knew if he had a family in Germany.

I was sitting on deck with Elli Rantala. The children were happy to play out here in the open and it wasn't too hot yet in the morning. It was a sort of breathing spell after the confinement of the cabin. One of the ship's workers walked painfully past us. There was a cast on his hand, his face swollen and his eyes blackened, and he was dragging his left leg badly.

"What do you think of that?" said Elli. "It looks to me as if a whole gang worked him over."

"Well, something happened to him," I said softly. "He certainly doesn't look as if his mother patted him on the back. He will surely remember this New Year's party for years to come."

"Have you been to Tommila's morning devotionals?" asked Elli.

"A couple of times. Have you been to hear him?"

"I went once, but our youngest is napping at the same time. He sounded like a lay preacher. I don't care much for him, and I won't start changing my schedule for his sake."

"I went just to pass the time. He must be a sectarian, but I don't yet know what sect he belongs to. If he were a good speaker I'd be glad to listen as long as the Bible is the subject of the sermon. The Germans have a service every Sunday in that big salon. They have a Catholic priest with them. And I've been to the English class a couple of times. You probably haven't had the time," I said to Elli.

"I just can't make it. Jallu's been going. He'll know enough to get by at first, and he's the breadwinner."

"Very few seem to be going to the class. Lepistö, who has studied at home, says that Joni is teaching wrong, that he's teaching the Australian dialect. But what's the difference, that's where we're going. I think the main thing is to learn something. I've often seen how stupid a person is when he doesn't understand what another is saying. Saul says we're sure to catch on. We'll see. I doubt it. Time will tell."

"Yaah, I don't know," Elli said. "I come from a Swedish family, but when I was only a child I learned Finnish from the neighbors' kids. For years I sold things at the Vaasa market, and there you had to speak both languages, otherwise you couldn't get by. That English still sounds like Hebrew to me at least. I haven't been able to get the girls to learn Swedish even though I've really tried. Listen Elsie, there are all kinds on this trip. Have you noticed that Jauhiainen complains about absolutely everything? His wife must have to put up with a lot."

"I noticed. I've heard that he complains to others but is good at home. They say he even washes the dishes," I said.

"Don't tell me. That is rare in a Finnish man. I can't believe at all that he changes to a lamb at home. He has such piercing eyes that he looks right through a person."

"Well, one never knows what happens within the four walls at home," I said thoughtfully.

Our ship anchored near the city of Colombo on the Island of Ceylon (now Sri Lanka). The mainland loomed up far away beyond the fog. The ship did not go into the harbor, but people who wanted to go to the city were taken there on motor launches. There was a moderate wind, and small craft were bobbing disconcertingly alongside the big ship.

"I'm not going into that kind of tub," Saul said. "You can go if you want to."

"I'm not going alone," I said. "I was terrified by the Egyptians in Port Said. Aren't the Indians even blacker?"

"Yaah, it's much safer to stay on board," Saul added.

In the evening we heard the most amazing stories about Colombo. Someone said it was so dirty in the cafés that he couldn't eat and began to retch. Another said that he had been in the rich section of the city where everything was so elegant he could never have imagined anything like it to exist. The poor were not allowed access there. People had to wear a red caste mark painted on their forehead. Jauhiainen had begun to complain to a snake charmer that his snake had not risen high enough and to demand his money back. The Indian had come at him with his fists, but Jauhiainen had managed to duck and run away. "It would have served him right for complaining," I thought. Most of us were tired of his grumbling.

Our ship left Colombo during the night. Our next stop was Fremantle on the west coast of Australia. The trip was expected to take ten days, and there would be no land in sight for the entire time.

On the second evening there were banging sounds. The men rushed up to the deck, but there was nothing out of the ordinary to be seen. It was quite late and very dark.

In the morning it felt as if the sun were rising from the wrong direction. We discussed it with one another, and everyone was of the same opinion. Lehvistö got a compass from his cabin so that we could see if we were right.

"Look, we're going northwest," said Lehvistö. "The ship has turned back. I just looked yesterday, and we were traveling southeast."

I went to look for Joni. "He'll be able to explain what this is all about," grumbled Jauhiainen and went hurriedly to the ship's office. He soon found Joni there, and the two returned at a half-run.

"What the hell is this? We'll never get to Australia this way," blustered Jauhiainen.

"I was just on the way to tell you the news," Joni began. "You are right, we are going back. By tomorrow evening we'll probably be back in Colombo. The banging sound you must have heard late at night was the drinking water storage tank bursting. The bath and drinking water are now mixed up. They have a small reserve tank, so there is no emergency. But don't get excited if the water doesn't run. Just stay calm, you don't have anything to worry about. You'll have plenty of time to spend in Australia."

The next day we had a real feast for supper. The dessert was that delightful burning pancake. We wondered what the cause of all this was. Were they trying to keep our morale up? Was the situation so dangerous that this was a harbinger of the end? *Calm down, all is well.* This feast had been prepared for the crossing of the equator. Now that we had turned back, we could feast on the food. Well, this was to our benefit—even Jauhiainen couldn't object.

When we woke up in the morning we already were in the harbor of Colombo, not out at sea, as on the previous day. The ship had been raised higher, but the bottom was still under water. Divers were at work along the side of the ship. Was something else in need of repair, not just the water tank? The question was on the minds of many of us. One would think a water tank would be repaired inside the ship. The ship was really at the end of its days, which is why it was used to transport refugees. The rail was lined with travelers watching the divers at work.

Splash! Someone had leaned over too far and fallen into the water. On deck, someone shouted at the top of his lungs and pointed down at the water. One of the divers happened to be near the ship and noticed what had happened. He dived into the dirty water and came up with a six-year-old boy who spluttered and opened his eyes. Then he began to scream as loudly as he could. He was in no danger since his voice was so clear.

The diver carried the boy, who was kicking and screaming with fear, toward the shore. An oldish couple hurried to meet him as a sailor carried him up the gangplank. The boy tore himself loose and began to run when he saw his grandma and grandpa. It was a happy ending to his adventure. We heard that the couple were the boy's grandparents and were taking him to their daughter in Australia. They caught a flight for the rest of the journey. They had had enough of the *S.S. Skaubryn.*

On the first day, we were not permitted to leave the ship, nor, of course, were people from Colombo permitted on board. Residents of the island began to gather near the ship: men, women, and even naked children. People on board began to throw clothing and goods of all kinds to those waiting below. I couldn't help but laugh when the children put on woolen bonnets even though the temperature was thirty-five degrees Centigrade. I went to get the children's winter clothing, which were snatched up eagerly. Our children would not need them—we were going to a land of summer. The children also felt pity for the poor naked ones. They fetched their carnival hats and everything else they had gotten on board ship and tossed them down. The poor things waited even in the dark in case someone might throw something down to them.

These people belonged to the poor class. They wore no caste marks. The bigger children had a rag of sorts wrapped around them, and their heads were covered with the same sort of fabric; it had probably been a sari originally, that is, a piece of cloth ten meters long which is wrapped artfully around the body. Now it was torn and ragged. The men were bare from the waist up. Below the waist was wrapped a piece of cloth some two meters long. With some it was long, reaching to the ankles, with others it came only to the knees. A few had silken cloths with bright patterns, and seemed to be proud of their dress.

One man stood with his back toward us. He seemed to be wearing nothing at all. But looking more closely, one could see a rope around his waist, which ran down between his legs. Now he turned toward us. It looked as if he wore a leather sack in front, which covered the best place. We looked at each other, and I thought that this, too, was probably a question of style.

There were many policemen here in the port area. One was always on guard at the foot of the gangplank. The uniform brought a smile to my lips. The policemen wore a broad-brimmed hat, the left brim of which was raised and buttoned to the hat itself, along with a short-sleeved shirt and knee-length pants. The hat and the rest of the clothing were sand-colored. They also wore dark blue knee-length socks and black shoes. The whole ensemble was neat and respectable looking.

The next day we had permission to go ashore. Three families set out together, with Elli Rantala pushing her youngest in a carriage. The beggars from the day before were waiting outside the fence; they had not been admitted into the harbor area. They extended a hand in greeting. Trying to be friendly, we shook hands with them. We've been vaccinated, I thought, as I looked at those dirty hands. One girl wanted especially to greet Little-Sisko. She showed us her carnival hat; it was the one which Little-Sisko had tossed down from the ship. Little-Sisko had pure white hair, and the girl wanted to touch it. She thanked us profusely, and we left her behind, proudly showing off her colorful hat. The poor children there needed very little to make their eyes shine with joy.

The farther we walked, the larger the group following us became. They were peaceful people. The streets were quite messy, with ragged clothing strewn about in many places. It looked as if the people spent their nights by the side of the streets. The houses were huts of clay roofed with palm branches.

We had probably come to the poorer section of town, so we turned in another direction. Now we began to see better houses, tile-roofed, in the shade of magnificent palm trees. The crowd in back of us disappeared little by little; only one better-dressed boy kept following us. The poor were forbidden to come into the rich district. It was hard to tell what the houses were built of, for a high wall of adobe brick fronted the street. Only the roofs and the palm trees were visible.

Now shops began to appear along the street, many of them with wares displayed out on the street. The women wore saris of fine silk. On one there was an exceptionally beautiful pattern of gold and green leaf; it was so long that only the woman's ankles could be seen. She wore sandals on her feet, or should I say soles tied to her toes and ankles with brightly colored thongs to keep them on. Rings glittered on her toes. She was indeed a beautiful woman. Her skin was a dull ash-gray, her black hair was parted in the middle, and she bore the red-painted caste mark just at the hairline. We probably looked at her too curiously. She smiled and nodded at us, and went tripping away with light, short steps.

During the entire walk, we saw only one automobile. It was quite an old model, and rattled along noisily. Instead of cars there were many four-wheeled ox-carts with remarkable roofs made of bamboo shoots and leaves. The oxen were thin, but had powerful shoulder muscles, and their yoke was very big. Their gait was always slow; it seemed as if time had stopped and no one was in a hurry.

A few of the men and women carried huge baskets on their heads. On one man's head we saw a wicker basket the size of a wash tub, and the man was not even holding on to it. A master of the art of balancing, he was talking away and waving his hands. A few people sat at the side of the street selling bananas. We had been forbidden to buy anything to eat here, for the danger of stomach ailments was great. All kinds of bacteria lived in this warm land, kept humid by sea breezes.

We got back to the ship, tired and depressed by all we had seen. Why was there so great a disparity between the rich and the poor here? What was wrong, and could nothing be done about it? Question succeeded question in my mind. It was eternal summer here—one would have thought that life would be easy. The earth yielded crops the year round. Of course, it had to be worked. Was human laziness the cause, or was it just that they were unable to do anything? Behind us walked young and strong-looking men, waiting for us to throw them coins.

The house painter Tamminen was one of the most colorful members of our group. We were warned that we should not go anywhere at night, but Tamminen evidently had a thirst for alcohol and a desire for adventure. He went ashore alone at night and into a bar. Naturally one can find friends when one has money, even if he doesn't understand the language. When he decided to head back to the ship, a couple of men offered to go with him. That was all he remembered. He was found unconscious in the gutter. His passport and papers lay nearby, but his wallet and money were gone.

There was a hospital on board ship, and he was carried there. In his family were his wife and a grown-up daughter. He soon began to recover; there were, after all, no broken bones. His daughter had some surprising news for her father. She approached his bedside tenderly and began, "Listen Daddy, I have news for you."

"What news? Tell Daddy."

"You're going to be a 'Grandpa.' Isn't that nice?" said the girl, patting her waistline, which still showed little sign that she would have a baby.

"Hell, no. Whose is it? Who is the father?" shouted Tamminen, enraged. Fists clenched, he tried to get up from the bed, but things went black before his eyes.

"Don't be upset, Daddy. Esko is in the army, and when he gets out he'll follow us."

"Why didn't you say so. Then you could have stayed in Finland," her father snapped.

"Well, I had the papers all ready and everything, and this happened in the fall."

"Oh, God. A single child. I'm going to divorce both of you, you and your mother."

But everything simmered down, and the family stayed together. In time, Esko arrived in Australia and the two were together.

After six days of ship repairs, it was announced one evening that we would leave some time during the night. Ahead of us there was now a journey of ten days during which we would be out of sight of land. Within a couple of days, we had already reached the Equator. It was a great event; in the afternoon there was a big celebration on deck. It was announced that Neptune himself, the King of the Waves, and his helpers would board the ship and baptize everyone who was crossing the Equator for the first time.

There was now water in the swimming pool for the first time. It had been rather cold, too. People were crowded around the edge of the pool, and we, too, waited there excitedly.

"Hey, he's coming, I see his trident," someone shouted.

Over the side clambered a big, frightful-looking man with a trident in his hand, followed by several less fearsome men. His flaxen-gray hair hung long and wet over his shoulders, and his reedy, knee-length skirt flapped in the wind. His upper body was bare, and looked as if it had been brushed with tar. The same war paint was on his face and legs. Looking grim, the ruler of the waves stood at the edge of the pool, his trident's points upward, and shouted in a loud voice. His helpers ran off and began throwing people into the pool, especially the women. I started running quickly toward the stairs, but someone seized me from behind, and I was in the water along with the rest. It all happened very quickly; in a couple of minutes most of the people were floundering in the water. Neptune's helpers stood in a ring around the pool, thumbing their noses and making faces at us. Little by little they disappeared "back into the sea," as we climbed ingloriously out of the pool, our clothes dripping wet. The disgusting tar was almost impossible to get off our skin. My white summer dress bore streaks of tar forever afterwards.

The festival dinner after the crossing of the Equator was indeed a sumptuous one, as we had heard earlier that it would be. In a sense, we got to enjoy the crossing twice. A few days later we all received handsome, official baptismal papers for having made the crossing. Even the children got one of their own.

The crew took remarkably good care of all of us, including the children. Elli Rantala was astonished by a knock at her door one morning. A waiter appeared, bringing them a cake with three candles. She had not remembered that it was little Virvi's birthday. It was a pleasant surprise for the whole family. It was not easy to travel with five children, the youngest of whom was less than a year. Jallu, the husband, was helpful and energetic, but they both had their hands full.

One day Jallu came to us and said: "Now the kitchen police blew a fuse."

We did not ask why but chatted about other happenings of the day. After a while, Jallu said: "I have to go and see if the storm has died down."

The laundry was a busy place. There were no washing machines; everyone had to do the washing by hand. The drying room was to one side, but the lines were usually full. There was, however, another clothesline on the deck between smokestacks. Elli went there early one morning to get her washing, but to her astonishment she saw a young man between the clotheslines. She stepped back a little to watch what he was doing. Was he planning to steal the laundry or what? No, this was weird. Silently the man felt the crotch of all the women's pants on the lines. Having done that, he went away. "It wasn't easy to keep from laughing," Elli explained to me. "Everyone has his own way of getting his kicks."

We got to know the Nortamo family. They also had four children, exactly the same age as ours. The father of the family, Toivo, told us about his experiences. He had worked for a company that built wooden houses, for which he had had to travel to different parts of the world. He had last been in Colombia, South America.

"Colombia. Did you see any coffee plantations there?" asked Saul.

"More than enough. After that I didn't care for coffee."

"No! How come?" asked Saul, who was curious.

"Their plantings are all around worthless little dwellings. They go up on the slopes of the mountains with mules daily to harvest the coffee beans. At home they spread them out on rags to dry in their cramped yards, where the kids play. The bigger children stir them up all day with their bare feet—that's how they dry the beans. Some of the children are so small that some piss must get into the mix. I really lost my taste for coffee when I saw what it was truly like," he said. He had photos, and showed us the way the beans were dried.

We attended the English classes diligently. It wasn't easy: one needed a good memory, and some of the words were terribly difficult to pronounce. One practically had to tie her tongue into knots to get them to sound remotely correct. One morning Vieno Nortamo had a black eye. Someone teased her, saying they were a strange pair. Nortamo said she had collided with the edge of a cabinet. In those cramped quarters it was possible.

The last two days of the voyage were windy, but no one got sick. We had already become accustomed to the rolling. When we were sitting in the salon, someone said these were groundswells. The orchestra tried to rehearse, but nothing came of it: the instruments would not stay in place. Every time a wave hit, the windows were under water. Between waves the sun always flashed into view. No going out on deck; the water was splashing everywhere.

At last we were in Fremantle, the harbor city of Perth, the largest city in western Australia. Our voyage on the open sea lasted twelve days, although the program called for only ten. The side wind had rocked our ship and slowed us down. In any case, it felt good to have solid ground underfoot again, although it actually still seemed to be rocking.

We and our acquaintances took a couple of walks around the city. Everything was exceptionally neat. The shops were European-style, and all the people were white. A few families went into Perth and said it was a very modern city. We were content to look at its tall buildings as silhouettes against the open spaces. After Ceylon, we had wondered if Australia would be like Colombo.

In a couple of days we would probably reach our destination. On January 23, 1958, we awoke in the harbor of Melbourne. Here ended our journey by ship. We ate breakfast on board, and after our papers were checked, we were loaded directly from the ship onto a train. Melbourne is a beautiful city—splendid tall buildings and many green parks. The train went slowly in the city, so that we got a general picture of the place where the last Olympics had been held a couple of years ago.

What a mighty bridge, but why was the water so dirty. Ahaa, this was the Yarra River, which flows upside down, that is, with the bottom mud on top.

We were now in the country. Gentle slopes of wild grass. No trees to be seen, except for a few on the banks of streams. They looked bare, as if the bark had fallen off. Could they be eucalyptus trees? From a distance they looked blue-green. The only leaves grew high up at the top.

Finally we saw the sheep for which this country was famous. When we left, they had scared us by saying we would have to become sheepherders. There were thousands of the animals. Where did they get food and water, since the earth seemed to be a parched red? Perhaps it was red ocher.

We were in the state of Victoria. We had already been in the train for many hours. Distances seemed to be great, and so they are in large countries. Our destination was a former military training camp named Bonegilla. Finally after a four- to five-hour trip on the train, we stopped at a station from which buses would take us to our destination.

It was truly a ridiculous-looking village. The lodgings were in the shape of a half-moon and were made of corrugated sheet metal. In their midst was a tall building on which only the roof was sheet metal. After a brief period to get organized, we were taken to one of the half-moon buildings. Each family got three rooms, which took up half of the lodging. Soon we were given eating utensils, plates, knives, spoons, and forks, along with trays. We had to take care of them and carry them with us to the dining hall, which was the large building. We were also told when food would be served, and we lined up at the appointed hour. Some of our acquaintances were in the line with us.

The food tasted good, although we were not really sure what it was. After eating, all the people gathered their own dishes and washed them in the same room where the showers were. Later that evening, there was a severe thunderstorm. We were tired, but happy to have finally reached our destination. The trip had taken longer than expected, that is, five weeks and four days.

For once life was carefree and easy, from my point of view. No cooking, no shopping trips, as long as one could put up with standing in a food line three times a day. There was nothing to complain about in the food, although it was not homey. The cooks were Germans. The men had language study two hours a day, and school-age children attended their classes for the same two hours. Mothers with small children had language lessons one hour out of each day.

This was all at Australia's expense, in addition to a small daily allowance, which was referred to as "cigarette money." At the same time, efforts were being made to find employment for the men.

"It's hot as hell here," someone said painfully. February there was still like June, for we were in the Southern Hemisphere. What of it—let the sun shine, and let's enjoy life. We went swimming with the children every day in nearby Lake Hume, and still took a shower in the evening. The dry dust seemed to cling to our skin and clothing, so that we had to put on clean clothes every morning, yet in the evening we always felt dirty. Well, what of it, we had plenty of time to wash. We did not have to carry water or hang clothes out in the cold to dry. Gone were the fur caps with earflaps and the felt boots. The girls wore only panties and a smock, and Poju only shorts.

Perhaps it was a turn for the better in our lives, coming here, where everything seemed easy and carefree. It seemed to be an ideal vacation. And we even had Finnish company on all sides.

Rantala stopped in one night to chat.

"How are things with our neighbor?" Saul asked.

"Well," Jallu laughed. "At least it's warm enough here. And we have no money worries, the state supports us. Even the kitchen police are getting a real vacation. They have really earned it. Our mama likes this life so damn much."

"How long do you think they'll keep us here?" asked Saul.

"I went to the office today, and a Finnish interpreter happened to be there. I hear he's there every Monday. I asked him a little about everything. He said they are trying to find us jobs but not to worry. You don't even have to take the first job they offer. Now they are offering temporary jobs for a few weeks, picking grapes in southern Australia. The families can stay here."

"In vineyards," said Saul, stretching lazily. "Out in the fields the whole hot day long. It won't do. Elsie could go, since she likes grapes so much. Do you plan to go?"

"No, unless they force me to. No, I won't leave my family alone. It's too much for Elli to cope with, when three of the children are still so small they have to be watched all the time. Lepistö put his name on the list, though."

"Really? Does he plan to go? Well, all he knows is chicken farming, and at least he'll get to be a farmer. He does know the language a little, but will that help much in anything?"

"Lepistö claimed that if he goes there, they'll see that he gets a good job. Jauhiainen and a few other young men have signed up too," Jallu continued.

"It's good that Jauhiainen is going. We're all tired of his grumbling. I would get a kick out of seeing him breaking his butt in a vineyard when he is used to work in a Helsinki print shop."

"I heard," said Jallu, "that you can stay here just like this for at least a year. Then if you don't find a job, they put you to work here, emptying garbage cans, if nothing else. None of the older men are leaving. I heard a rumor that the younger men have run out of money."

"Yaah, yaah, I'm sure not going to work picking berries," said Saul.

The hot weather continued, and it was March already. Now and then a sudden thundershower made the air fresh again. Two weeks had passed since the grape pickers had left when Jauhiainen and a couple of the younger men returned. According to Jauhiainen, it had been completely unbearable there. They had stayed long enough to collect their first wages and money for a train ticket. Lepistö and a few others stayed the six weeks to which they had agreed.

At the end of March, we had already been in the camp for eight weeks when jobs on the east coast were offered to the whole group of Finns. The men conferred with one another about what to do. The work was in an iron plant some one hundred miles south of Sydney in a city named Wollongong.

The majority decided to go. Many were already tired of this vacation. Lepistö stayed on at the camp with his family. He had just returned from picking grapes and needed a rest.

Buses drove us to the station. With us was the same group of Norwegians and Germans who had come on the ship. We were three hundred people in all. The faces were familiar, but we could still not understand each other, except for the few words we had learned in the language class.

Boarding the train reminded me of the wartime evacuation. After two hours on the way, we stopped and were ordered to change to another train. It was a complete mess, for the children had just begun to calm down, and it was already midnight. In time, everything was sorted out. Nortamo, who knew a little of the language, was able to get information. "We're at the border of Victoria and New South Wales. The tracks in Victoria are a narrower gauge than here, so we can't continue on the same train. Everything has to be switched to another train in the next state. Long ago when the railroads were built, the states could not agree on a common gauge, and so here we are. Just think, even freight trains have to be emptied every time. Think of the extra work."

The switch took more than an hour. It was already beginning to dawn when we began slowly to jerk ahead. The landscape was almost entirely covered with hay burned to a reddish brown. That must have been one of the famous kangaroos hopping over there. Huge bounds, at least six meters high and hard to guess how long. It looked just as if they got a spring from that enormously long tail. Were there young in their pouches, as the stories said?

Soon a bluish gray began to loom in the distance. We were coming into some craggy mountains. These were the blue hills which separated the coast from the interior. Joni had told us about them on board ship already. The interior is dry, and east of the mountains, it rains a lot. The story goes that here in the interior there lived a thirty-six-year-old man. One of the new settlers asked him, "Does it ever rain here."

"Sure it does," he said. "I haven't seen it rain, but my father did once."

The train wound around the sides of the mountains like a wriggling snake. From time to time it dived into a tunnel. Finally we made it over or down the mountains, whichever might be said, for before us opened a vista of houses surrounded by green trees and shrubbery. The air too seemed fresh and pure. In the distance we saw tall buildings as well. As the train slowed, we saw the name, Blackdown. We began to head straight north, so we were not going to Sydney, which was due east.

We were taken to another military barracks named Concord, on the outskirts of Sydney. The men parted from us and were taken straight to Wollongong. Women would follow in some ten days.

Here all the buildings were of the barracks type, and we did not even have to wash dishes. The place was called a hostel. There were a few residents, but we were unable to speak to them yet. None of them could speak Finnish, but Elli Rantala could speak Swedish, and by that route we were able to get the help we needed.

We were given two spacious rooms, which obviously had not been used for a long time. The rooms were full of mosquitoes. I opened the windows and doors and tried to drive them out, probably succeeding in part. We were very tired and fell asleep at once. When we awoke in the morning, our faces were full of red spots. We did not have a mirror, and I asked the children if my face looked the same.

"It does. You look as if you had some kind of pox."

Those darned mosquitoes tried to eat us alive. Poju was completely covered with those spots from the waist up. In the dining hall every one stared at us with a frightened look on their faces. A bolder Finn dared to ask what the spots were. They thought we had something contagious.

While we were eating, a nurse came to ask questions. I did my best to imitate the buzzing of the mosquitoes, which she did understand, and she brought us some salve to soothe the itching. No one gave us any advice on how to rid the room of the insects.

The same thing had happened to the Nortamo family, although they were not bitten as badly. We heard that there was a store somewhere a kilometer away and headed for it with Vieno and eight children. The storekeeper looked at us apprehensively at first, until I began to explain:

"Mosquito—mosquito eat. Mosquito eat."

"Oh-oh-oh, me understand," he said, and took some kind of sprayer from a shelf, along with a bottle of some liquid poison. He showed me how the sprayer worked and warned me to keep the bottle away from children.

"No kids, no kids," he said, pointing to the picture of the skull on the bottle.

I had copied the word "mirror" from the dictionary, and we found one in the store as well. That was the sum total of our purchases. The storekeeper asked me another question, which I did not understand. He went and started to scoop ice cream into cones, and that the children did understand. Each time he handed out a cone, he repeated, "Ice cream, ice cream," so we learned at least one English word on that trip.

That was how we got rid of the mosquitoes, and soon the earlier bites got better. The weather here was cooler, but somehow humid and tiring. It was already April, and the weather should have been cooling off. "Winter" was coming to the Southern Hemisphere.

In large groups we took long walks. We had just returned from one when Poju shouted, "Father!" and began to run. It was a pleasant surprise. The men had two days off and had taken a taxi to come and see how we were doing. There was a lot to talk about, for we had been separated for over a week.

"How are things going? What is the work like?" I asked.

"It's easy. All I do is push a broom. They put us in a cleaning crew while we are learning the language."

"Well, what does it matter, as long as the work isn't hard."

"No one is complaining except for Jauhiainen. The whole gang decided to pull a stunt on him. It will really gripe him when he finds out that we came here. No one told him about it."

"You don't say! Didn't even Laitinen say anything? They knew each other even in Finland," I laughed.

"Laitinen is as tired of him as the rest of us. We've heard that you will get to join us there in a week. The hostel is on the seashore, and there's a really clean sand beach close by," said Saul.

The day went by quickly. The men had to leave in the afternoon, for the trip took four hours. I was hoping that the week would pass quickly and that the whole family could be together again. He had been so nice during the entire trip. I was hoping that the devil in his mind would not be able to plot more wickedness. If only he were permanently cured of his delusions, I prayed.

Evenings the weather was cool. The whole group of us was on a long walk again. Far off to our west we could see the blue hills. They looked so romantic with a blue mist hovering over them, but we knew that beyond them was a dry desert, where it had rained only once in the memory of a grown man.

There was a nursery where we could leave the smaller children for an hour each day while we went to the language classes with the bigger children. It wasn't easy for the children either, for they could not understand anything. The Kangases' boy came home one day with his pants wet, because he was afraid and did not know how to ask to go to the bathroom. The poor kids.

We were now on the way to Wollongong, in three chock-full buses. The land was hilly but really beautiful and fertile. Wherever there was the least bit of level land, there were houses. There were enormously long climbs and descents. We were nearly at the bottom of one hill when the bus behind us tooted loudly. Our bus stopped, and we could see that it was smoking in back. Everyone got out quickly. The driver went to spray it with a fire extinguisher, but there was only smoke, no flame.

The bus started off again, although a little more slowly, and the driver stopped to check at the next gas station. The brakes had begun to smoke on a long downhill stretch, but otherwise the bus was in good condition. We drove quite slowly, and arrived much later than the others.

The men were waiting for us, looking upset. A rumor had already arisen that the bus had caught fire. Even here news seemed to travel with the speed of an airplane.

The men had been assigned family lodgings in semi-circular, corrugated sheet-metal barracks. The whole environment here seemed much neater than that in Bonegilla. There the barracks had been close together on the bare sand, which blew inside with the slightest wind. Here they were farther from one another, and there was even grass between the buildings.

It seemed as if there were more people here, because the food lines were longer. Food for the men was prepared in the dining hall, and it was ready when they came for breakfast and left for work. The organization was exceptionally good. The food was varied and suited even Finnish palates. Of course one always heard complaints. But in fact, things were much better than we had expected. We had reached our destination and were beginning life in our new country, in the Southern Hemisphere, where even the Man in the Moon was upside down.

Remember always to take a rainbow with you. It brightens your thoughts.

Stick a geranium in your hat and be happy.

Quotes from The Best of Barbara Johnson, by Barbara Johnson, Inspirational Press: New York, 1996.

CHAPTER X

Every morning the sun shines from a clear sky. Rugged mountains surround us, and on one side is the blue Pacific. It is May, and it ought to be winter, but the only sign of it is an occasional chill wind. Is there a more delightful place in the world than this? And the women still didn't have any household cares. We didn't even have to wash the dishes, but only the knives, forks, and spoons. On the other hand, this is our best chance to learn the customs and the marketing habits of the country. It would be very difficult for us to start preparing food when everything was completely strange and new. But let us enjoy life while we can.

We were paying for our keep now, but the price was very reasonable. Those with large families received assistance from the state. The wages were small, but a certain amount of it had to be left for the family's private use. In other words, those with larger families paid less than those with smaller ones. This irritated Jauhiainen, who had only two children.

"Well, just go ahead and get a bigger family."

"Hell, I have enough to do supporting these two. The old lady has so much fun with money that she never has enough."

"You have to hold the purse strings tighter," jeered Laitinen.

We enjoyed life on the seashore, for we had never lived there before. That enormous mass of waters had its own appeal. It was almost always a beautiful blue. Every wave that struck the sandy shore was different from every other. One could watch them for hours without being bored. During storms, the sea was frightening, a gray-green in color, and it literally howled. Everything here was so mighty and powerful. For example, if you happened to be outside in a storm, you had to hold on to a fence or a tree to keep from being swept away by the wind.

I often sat on the shore with the little ones. The children could always occupy themselves building sandcastles. I sat deep in thought, dreaming of everything under the sun—Just think, that wave had come from South America, perhaps from Chile. This one was surely from Mexico or California. Perhaps that drop of water had touched the leg of some film star. The Pacific Ocean did not live up to its name. It was never calm. It tried to storm even when the ebbing tide seemed to be drawing the water into the bosom of the ocean.

"Hey, look at this," Laitinen came up in a dither, a newspaper in his hand.

"The *S.S. Skaubryn* has sunk. We came here at the end of January. It went back and was returning with a load of refugees. It caught fire and went down in the Indian Ocean," Laitinen continued.

"How awful! What happened to the people?" I said, horrified.

"They managed to save them, except for a German who suffered a heart attack. That was after they had all been rescued by a passing ship and taken to Aden. You remember the place to the north when we came from the Red Sea onto the Indian Ocean."

Laitinen left with his newspaper.

Saul went out to get the paper from the nearest store. We wanted to learn more about how it had really happened.

"There's a good picture of it on the first page," said Saul, spreading out the paper. He went to get a dictionary to help with the reading.

"There were about 1,500 passengers and a crew of from 500 to 600. It was lucky that we got to go in December. If we hadn't been able to sell the house, we would be in that mess now," he said, pleased.

"Yaah, I remember how we often used to look at those lifeboats. They were supposed to hold eighty-five people, but they looked so miserably small. We were supposed to go to those life-saving drills every week. I used to think about it and pray that the real thing would never happen. The Germans were always so selfish and tried to get in first."

"And those people had to stay in the lifeboats from four to six hours," Saul said, studying the paper with the aid of the dictionary.

"All of their luggage went to the bottom of the sea, if it didn't burn with the ship. When this paper went to press, the ship was still burning."

"The people will be brought to the airfield here. It says that there were Finns among them. Most of them, though, were refugees from East Germany, like last time—Wow, that was a close call. We had been planning not to leave until this shipload left, but you kept rushing things so much. It's good that we got out of the cold there."

"Well, here we are now, and here we stay," I said determinedly.

"That ship was really an old wreck," said Saul.

"They tried to make it look good on the outside. Whenever we were in port, the crew was busy with the paint brushes," I said.

"It was a trip we'll never forget. It's awful to think of the ship at the bottom of the sea and of what the people suffered. Just think of the creatures that are wriggling through our cabin now."

"It was a terrible thing to happen. I wonder if the women even managed to get their pocketbooks with them, not to mention their other things?" I said.

"It happened at ten o'clock in the evening. Most of the people were already asleep. It sure would have been a mess if we'd had to rush out into the night like that. 'The sea was calm,' it says here."

Nortamo, who was a cabinetmaker, was the first to leave his job at the factory. He got a construction job in the neighborhood. The couple lived near us with their four children. We got to know them better as people who could be depended upon.

However, Nortamo was not satisfied with his lot. It was rumored that there were good job prospects for cabinetmakers in Queensland. It was to the north, and thus in a hot, tropical climate. He did not seem to take that into account, but spoke enthusiastically of moving there.

A few days later the couple came to visit us in the evening to talk about their plans. Toivo had already bought a train ticket to the city of Brisbane in the state of Queensland. He had everything all ready to go on an early morning train. When he got a start there, the family was to follow. We said goodbye when it was already quite late. We wished him luck on his journey. "We'll see you again some day," I called out after him.

Saul rose at five, went to breakfast, and left for work on the six o'clock train. When he had left, I heard a frantic knocking at the door. I ran to open it. Vieno Nortamo stood there with her face a dead white. She had trouble getting her words out:

"Toivo . . . Toivo committed suicide. I don't know where I should go to let them know. It just happened."

"Oh my God!" I said softly. "The office won't be open for many hours. I think there's a phone in the dining hall kitchen."

"I'll go there," said Vieno, and set off at a run.

Sisu Mother

I dressed quickly and went to the Nortamos'. I wish I had not. I'll never forget that sight. Toivo had slit his throat with his Kauhava knife. He was lying in the center of the room, and the blood had spread all over the floor. At the far edges it had begun to congeal into a dark slime. The two oldest children were peering through the door of the next room, their faces deathly pale.

"Pick up your clothes and run over to our place," I managed to say. They went out quickly, and I closed the door. I saw Vieno returning with someone. She saw the children going to our place.

"It's good that they're gone. The ambulance will come soon. I'll go into Vesa and Arja's room, and stay until everything is cleaned up. I won't let them see any of this chaos. Why did this have to happen?" Vieno managed to say, and then she burst into uncontrolled weeping.

I went to my own lodging and saw that the ambulance was already at the end of the lane. Anni and Pauli sat crouched over on a chair in the doorway, silent, their clothes in their arms. I could say nothing to console them. Poor kids.

"Mother will come right away," I said. "You go into our room and dress, Anni," I said in a whisper, for Poju was still asleep.

Gradually my children woke up, too. Vieno also came with her younger children when everything was over. She had told Vesa and Arja nothing about what had happened. Our children were amazed that their playmates had come so early.

"They came to get us for breakfast," I explained. We usually went to breakfast together, and now we did all go in a group. I took something for appearance' sake only; I could not even think of eating. My stomach was heaving as if I were about to throw up. No one said a word; Vieno drank some coffee, her face gray and tears running down her face, even though she strove heroically to repress them. Her youngest children and our children sensed something, but did not ask any questions. Everyone was very grave, and there was none of the usual tittering.

"Can we come to your place again?" asked Vieno as we left the dining hall.

"Of course," I said emphatically. Our bigger children left for school, but the Nortamo children did not go.

"I'll go to the office to let them know where I am. I assume they'll want to ask questions. I'll give them your building number."

On her return, Vieno said: "Well, they're moving us into another apartment. I already have the number. The movers are coming. They told me not to go back there any more."

"That's a good idea. The bigger children went for a walk along the shore. Poju and Arja are playing in the other room. They get along very well together; they're exactly the same age. Did Toivo say anything to you before it happened?"

"Not much. He slept very little. He would pace the floor and sit down, and stretch out on the bed sometimes. He was terribly upset. I asked him what was wrong, but he wouldn't answer."

There was a knock at the door. The girl from the office wanted Vieno to go with her. Vieno gave me a significant nod and left. I promised to take care of the children. When she returned she looked upset. I did not want to ask questions, but waited for her to speak.

"Can you imagine? They questioned me as if I were a criminal. Two policemen grilled me up and down. They thought I was to blame for this."

"Don't tell me. How could they? Didn't they see that the knife was still clamped tightly in his hand?"

"They didn't accuse me of murder, but they thought we had been quarreling, and that's why Toivo did it. We didn't argue at all that night. But he was very upset, though he said nothing."

"Did you understand everything they asked?"

"Well, almost everything. I would say that I didn't understand, and they would find an easier way to ask. It was hard for me to give the answers. When they realized that, they began to ask the questions so that I could answer yes or no."

"Well, our lessons were of some help. You had some preparation for them, since you went to middle school."

"Yes, but I was surprised myself at how well I understood. Listen, I think I know why Toivo did it."

"Well why?" I asked, curious now.

"You know, he was so pathologically jealous that he found it hard to leave us here," Vieno said, and she began to sob.

"Yes, I know. It's an awful disease, but he himself wanted to go there. You didn't drive him to it. He could have stayed at the iron plant at least until he had learned the language well."

"He could have kept working on construction here. He drew his last pay when he got all steamed up about going to Queensland. I didn't say anything one way or the other—you couldn't to that man. You remember when I had that black eye on the ship? Toivo had hit me."

"Don't tell me. Did he have such a temper?" I asked uneasily.

"Mmmhmh," Vieno nodded. "And that wasn't the first time."

"Listen, Vieno, I'll tell you now that Saul is delusional, too, but only at times. Sometimes a couple of years will go by without any symptoms of it. He has never hit me. Once he had a strap in his hand, but I said I would leave once and for all, and he didn't touch me."

"We are the same hard-luck children," said Vieno. She came over and we hugged each other.

"Did he imagine anything else except that you were chasing around with other men? I know you're not guilty of that."

"I can say the same of you, Elsie. He didn't imagine anything else, but he watched every step I took. That's why he took the job nearby, so that he could come and eat here during the day."

"How awful! What a terrible time you've had. Saul gets the wildest ideas. I still have to laugh about the business of the sheepskin coat. He once bought a sheepskin and a fine piece of gabardine for a man's jacket. There was a tailor nearby who made it for him. When he got it, he inspected every seam and corner and said angrily that the old man had switched the hides. The sheepskin was white, but he found a black hair here and there. I thought the sheepskin looked better than when he took it there. Of course it was the same one, but he did not believe it. He went to the tailor and began to rant at him. The poor old man could do nothing about it, and I felt sorry for both of them. Saul never wore the coat, although I thought it really looked good.

"He often imagined he was deathly ill. He was even checked in Helsinki once, by many doctors and with all possible machines. They found nothing, and he soon forgot it himself."

"You've had to put up with all kinds of things, too," said Vieno. "It's hard to believe: on the surface it looks like you get along so well. How long have you been married?"

"Soon it will be twelve years. A person never knows in advance what fate will bring her. Beautiful dreams can collapse so suddenly. How many years have you been together?" I asked Vieno.

"The same length of time. It was twelve years just last week. I didn't even dare think of a divorce, even though every day was difficult. Toivo threatened to kill me if I divorced him."

"How awful! How could you go on from one day to the next."

"The bigger children knew about it, and they were on my side. It was easier now than it was a few years ago," Vieno sobbed.

There was another knock on the door. It was a girl from the office, who explained that the rooms were ready. She gave us the keys and showed us where the new apartment was, even taking us to the door. The children left the playground and came with us.

The rooms were a little different, but they too were spacious. The children began enthusiastically to arrange the furniture. The boys got their own room, and so did the girls. Vieno took the first room for herself. "I'm the first one to get up anyway, and the last to go to bed. This can be the living room. I'll sleep on that sofa; it's wide enough for me without being opened."

It looked as if she had forgotten for the moment everything that had happened that day. Or was it so unnatural that it had not yet found a permanent place in her heart. I left them arranging their new apartment. It was time for Saul to come home from work too. As soon as he opened the door, I saw by his face that he knew what had happened.

"How did you find out?" I asked at once,

"Jauhiainen blabbed about it first, when he came to work for the evening shift. We didn't believe him because he talks such rot. Then Rantala came and told us about it. How could Toivo do that? When he left in the evening I didn't notice anything unusual. He was so enthusiastic about going," said Saul.

I told him the story in detail. "Vieno told me that Toivo had a very hot temper," I began. "And he was insanely jealous; that's probably why his nerves failed him," I added.

"Toivo couldn't have accused her for no reason," Saul said abruptly.

"Do you think Vieno was chasing around with others?—Never!" I said hotly. "We've known and seen each other every day for the past six months. Neither you nor I have seen anything that even suggests it."

"You're just sticking up for her. You're all in it together."

"Well, damn it, what can I say? You sing the same song as Toivo. Don't you remember on board ship when Pajunen's wife started fooling around with those sailors? Everyone noticed it right off. Have you heard a single word about Vieno or me? Now have you?" I stormed.

"I haven't heard anything here, but I did earlier," he said in a low voice.

"I think something went wrong with Toivo's nerves. But he didn't say anything about being homesick."

There was a short knock at the door. Saul looked at me strangely but went to open it.

"Just come on in, Vieno and you children too," he said in a kindly voice.

"I started to feel so bad that I had to come," said Vieno, with tears in her eyes.

"It's hard to say anything," said Saul gloomily and took Vieno's hand. "You're always welcome here, if it helps," he added. "We're friends, and we'll try to help as much as possible."

"Thanks, it's nice to have a place to go to," said Vieno timidly, still teary-eyed.

"Yaah, it's hard, especially here in a foreign country when you don't know the language well," said Saul.

"I've learned a lot today," Vieno said, sniffling.

"Well, no matter how hard it is, crying doesn't help. If people could only learn from nature. When you watch ants at work, for instance, when one dies, the others just keep on going. We have to go on living, too. We can't just let life come to a stop. It's probably easy for me to talk, since it hasn't happened to us. You just have to hope that you stay healthy. How are the children taking it?" asked Saul.

"It was awful for the bigger ones; they woke up when he crashed to the floor. I haven't said anything to them about it. Vesa started to ask questions when he heard that his father was dead. I don't think he believes yet that his father is gone forever. Arja doesn't really understand yet."

"Have you been able to think about the future at all? Will you stay here or will you go back to Finland?"

"No, I won't go back to Finland, I've decided that. I think I'll get along better here. I won't go back and be dependent on my relatives for help. Everyone has his own worries in Finland, too. And I don't have any trade there; it's all the same if I stay here, even as a cleaning woman. Let the state help me if I can't manage on my own. A minister visited us early in the evening. I don't know what church he represented; they have so many beliefs here. He actually blamed me for what happened and actually pressured me to tell him what kind of quarrel we had. But there was nothing of the sort last night."

"Don't tell me. He should have been there to console you," I said, annoyed.

"What next? I certainly won't have that minister for the burial if I can find another," said Vieno bitterly.

The burial was on the third day following the death. It had rained during the night. There were no paved walks in the cemetery, and the ground was a clayey muck. A few of the Finnish men had stayed home from work as pallbearers, Saul among them. I was with the little children at the graveside along with the Nortamo family. A Lutheran minister read the blessing. We understood few of the words, but we knew their intent. The minister began to sing in English, but the melody was unfamiliar to us, and we could not even hum along with it. We had our hymnals with us, and at the end we sang Hymn 600.

> Oh Lord, if this earthly traveler,
> Could see Thee at his journey's end.
> If only I could see but once,
> The Lord in all His glory.

Thus ended the adventurous journey of one Finn in faraway Australia. It was a shock to all of us who had made the trip from Finland with him. It was natural that those of us who were his acquaintances would soon forget, but it would always be a sad memory in the Nortamo family.

Vieno came with her children to spend the evening with us. She already seemed much more animated. She began to talk in a soft voice:

"It seems a lot easier now that it's all over. These evenings are the saddest. Can you imagine, I have to open that sofa into a bed every evening. Before morning there are five of us under the same covers. Anni wakes up in fear many times a night. It's no wonder, since she saw everything that morning. I have nightmares, too, and wake up with my hair wet. But they say time heals all wounds. I managed to write to Toivo's mother and sister today about what happened. I tried earlier, but I couldn't get a word down on paper. I hope they understand, but what can you do? It happened, and it can't be changed. It was his fate to die here in this foreign country."

Vieno was able to get a job as a cleaning woman in a hotel, as she had foreseen. The three oldest children were in school. I took care of Arja, along with Poju, who was also four years old. They got along very well together. Life in the Nortamo family began to settle down. Vieno seemed relaxed;

sometimes we even giggled together. It occurred to me that she had been freed of a heavy burden, although by way of a grisly fate. We always had lunch together in the dining hall, where we had the opportunity to unburden ourselves to each other. Once she began to explain to me, "Listen, Elsie, I have to admit that my life is much easier than before. I am tired at night, but I sleep well. I have no great worries. My pay is reasonable; in a few years I may be able to buy a little house. There is always plenty of this kind of work. In private homes the pay is better. Of course I'll stay here until I learn the language better."

"It was your fate to succeed after going through that suffering. It wasn't easy, but you are brave and you try to do your best."

In these former military quarters there were common bathrooms with showers at one end. I went there one morning as usual. I opened the toilet door and turned pale, grabbing the door to keep from falling. The toilets in those days had a water tank above, with a rope which one pulled. A man hung from the rope, strangled. There wasn't a soul around, even in the laundry room. What should I do? I felt the man's leg cautiously—it was stiff. I ran back toward our dwelling. Saul was just dressing. He thought I'd had a heart attack because my face was absolutely white.

"A man . . . a man has hanged himself," I finally got the words out.

"Are you sure? Is he dead?"

"He's all stiff, I felt his leg. Come and see. There's no one there. He's in the women's bathroom."

We ran to the place. There was no one around. I opened the door timidly. Saul turned pale. The man was young, under thirty, his brown eyes open, staring senselessly.

"Stay here and watch. I'll go to the dining hall for help."

A German woman tried to come in, but I would not let her. She looked at me angrily and began to babble something. Finally it occurred to her to go to another bathroom. As she left, she was still shaking her fist at me.

Soon Saul returned with a kitchen helper. A quick look and the man put two garbage cans against the door so that no one could get in. We left; it was time for Saul to go to work. He said: "I can't eat breakfast, I'll just go and get my lunch bag."

It was learned later that the man's family was still in Germany. Perhaps homesickness and absence from his family had brought this about. It also turned out later that the woman who had shaken her fist at me was a relative of his. One day in the dining hall she came and extended a hand to me, speaking nicely to me in German which I of course did not understand. I took it as a plea for forgiveness.

There was a school holiday for a few days, and the Nortamo children were in my care. We decided to go on a trip, planning to take a train south for a couple of stations and then walk back along the sandy shore. We took lunch with us, for the trip would last the whole, long day.

We were the object of some slightly odd looks while we waited for the train. Eight children, the oldest of them eleven. They all looked very much alike, with round cheeks, blond-hair, and gray-blue eyes. Someone asked a question as he went by, but I was not able to answer.

Everyone found the trip really rewarding. We gathered seashells and sang Finnish folk songs as we walked along the shore of the Pacific. Perhaps these shores had never heard Finnish music before. Oh, how good these plain, ordinary sandwiches tasted as we sat on a rock on the shore. The water was cold, so no one felt like swimming. And it was so salty that if we got some on our clothes, it hardened at once, and salt rime formed on the surface.

We all went to night school diligently to learn the language. Our teacher was Mr. Brown, an older man with a sense of humor. He had taken care of many of Vieno's affairs since the death of Toivo. He never mocked anyone, even though many funny things happened. First he would point to parts of his body, and then we would say what they were. Once he pointed to his left leg above the knee, and Mrs. Törma answered, "It's you left egg."

The rest of us had trouble to keep from laughing, but Mr. Brown delicately changed the subject.

Saul began to feel like working at his own trade again. Wollongong was a small place, and the only job possibilities there were in the automobile plant. On one of his free days, we went to Sidney together. We had the address of a Finnish real-estate agent there. We found him, and he was able to spend a few hours with us. He showed us a few houses for sale, which proved very interesting to us. He even called the automobile plant about a job for Saul.

"Yes, there is work there. The first day you have free you can go there personally and put in an application. If you need help with the language, you can give me a call."

We paid the agent for his troubles and went home in a cheerful frame of mind. Now we could really see how the train wound around the mountain and through the many tunnels. A level space the width of a railroad track had been hacked out of the side of a steep mountain. When we looked from the rear end of the train, it looked as if the engine were headed straight for the sea. Phew, it made our heads swim to look. But it was not actually going into the sea, merely circling the peak of the mountain. It was only a one-way track, which eased our tension slightly. I noticed that Saul was really afraid.

We began planning a move to Sidney. Saul had already been working in the automobile plant a couple of weeks. They also had a similar hostel there named Villawood for the immigrants. It was not near the place where Saul was working, but there was no other possibility. We waited for a place there for the family to move into, a move that now had to be made at our own expense. We could live in the hostel for two years; by then one should have gotten a start in life in the new land, but we heard that even then we would not be driven out. We chatted with a pair that had lived there for five years, although usually everyone tired of the food there and wanted to get into their own home.

We were sad to leave Wollongong. It was a beautiful area, with the constant surging of the sea, of which one never tired, and the rural atmosphere around us, even though the city was within walking distance. Saddest of all was leaving the Nortamo family. We had grown to be close during these last months. Arja was able to stay with another Finnish family during the day, but she cried when we left because we weren't taking her with us. I cried too, but there was nothing I could do.

There were many other Finns in the Villawood hostel, a few of whom had been there for more than a year. The housing was the same half-moon lodgings of corrugated sheet metal. In size this was the next largest immigrant living site after Bonegilla. One could say there were people from all the

European countries, and everything was arranged accordingly. It was like a little city in itself. It had its own post office, bank, store, and school for the children in the hostel area, with the same food system: everyone ate the food which was prepared and served in the dining hall. Everyone saw to the cleaning of their own lodging, and sheets and towels were exchanged weekly at the supply room.

In a small town nearby, we saw our former acquaintance, Lehvistö, and his plump, energetic wife come walking toward us down the street.

"Well, hey, friends," Kerttu shouted from a distance, "if I could just remember your name. Let me think. Elsie, yeah, and Saul. You're here now, too."

"Yaah, we came a couple of weeks ago. I got a job in the automobile plant. Hey, how come we didn't meet at the hostel," said Saul.

"We're not in the hostel anymore," said Ville. "I bought a lot the week after we came, and then I bought a prefab garage. Me and Kerttu put it up. We had a Finn help us a couple of days. We finished it up after we moved in."

"You're really something, going at it like that," Saul marveled.

"Yeah, we were in the hostel only six weeks when we moved here," said Kerttu. "It wasn't so great, but it's so warm here that everything worked out just fine."

"Yaah, you can really save when you live on your own," said Saul. "That hostel takes a huge chunk out of your pay, especially with a big family."

"Oh, so you got into the auto plant Well, that has something to do with cars," said Ville. "That Lidcombe got me a job cleaning state offices. Nothing to it. It's light work, and you can be inside all the time. You don't get days off, like in the building trade. I knew I couldn't get into farming here. I bought a bicycle, so I don't even have to go to that station. It's a three-mile ride there, and I get enough open air that way. They taught me how to run the floor-cleaning and polishing machines. I'm very happy with my job," Ville concluded.

"Come and visit us," Kerttu urged. "Ville can draw a map, so you can find us."

"You just turn right there," said Ville, beginning to sketch on a slip of paper. "Why not come on Saturday. There'll be time then."

The whole family was going to see the Lehvistos' new home. I had bought bread and salt as a housewarming present, to bring good luck to the new home. Kerttu was fussing busily around the stove. It was a small place, but there were only four of them. The children went out to play. In back there was a large tree, which would keep them occupied.

"We were the first of the gang on board ship to get under our own roof," said Kerttu. "We've heard that Keppo bought a house in North Sydney. He used to boast about all his money on the trip. We started with little, and didn't borrow much. When we get this lot paid for, we can even put up a house on it and rent it out. That's what we're planning. The rents here are sky high."

"Yaah, that's a good idea. Then the house will pay for itself. You and Kerttu are business people."

"Yaah, you can't get ahead much living in that hostel. Many yell and complain about the Australian government but do nothing at all themselves. The state has given them enough to begin with; now everyone has to try to do it himself from now on."

"We came here to shave off that gold, but we have to start off small. You can't knock around for long with the money you brought from Finland if you don't start getting more in. It costs money to live everywhere."

"I've never got it straight about the prices of food. Are they higher or lower here than in Finland?" I asked.

"They're much lower here, especially for fruits and vegetables. But we haven't learned to eat much of that fodder," said Kerttu.

"We've eaten a lot of these salads in the hostel; I've learned to like them a lot," I said. "They seem to be just right in such a hot country. We've bought a lot of fruit as a kind of delicacy, and here you can get all you want at a reasonable price."

"You should learn to eat salads," Saul urged them. "They're not as heavy as meats."

"I suppose you heard about the sinking of the *Skaubryn*," said Ville.

"Yes, we did, that was at the end of April already," said Saul.

"There's a rumor going around now that it was done on purpose."

"Don't tell me. Where did you hear that?" asked Saul, interested.

"Well, you remember what an old tub it was. It was well insured, and repairs would have cost an awful lot When they set fire to it, they got a lot of insurance money. It wasn't good for anything else but transporting those war refugees."

"Well, darn it all. Is this what you think?"

"That's what the Germans said was the absolute truth. You see, I understand German better than English."

"Well, are they paying any reparations to the people who lost everything?" I asked, flabbergasted.

"I'm sure the shipping company won't pay anything at all. If the people had their own insurance, they got paid from that. I've heard that the Red Cross helped those who were saved."

"The weather was smooth and the sea was calm, and they weren't far from Aden, so everyone was saved. Someone said they tried it already when we were coming, but it didn't work out. You remember that night when there was a crash, and the ship turned back to Ceylon."

"Yaah, yaah. We wondered why the divers were repairing the bottom of the ship when the water tanks were supposed to be ruptured."

"These are rumors, but you hear everything," said Ville. "If they had tried to split the ship in two then, there would have been no chance to save anyone. We had already sailed for two days, and there was no land anywhere. We would be in the fishes' kingdom now."

"Yaah, remember those big schools of sharks. They would have had a tasty meal if 1,500 people had splashed into the sea."

"I tell you, we all would have been fish food," said Kerttu. "It was by God's good fortune that we got out of there."

"Is there anyone in that hostel who was in the disaster?"

"I haven't heard of anyone. I usually go there once a week to speak Finnish. I'm not too good at English yet, and we're among Greeks here. I can't talk to them. The boy goes to play with their kids and can say a few things in Greek."

"Don't tell me. Why that's fun," I said. "Does he understand English yet?"

"He tries to. They learn quickly in school because there's no one there who can speak Finnish, so they have to learn."

"To change the subject," said Ville. "There are still lots for sale here. Come and buy one from our neighbor here, set up a garage to live in, and you'll get away from that hostel."

"Yaah, it's something to think about," said Saul cautiously. "But my job is so far away. If I mean to work there I should get a place to live that is closer. When I learn more of the language, I'll try to get into an auto repair shop. I've found out about wages, and they're a lot higher there. The work I'm doing now is Charlie Chaplin stuff. A car is put together on a belt that travels slowly, and everyone adds something to it."

"Hey look, that's neat. What do you add? Do you have to rush?"

"I put on the door on the right side. I'm in no hurry at all. I'm used to handling the screws. I have an electric screwdriver. The work is easy, but monotonous. I don't even try to rush. If I do the work too quickly, they speed up the belt, and then the others can't keep up with it."

We settled in at Villawood, but we missed Wollongong, it's sea and sand beach. A letter came from Vieno, saying: "Things seemed odd after you left. Arja cries often and asks when you are coming back. She just doesn't want to go to that other family at all, and often runs off to come and see me at work, where she traipses along after me. She'll start school in a half year, and things will be easier then. I haven't found any friends like you among the other Finns. Everyone has his own pressures, and hardly anyone remembers what happened to me, or at least no one talks about it. I've kept on trying to go to the language classes all the time. Mr. Brown has helped me a lot with official matters."

"What do you think about buying a lot?" I said to Saul one evening.

"Not from Lehvisto's neighbor, at any rate. It's way out in the boondocks. It's at least a mile to the station. A person always has to go to work, and he needs good travel connections. We really have to start looking for a place of our own. We're not going to live in this hostel for the rest of our lives."

"I don't favor that lot of Lehvisto's either. We don't even know how far away the school is, and that has to be taken into account, too. I'm tired of those Italians on the other side of that wall. They're such a fiery bunch. Yesterday the man was beating his wife. I was just about to go to the office for help; they were making such a huge racket. Then it could hardly have been fifteen minutes later that they were hugging and kissing each other there outside. I don't understand how they can be so lovey-dovey after such a row."

"Have you ever heard that jouncing at night," said Saul, with a grin.

"I've waked up many times when the whole barrack was rocking. They enjoy all of life's gifts to the fullest. The man still doesn't seem to have a job, since he hangs around here all day. The other day the kids were crying outside the door when I came home. Judging by the sounds, there was no doubt about what was going on. They had driven the children out into the yard and locked the door. Those southerners are hot lovers."

"Isn't that guy working anywhere?" Saul said suspiciously.

"He was for a few weeks at first, but now I've seen him hanging around the hostel every day."

"We have to get out of here, when there are men hanging around with nothing else to do than come around and paw these lazy wives," said Saul angrily.

Realizing that I was in the devil's net once again, I said nothing more. We began to look for our own place in earnest The matter was expedited by the fact that Saul wanted to get out of the hostel because of those idle men. I could see all the signs of what was on his mind: his silence, his long periods deep in thought, his angry glances. I acted as if I noticed nothing and chatted as usual. Often he did not answer, merely growled something.

I was surprised when he arrived home one evening and began to talk.

"I had to wait for a train at the Regents Park station. To pass the time, I went for a walk to see what the place was like."

"Is that where you get the train to Banksdown?"

"Exactly. There are stores close by, and a big school. There's a lot for sale behind the school. All the others have been built on, and the houses are really nice. There's already a garage and a rock footing on the lot."

"That sounds as if it were made for us," I said. "Let's go and look at it on Saturday. The children can get along by themselves for a couple of hours. It's only a couple of stops on the train from here."

From the train we walked past the post office, and then by a huge brick building which looked like a school. Around it were smaller, barracks-like buildings which looked as if they had been added later. A slight turn to the left, and there it was, a "For Sale" sign. A good-looking square plot of land on which uncut hay had been flattened to the ground. New green grass thrust bravely up through the old rotting hay. We tramped around the lot and got our feet wet The grass was still soaked from the rain the day before. On three sides of the lot was a two-meter-high board fence. A small path ran through the hay, and three boards had been removed from the back fence. Someone used the path as a shortcut.

Through the window of the garage, we could see that there were no inner walls or electricity in the building. It looked as if someone had once lived here, for there was worn linoleum on the floor. There were no water pipes in the building either. We took down the phone number and the address from the ad as we left.

"We'll see what the price is like, since it's in such a good location."

"Yes, It's bound to cost more than the Lehvistos'," I said. "And it should. It's so close to a railroad junction and it's on a hill. It slopes a little to the rear, so that water won't stand on it, and there's no danger of flooding."

"It's only a half-kilometer from the station, and the railway is off in the other direction, so that we won't hear that racket," said Saul enthusiastically.

When we got back to the hostel, I tried to place a call with my poor English. I managed to get across enough so that we arranged a meeting for Tuesday at five in the agent's office.

"It's best if we go to Lehvisto tomorrow and ask him to come along. I don't trust my own English," I said uncertainly.

"I think you'll get along somehow," said Saul. "I can't seem to get many words right"

"What will Ville say when we aren't looking for a lot out his way?"

"Let him say whatever he wants. This is our business. But I think he'll come and help us with the language since he works so near the place."

The agent took us to look at the lot. Lehvisto was amazed and praised the lot as a good one. We decided to think the matter over for a few days. As we left the place, Ville began to talk. "It's a good lot, but the price is high —at least triple our lot's. But the garage is ready. You can start living there right away, if they let you, since this is within the city. Find out before you buy it; otherwise you'll be in the soup."

The following day I went with Poju to Banksdown, where all the offices were. I had written down all the questions we had. The main thing was to find the building office. I showed a passerby my slip of paper. He pointed to the left and said something I did not understand. Soon I saw a sign, "Wood Coffins." Well, it did mention wood, but the man had pointed to the left, and this was to the right. Nevertheless I went inside.

It was a small office, with no one there. There was a small bell on the counter, and I understood from a slip there that it was to be rung if necessary. A jingle, and a man appeared in the doorway. I showed him my papers, and he came out to direct us courteously to a small, low building to the left. "Thank you, thank you," I tried to express my gratitude, at which he smiled politely and returned to his office.

At the building office, we managed remarkably well. All we needed do was bring them the plans for our house, and we could move to the lot and live there. Just to be absolutely sure, I had them write it down on paper. Riding home on the train with Poju, I was in a good mood, and answered his questions about the landscape gliding by. At home I checked the dictionary at once to see what the first office had been. I found that out, too. Wooden coffins. Ugh, what a mistake.

We were busy moving under our own roof in February of 1959. We had been in Australia a little more than a year. When we left Finland, we had only clothing with us, so there was much that had to be bought now that we would be living on our own. Saul kept the purse strings to himself, and they were always tightly tied. Every morning I literally begged him for money for what was absolutely necessary. In the evening I showed him in my account book what I had bought. "Where the hell is that money really going?" he stormed.

"Here it is, down to the last penny," I said, and showed him the book. "You forgot that we had no household utensils with us when we left, and we need everything from spoons on up. We'll get water there on Friday, so we can even move in this weekend."

"But we can't have pipes run indoors. It'll be too expensive."

"No, we can't There isn't even a kitchen counter inside. I don't know what we'll use for cooking when there isn't even any electricity."

"Ville said they cooked with a Primus until they got electricity."

We were now under our own roof, although we could not really call it a home. There was no furniture, and we slept on mattresses laid along two walls. The table was cardboard cartons stacked atop one another when the man of the house came home from work on the first night. A salad, canned fish, bread, and milk were set out on the cloth over the makeshift table. I could not cook without a stove, of course, but everyone ate with a good appetite. We all sat on the floor, since there was nothing else to sit on. The children were full of enthusiasm, for we were in our own home at last. Saul stood up slowly and said, "The first lousy meal in a long time."

I went outside and wept bitterly for a long time behind the corner between the wall and the fence. I was tired, and I had done my best. How could a person be so mean? It wasn't my fault that I couldn't cook; I had learned to be quite a good cook, so there was no reason to grumble on that score. That man was lacking in brains at times; not only were the screws loose, some of them had fallen out already. Then and there I decided that when the children were grown up, I would get a divorce. I was tired that evening, but I could not get to sleep. Wearily I tossed in bed, listening to everyone else sleeping peacefully.

The weather cooled off in the evening and the room felt cold. Saul drank milk for breakfast when he left for work and promised to bring a Primus stove on his way home. When the children woke up, there was nothing to do but dress them quickly and send them out to play. Luckily it was still the summer vacation from school, which would begin the following week. Perhaps by then we would have electricity and possibly a place to wash.

At midday I said to the children, "What if we take a train back to the hostel. Everyone was eager to go. I explained that we would eat in the dining room there as we had done before. I knew it wasn't allowed, since we no longer belonged there and were not paying, but we ate as we had done before and went to visit acquaintances. I made the children swear not to say a word about the meal, and I felt my conscience upbraiding me when we came home. In the evening I told Saul about it, expecting him to scold me.

"That's good," he said. "Go there to eat every day and we'll save money. The train fare isn't much. Hey, you are good for something after all."

"Listen, friend. I'm not going to make a habit of this. I still feel as if I've done wrong. I may be poor, but no one has ever had to pay my way. And I don't want to feel like a criminal now either. Sooner or later you always get caught at something like this. And it's a bad example for the children."

"What of it. All the others get whatever they can from the government."

"Let the others do whatever they want, but I can't," I said glumly.

We got started living somehow, but our conditions were really limited. I cooked on the Primus, which I hated and feared. In our cramped quarters, I used it for heating in the morning, always fearing a fire, for the danger was great in the small space we had. We already had electricity, and without his being aware of it, I guided my husband to look at stoves.

"This is just the size stove we need," I said.

"It's terribly expensive. Look at the price. We have a Primus; that's all we need," he said, pleased with himself.

"That Primus was supposed to be only a temporary solution," I said tartly. "It's been many months now. I didn't come to Australia to cook on a Primus for the rest of my life. We came here to find a better life. I've never lived in such limited conditions, not even in Finland."

"Everything costs so much," he said unhappily. "I've hardly been able to save anything."

"Well, there is certainly enough so that we won't have to go into debt if we buy a stove," I said angrily.

We did not get the stove that time. I saved a little from the state support payments for children and put a down payment on a stove. It was delivered on a Saturday. I had said nothing to Saul about the purchase. A truck drove into the yard, the men checked the address, and they delivered the stove. Saul gave me a dirty look but said nothing. The man handed him the bill. To my wonder, he paid it without saying a word.

"Well, there's a plaything for the old lady now," he muttered to himself.

I was surprised that it had been even this easy. I had spent sleepless nights over this Saturday. We had even managed to get washing facilities of a sort, so this was a kind of progress.

Saul had gotten a job in his field, that is in an auto repair shop, one that was close to us as well, only a couple of stations away. To my amazement, he bought a used refrigerator without my even asking. It was absolutely indispensable here. Summer was just coming. I wondered if someone had been telling him about the necessities of life. We were still going to the language lessons once a week. It felt as if we were always learning something new. I really tried to speak it as much as possible. The day before, I went to the store and said I wanted a pound of wieners. The clerk asked if I wanted large or small. Trying to be polite, I said I liked big wieners. As I left, I said, "Bye-bye." thinking the clerk very courteous, for he was grinning from ear to ear. Before I made it out the door, I heard loud laughter from in back of the counter. I must have said something awfully funny. A-haa, my "politeness." "I liked big wieners—ha, ha."

Again the weather started to get warm; summer was coming, and Christmas, at the very hottest time of the year. In the morning it was steamy hot, in the afternoon it always thundered and poured down rain. We had been away from Finland for two Christmases, with no real preparations for the day. Now that we were under our own roof, I felt that an attempt should be made. I bought candles, but they warped very badly in the heat. Santa Claus was expected to drop his bag from a helicopter. At least that's what Poju believed.

Our Christmas tree was a thirty-centimeter-high artificial one, and Santa Claus did drop his bag of presents out in back of our shanty unobserved. The temperature was thirty-seven degrees Centigrade in the shade. I had tried to make it a Christmas, but the heat dampened the mood. No, for Christmas one had to have cold, snow, and a Christmas church service.

The year 1960 was approaching. What would it bring with it? The girls had a summer vacation from school now, and Poju too would start going to school at the end of February. Since all the children would be in school, and we lived directly opposite it, perhaps I would try to get some kind of a job. A few of the Finnish women worked as housecleaners in private homes. I didn't want to look for that kind of work. I got enough of it at home. One could keep cleaning this little house constantly, but it was never clean.

I had sewn a lot at home, but I heard that in factories the system was completely different It was piecework, and you were paid on a contract basis. One had to have experience, but where could one get it?

I saw an ad in the paper for a two-week machine-sewing course, which guaranteed employment on its completion. Saul was highly enthusiastic at the idea. The children were still on vacation from the school, and were learning to stay at home by themselves for a few hours at a time. The oldest was thirteen and the youngest five. The course was in downtown Sydney and the journey there was a full half-hour on the electric train. In the course one was taught speed and the many tricks one needed to sew in a factory.

I stayed at home for the first few days after school began, and everything went smoothly. Then I began to search for jobs in the paper, and there was no shortage of them. On Monday morning I set out to try my luck.

I had already been to three places, but when they looked at my credentials, they shook their heads and said, "More experience." What should I do now? The credentials were only a hindrance. If they would only let me sit down at a sewing machine and try. I was in another office now. I did not show my credentials, but said I had been a seamstress years ago, but that I had been at home while the children were small. "Well, let's give it a try," was the response.

Ahaa, now I pulled the right string, I thought, as I followed the foreman to the factory section of the building. I estimated that a hundred sewing machines were going at the same time, and everyone was working at top speed. I was possessed by the same terror that had gripped me in the furniture factory when I was young. Run away. No, if I got a job here, I would stay, if only on guts alone.

A bundle of ready-cut fabric was brought to me. "We make light, short coats here," an elderly woman began explaining to me. There were ten coats in the bundle. First I was to sew all the collars, which would be sent for pressing. I did what I could, but then I ran into a wall. Those pretty pockets, the corners of which had to be sewn like those on a large buttonhole. I gestured for help.

"Don't you know how to do this? Take your scissors and handbag and follow me." Again I found myself out on the street.

I got to start work at another place where they made sunsuits, with a lot of long, straight seams. I did my best It was time to go home, and the foreman came sailing over to me and looked at my results. "Your work is okay, but you're too slow. This is contract work, and you haven't finished half of your quota." He handed me seventy-five cents and said good-bye.

I got on the train feeling stupid and depressed. "Well, anyway you earned the price of a train ticket," I consoled myself. If I knew that I would get a job tomorrow, I would say nothing of today's experiences at home. But if I didn't get work I would have to confess. All kinds of thoughts passed through my mind as I sat there on the seat of the train. Saul was already at home when I finally came wearily into the yard. I shook my head despairingly.

"Well, where the hell have you been dragging around all day if you didn't fmd work," he demanded. I explained everything in detail.

"You have to go back to that school; they guaranteed you a job," he said.

"Not tomorrow, at least. There are many places in the paper where I can go and ask," I said. I saw that Saul was beginning to believe in me and to calm down.

In the morning I was taken on at the very first place I tried. To my astonishment, they showed me all the phases of the work. I began to sew on long blouse sleeves. The place was small compared to the one I had tried the day before, with only about a dozen seamstresses. Naturally things were just as hurried here, and it was contract work, but I was allowed to practice a few days, since I had been away from the work so long.

I came home tired in the evening, with the hum of the machines still sounding in my ears. Saul was satisfied because I had found work, but I was so tense that I could not sleep, and the machines kept humming in my ears. I was tired in the morning, but determination kept me at work. At least I would get experience here, since that seemed to be the alpha and omega in everything. If they fired me from this job, I would have learned a good deal.

At the end of two weeks I was called into the office. I was startled, for I had thought I was on firm ground. "We are satisfied with your work, but you haven't reached the minimum speed, which is absolutely essential. We can't keep you on longer," said the elderly man who worked as a cutter there.

"It would have been better if she hadn't started," I heard some of the others whisper as they looked at me scornfully.

I felt downcast. I would have to come back the next day, to collect my first and last paycheck from the place. But why concern myself with what others thought? They had been beginners once themselves.

On Monday morning I started out eagerly to look for work again. I had already learned a good deal, and I thought that I had probably worked too carefully in the last place. Now I got started in a building right next to the one where I had been the week before. Here children's clothing was made, and it was not contract work. The friendly foreman showed me all the phases of the work. It seemed so easy. In the evening I asked the foreman, "Should I come back tomorrow?"

"Of course, of course," was the friendly response. My two-week trial had done me a lot of good, I thought.

I followed the work of the other seamstresses, and on the second day, I was able to finish my bundle at the same time as they did. Here they did very careful work. It was a big factory, and the atmosphere was pleasant. Everyone was friendly, and I didn't notice the envy I had seen in the first place.

In the evening, the sound of the factory still buzzed in my ears. "I have to get used to it; I will not give in, I said to myself. On the other hand, things were peaceful at home when I didn't have to beg for money to go shopping. Saul had become even more stingy lately. It seemed as if he just could not understand that as the children grew bigger, their expenses became greater. I still sewed all of their clothing, which was a large saving in itself. I even sewed Saul's work shirts for him.

On weekends, I began to sew a number of smocks for myself. I wanted to change into clean clothes every day, as all the others did. In addition it was so hot that I hated to put on yesterday's clothing. Fabric was cheap, so I tried to be neatly dressed.

"Do you have to be so fancy? You're putting all your money into clothes," Saul began to rant at me.

"These are nothing fancy. They are of the cheapest cloth I could find, washable cretonne. I can't go to work dirty and sweaty, and since I don't have time to wash in the evening, I have to have enough for the week. You have shop coveralls to wear, and can wear whatever you like underneath. And it's as hot as hell where we work."

I managed to calm him down that time, and life began to go on quite pleasantly. Saul began to make sketches of plans for the house. He still did not trust his own skill in the language, so I had to buy all the building materials. Sometimes I had to take a day off from work for that reason. I had to make up excuses to the foreman for my absences.

"My leg was sick yesterday, and I couldn't get to work," I said once. I saw his lips spread in a broad smile.

"Elsie, your leg doesn't get sick; it gets sore," he said, and patted me on the shoulder.

It was so pleasant when everyone was on a first-name basis, the foreman as well. No one had a title of any sort.

Twice a year, a Finnish seamen's pastor visited Sydney. The service closest to us was in the grand ballroom of our former hostel. The room was anything but grand. The different nationalities held their affairs and dances in it. Sunday school was also held there. I took the children with me whenever the pastor was there.

We had sung the opening hymn and said the prayers. The pastor began his sermon on the text for the day. "All else perishes, but the kingdom of heaven endures."

From outside a voice could be heard through the thin walls: "Like sh— it endures."

"It does endure," said the pastor more loudly.

"Like sh— it endures."

"It endures. You can believe it." the pastor answered.

"Like sh— it endures," said the voice even more clearly. The pastor gave in. He picked up the hymnal, gestured to the accompanist, and began to sing, with the congregation joining in. We sang a few more hymns, and the pastor began cautiously to continue his explication of the text There was no longer a reply from outside. The harasser had gone on his way, most likely to find more to drink.

I felt ashamed on behalf of the Finns, although not everyone understood what had happened. God did, however.

From then on the pastor used the church downtown on his visits. I never found out who the blasphemer was. For those given to drink, Australia was a paradise. Liquor stores were open late into the evening, and they were to be found in every little place. The same was true of taverns, which had two sides, one of them for women. Sometimes I saw them going in during the day, pushing their baby buggies. The women were not allowed on the men's side. Sometimes on the way from shopping I would pass a tavern with the door open. The men inside would be sitting on high stools leaning on a circular bar. Near the bartender were three barrels, from the taps of which the joy juice was drawn into large mugs. A small light flickered amidst the cigarette smoke.

"There are no windows," Ville was able to explain to me. "If a fight starts none will be broken. That's why there are none."

The women's salon, the more elegant side, was well lighted and neat looking. Sometimes the entire family would go there for dinner, but soon the man would slip off to the other side.

Australians loved horses, horse shows, and horse races. The horse shows opened with a style show and wound up with elegant dances. The following day the papers had page after page of stories and photos about the elite women in their fine gowns.

The Lehvistös had had a house built on their lot. It was a duplex, and they rented it to two newlywed Finnish couples. They themselves bought another lot and moved to live on it. Here they began to build a house themselves. It was a good idea. Now they had an income from three rental dwellings. We got to know one of the young couples, the Saarnos from Helsinki. They often talked of going to America.

"Do you have relatives there?" I asked, interested.

"We don't, but you don't need them as long as you know the language," Kalle declared.

"Yaah, that's a good idea," said Saul. "I've heard too that living there is cheap. We could raise this family of ours cheaper there than here."

I got busy. The next day I left work early and went to the American embassy to find out about the matter. I was told that one could go there even without a guarantor, but that some funds were needed, although no amount was specified. They were happy to give us application blanks, but told us we might have to wait perhaps for several years.

We filled out the forms and sent them in. The next time when the Saarnos began to speak of the matter, I asked, "Have you submitted the papers?"

"No, not yet. We won't be ready to go for a couple of years. By that time we'll have the money for the trip," said Hilkka.

We did not mention a word of our going to America. I began to mention the business of building our house from time to time, since there had been very little progress on it. Saul did not seem at all interested in it.

"We would get a better price with a house if we were able to go to America. What do you think?" I said to him one evening.

"Yaah, maybe so. All there is now is the new footing, but that won't sell for anything. Everything is all Hebrew to me here, when it's all inches and yards. I've learned everything in meters and centimeters."

"Well, make your estimates in Finnish, I think I can convert them to feet and inches," I said a little uncertainly.

I had more than enough to do with keeping house in addition to working. I had no washing machine, and there was a lot of laundry to do. In those days, all the clothing had to be ironed, and that was my Sunday job. I really had no time to see the city. One Sunday we went to the zoo. It was fun because the last part of the trip was by ferry. As soon as we entered the door, a parrot cried out "Hello, Santa Claus" in pure Finnish. We were astonished at first, but then burst out laughing. Some Finnish joker had been at work there.

Once our old acquaintances from the ship, the Laitinens, stopped in to visit us, and we chatted about our visit to the zoo. Laitinen said with a mischievous twinkle in his eye: "Does the parrot there still speak Finnish?"

"Well, yaah, it did say 'Hello Santa Claus.' Was it you who taught it to?"

"It learned so easily. The children repeated it a few times, and that's all it needed. I guess you've heard that the Jauhiainens have gone back to Finland."

"Why, no," said Saul. "We did hear that he thought everything here was shitty. He said that half the people in Sydney lived in garages and lousy shacks."

"He never did get a roof of his own over his head, neither here nor in Finland. He could have gotten one here; we've been here for three years already," Laitinen continued. "No one will here will miss them."

"That's for sure. I heard enough of his moaning at Wollongong. Here I didn't have anything to do with him. Did he work at the same place as you did here?" asked Saul.

"No, I didn't want him there. He does work at bookbinding like me. It's his trade," said Laitinen.

I often worked late at night on planning the lumber for the house. Finally I had converted the centimeters to inches and the meters to feet.

"Saturday you'll go to the sawmill and put in the orders," said Saul.

"Don't you mean to come with me at all?" I asked.

"What would I do there? You know what you have to buy."

"This is such a large purchase that I won't go by myself. If I make a mistake, I'll hear about it for the rest of my life. I doubt that they would even trust me with an order for all the framing materials of a house. They'll think I'm some crazy woman," I said with a smile.

Saul went with me, and the purchase of the lumber went off well. We had planned to get the frame up and the roof on during the six-week Christmas vacation. The building began to rise slowly. I always had to be at the other end of a plank, and Tytti helped with the lighter work. Our real-estate agent stopped in now and then to see how we were doing. We were just planning to pour the cement back porch when he drove into the yard.

"I'll come to help you tomorrow," he promised.

He did come in the morning, bringing his four and five-year-old boys with him. Our children took care of the boys. It was a tough day for all of us. It was the very hottest time of the year, but luckily it did not rain. After some six hours the job was done. The two of us could never have finished it in one day. *Thanks Mr. Lovebridge; you were truly a friend.*

We decided to take the next morning off, which was a Sunday. Taking a lunch along with us, we went to see the botanical gardens of Sydney, which we had heard so much about. The children, of course, were bursting with enthusiasm.

It was extraordinarily interesting. That tree was from New Zealand, that shrub was from Malaya, there was a Chinese tea rose. The children went bounding from one place to another. An elderly couple stopped us and said, "What a pretty sight. Healthy, happy, blond children. Be proud of your children, Ma' am," the old man said in a shaky voice.

"Thank you, thank you," I said happily.

I felt moved. I was close to crying and had to hold back my tears. They probably had no children nearby. If only Saul would at some time find something good about his family, and not just consider the children and me a burden on him. I had been working for two years now, and during that time he had not offered a penny for household expenses. Nor had I asked for money. I had had too many years of begging.

At intervals we sat down on a bench to rest while the children ran around nearby. It was beautifully calm and quiet A happily laughing pair walked by; I took them to be Greeks. The man was well into middle age and the woman much younger. They seemed to care very much for each other. Just as they passed by us they kissed passionately.

We walked around, checking the names of different trees and bushes. My eyes happened to fall on the roots of a sheltering shrub. There a couple was making love so wildly that they were crushing the hay. I turned in another direction so that the children would not see them.

Animals, I thought. *They really are vile. Shame on them.* I felt almost like throwing up.

At that moment, the children came up, and PoJu looked at me. "Are you ill, Mother, your face is so white."

"I don't know what is making my stomach upset." I noticed that the couple were on their feet now and were walking off arm in arm.

The children were hungry, so we found a suitable spot and began to dig out our lunch bags. Everyone ate with a good appetite, yet I could not even think of eating. But a cup of coffee refreshed me. I couldn't get the recent occurrence out of my mind. If someone had told me such a story, I wouldn't have believed it.

We did not get as far with the building during the vacation as we had planned, but gradually the house rose to the stage at which I had to order the roof tiles. Here the roofs were generally of tile, and the more colorful they were, the better they looked. After more than two years, I had changed jobs. I was sewing sneakers and other fabric footwear and was permitted seven paid sick days a year, none of which I had taken. There was an amiable Russian doctor nearby who was willing to write medical reasons for sick days, so we both took sick leave in order to get the roof on.

That week was anything but a leave. The work was terribly hard. I was totally exhausted every evening. If one could die from overwork, I thought, I was on the verge of it. Every evening, I was dripping with sweat and felt as if I had been beaten. Never in my life have I done work as hard as putting on that roof.

Saul bought a somewhat dented automobile, a Morris. On weekends, he began to do body work and repairs on it. A number of Finns already had automobiles, and naturally we were excited about when it would be finished and we could go for a drive in it. The house was now relegated to second place—well, at least there was a roof on it, and it wouldn't rot.

The day finally dawned when we could go somewhere in the car. Here people drove on the left side of the road, and that too was strange. We tried to arrange a time on Sunday afternoons to go and see the surrounding landscape. We actually went for the whole day to Manly's sand beach. But the most fun was a day at the kangaroo park.

The ticket seller urged us to buy potato chips before entering the fenced-in area. Soon we were followed by a long train of tame kangaroos. When they heard the rustle of paper in our pockets, they quickly thrust their noses into them. A mature kangaroo is about two meters tall. Its tail is about a meter and a half long, and is very sturdy at its root The animal uses it to help as it bounds into the air.

"Hey, there's one with a pup in its pouch. Let's go and see it." The mother took a potato chip nicely in its front paw and gave it to its young. "How neat. They, too, take care of their young."

Off to one side was a smaller species, a wallaby, related to the kangaroo, but only about a meter tall. Tytti went to get more food to distribute to the animals. They gave us no peace; there was always one of them begging for something. They poked you in the arm if you paid no attention to them otherwise.

Koala bears sat on the limbs of trees holding on to one another. I was reminded of our sledding when we were children and also held on to each other. The koala also had a pouch in front for its young. When the cub grows a little larger, it rides continually on its mother's back. Koala bears eat eucalyptus leaves at night, leaves that contain many medicinal ingredients, camphor, for example. During the day they are half intoxicated, and sleep merely sitting on the tree limbs. Koala bears never come to the ground except when they move to another tree. They never have to drink, but get their fluid from the tree leaves.

Then came an emu, a bird nearly a meter and a half tall. Ugh, how angry it looked. It seemed to like potato chips, too. It has enormously large and powerful legs. It cannot fly, but can run at a speed of fifty kilometers an hour. Its feathers rustled like dry hay as it worked its way around us. It was good that we still had food left to give to it; I was afraid of that big, strong beak. I judged it to be at least fifteen centimeters long. The bird's head was small, except for that powerful beak. Its neck was thin and almost featherless. When it ran, its stride was almost two meters long. It would be exciting to see its eggs, but perhaps it was not that time of the year.

"Hey, what's that flying over there?" said little Sisko.

It had to be one of the flying squirrels we had heard about It was flying from tree to tree, looking like a rectangle in shape, with only its fuzzy tail floating behind it. When it leaped, it spread its wings, between which was stretched hide attached to its body, just like wings. Thus it could fly from tree to tree. Sitting it looks just like an ordinary squirrel.

Now it is best to head for the gate. A flock of emus was coming after us, and we had nothing more to give them. *Thanks neat park.*

It would surely be good to be a farmer here; everything grows so well. Lehvisto brought us a dried-up looking piece of twig and we stuck it into the earth. In two years it was producing grapes. We grew vegetables, which we never had to water. The rainfall was abundant: about 150 centimeters a year. Every time I pulled up the last of the carrots, I put new seeds into the ground, and so we got three crops in a year. We also grew potatoes on our own lot.

We had bought a television set about six months back. That satisfied our need for entertainment. On Friday evening, I wrote up a shopping list and put a small bag on the refrigerator. Tytti usually did the shopping before I came home from work. She was already fifteen, and a great help to me. One afternoon at work, they came to call me to the phone in the office. *Something has gone badly awry*, I thought as I half ran to the other end of the large plant. It was the first time anyone had called me there.

"Hello, this is the teacher. Poju came to the office and said that someone has broken into your home. It's best that you go straight to the police and let them know about the matter."

"Thank you for calling. I'll do that," I said with a sigh of relief. Thank God nothing had happened to the children.

The police station was within walking distance. A couple of policemen took me home in a car. When we arrived in the yard, the door was open. One small pane in the back window had been unscrewed, hinges and all, and was still standing against the wall. There were tire tracks in front of the door. What was there to take, except for the television set, the sewing machine already in its case, and the small purse on top of the refrigerator? "Look carefully to see if anything else is missing," the policeman urged me.

Even drawers had been ransacked, but yesterday's wages, which were then paid in cash, were safe. I had hidden them well. What had the robbers expected to find in a little shack like this?

"What time do you think the robbers were here?" asked the policeman, who was writing a report.

"In the morning, before twelve. The children come home then to eat."

"Are you insured against theft?"

"We only have fire insurance. These things were all paid for, so we didn't think insurance was necessary. The people on our right are all at work during the day. I think the lady on our left is at home."

"I'll go and talk to her," said the other policeman.

"I'd like to know if the thief is able to read my shopping list. It was in the bag and was written in Finnish," I said with a laugh.

"How much money was in it?"

"Oh, I'd say about seven pounds and some coins to boot."

The other policeman came back and shook his head: "Mrs. Gaicer just got home. She has begun doing volunteer work at the hospital on Fridays. It looks as if the thieves have been keeping an eye on this neighborhood. I wonder, though, why they picked just this house when there are such expensive ones around here."

"We can't do any more now. Call us once a week in case we happen to find a cache of stolen goods somewhere. Right now it looks as if there's little chance of getting anything back."

I wondered as I sat waiting for the children to come home from school. I still could not believe that anyone would be such a scoundrel. When the children arrived, they told me about everything in detail. I was in such a funk that I had not even made supper when Saul came home. He could not get it into his head that such a thing had happened. He had to be told everything over and over again.

To Saul, this was an incredible blow. In recent years he had grown more and more tight-fisted. From the time I began working, I had paid for the food and clothing of the entire family. He had paid for the building supplies, but not one penny had been added to our joint bank account. I knew that he had not spent all his money, but I had no idea where he could be hiding it. I did not, however, complain. Tomorrow always brought its own problems to worry about.

Once when we went for a ride, Saul said: "Give me some money for gas. This car won't run without it, and the whole gang of you is always going for rides."

"Shame on you. Why did you go and get yourself a family if you're not willing to sacrifice a penny for us? I've been working for four years, and you haven't paid for food for yourself or your family during that time. That's a pretty big sum you've been able to stash away, God knows where. Not all of it has gone into the building. Now there will be bigger expenses when the plumbing and electricity has to be put in," I said indignantly.

Saul said nothing but walked away. I could see his face turn red. All in all, this had been a physically taxing, but mentally relaxing time for me. I had not needed to beg him for money, and he had not been jealous for years. Now he was interested only in money. I was not worried about tomorrow. I had a steady job, and I felt somehow free. The children were happy, too, for I was able to buy a little extra for them, which had been out of the question before. The bigger children were beginning to understand the situation, and they were automatically on my side where money was concerned.

It happened to be a Saturday, and it was pouring rain. Now I did believe that the goods had really been stolen and were gone forever. We all sat gloomily in the little shack. The children could not go out to play, and there was no television to watch. I usually sat sewing on rainy days, but now I could not, since the sewing machine had walked off. Saul sat glumly, with nothing to say. I began to weep, and the children came to console me.

"The police are sure to get the things back." "Don't cry, Mother, we'll get new ones." They hung around my neck, and I could not help but laugh. We had some ice cream and enjoyed every lick of it. When Saul had had charge of the purse strings, ice cream had been forbidden. He watched us with his mouth watering.

Poju came to whisper in my ear. "Father would like some ice cream."

"Oh, yaah? I thought you didn't like it since you never let us buy any," I said innocently, as I filled a cone.

The mailman brought us a totally insignificant-looking card. I was about to toss it into the wastebasket when I gave it a more careful glance—What! From the American Embassy?

"If you are still interested in emigrating to the United States, fill in the other side of this card and return it." I had completely forgotten the application to go to America. It must have been three years before that I had sent it in, yet it had not been lost along the way.

We filled out the card and sent it in the next day. This added a new spark to our lives. At the end of a month, Saul and I were called to the embassy for an interview, which turned out to be a pleasant chat. The consul explained the advantages and the drawbacks of life in America, and did not try in any way to sell it to us or urge us to go there.

"What do you think? Shall we start the 'paper war'?" he asked. We exchanged a meaningful glance and nodded.

"Yes, we do want to do it if we can get in," said Saul.

"You will need to get quite a number of testimonials from Finland. The United States has high requirements for immigrants. Getting admission is not as easy as here in Australia. They want immigrants here, but the United States already has problems with unemployment. As you know, you can get in without having anyone to vouch for you, but you need to have financial resources of your own," the official explained.

"Is there information about how much money one needs?" I asked, curious.

"Here are the forms. Fill out the required sheets and send them to this address. That's all I can say," said the official, handing us a large sheaf of papers.

We sat deep in thought on the way home. Would we actually be going? We had not been really serious when we sent in the first application.

I began to write official letters to Finland every evening. One had to get proof of a crime-free record from every place one had lived for more than three months after reaching the age of sixteen. It was just during those years that I had moved around so much as an evacuee. Saul had not lived in as many places as I.

In a week I got the letters off.

Within two months I had received a number of replies, all of which had to be translated into English. My English was still not great, and after sweating over the task for a few nights, I decided to take the papers to the Finnish embassy in Sydney.

I took another sick leave for a week. I had to have the documents filled out in triplicate with an official seal. An employee at the embassy took the papers and told me to take a seat in a nicely furnished room, where I began to admire a beautiful landscape, which lay spread out beneath a large window. The building was high up on a hill that sloped down to the sea. The water was a beautiful blue with a few brightly colored sailboats sailing peacefully on its small waves. The Finnish officials certainly had a fine place. There was small chance of their being homesick here. A young lady interrupted my daydreams. She had a stack of papers in her hand, and asked with a smile: "Who translated these?"

"I tried," I said.

"They are not right. They will all have to be done over again. Do you have time to wait? It will take about two hours. Or do you want to come and get them some other day?"

"I'd like to wait, if only you have the time to do them now. I live at the other end of the city, and it takes several hours to get here."

"Good. I'll get right to work. Come and get a cup of coffee from the office."

"Thanks. That would taste good," I said, and followed her into another room.

I was pleased with the day's results. Now all the papers were ready to send in. What if we were refused admission anyway, and all this work was wasted? *Well, if you don't try, you get nothing*, I thought to myself as I sat on the train on my way home. It was the height of the rush hour. Someone got off, and a young man quickly took the seat opposite me. Most of the passengers were absorbed in reading their newspapers.

I noticed that the young man's zippered fly was open. I had to let him know somehow, but without calling the fact to the attention of others, so I pressed down hard on the toe of his shoe. He did not look up, but shifted his foot. I did the same thing two more times. Now, he looked up angrily. I gestured with my hand to show why I was bothering him. Now he too noticed. Blushing a bright red, he covered himself with a newspaper and corrected the problem. Later he pressed gently on my toe. I looked up. His lips shaped a soundless "Thank you."

Facing us was a medical examination for the whole family—in Sydney of course. Everything went well, except that Saul had some round growths under the skin of his neck. The doctor was afraid that they might be cancer.

"Oh, how awful. Now we're in for it," I said in despair.

After a couple of days he went to the hospital, where they took a specimen. When he arrived home, he waved a small glass jar in which a reddish-gray glob floated in alcohol.

"Well, there's the enemy. They gave it to me as souvenir."

"Well, what is it?" I asked in panic.

"I don't know yet. They took two specimens and sent one to the lab."

We had to wait for two long days. "If it's a cancer, we can't leave, and all the rushing around will have been for nothing," I said disconsolately.

On the second day, Saul went directly to the hospital from work to hear the news. It was later than usual when he finally came home. I could tell at once by his face that all was well. It felt as if the sun had begun to shine on a dark evening.

"They were only swollen glands," he explained.

When the children had gone to bed, I brought out a bottle of champagne I had bought during the day. Waving it in one hand, I said, "Now we're going to celebrate. We have good reason to."

"You shouldn't. It's too expensive."

"Not so expensive that we can't buy it when it's needed," I said, and began to pour the champagne into ordinary water glasses. We had no such extravagances as champagne glasses. The place was so small that we had room for only the absolute necessities.

"It really is good," said Saul. "Give me some more."

"Yeah, we have to drink it all down once the bottle is opened. Cheers!" We clicked glasses.

Saul came over to me, took me by the shoulders and kissed me gently. I felt like a young bride. All the hopeless years seemed to be wiped away in that moment.

"Thanks for buying the champagne," he said. "It makes you feel so light." I could tell by his speech that the alcohol had gone to his head. Actually he had drunk most of the bottle. I didn't really care for the champagne, but tried to play along with him.

"Things have gone well for us here in Australia," he said. "We should do even better with the finances in America. Getting there will cost a lot, since America doesn't help immigrants at all with that. But the children are big now, compared to when we came here. Just think, Tytti is already sixteen. She's a young lady already, and the youngest is nine. And you haven't aged at all in the last ten years."

"Don't talk nonsense. Maybe it's just that I dress like a younger person," I said, blushing.

"Whatever it is, you're still young and pretty. Saarno noticed it too. He said you were just as young-looking as the girls. You've done so much for the family, and I haven't even thanked you for it. Forgive me for treating you so badly. I love you as much as when you were young. That's why I'm so jealous, when I think that someone will take you away from me."

"Pooh, stop talking such nonsense. We've been married for seventeen years already, and I've never even thought of anyone else."

Later I lay in bed, unable to sleep even though I was tired. Saul was already snoring, and I thought, "That bottle of champagne was a good idea. I should have thought of it earlier. He was like another person after a few drinks. If it's true that a person shows his real nature when he's drinking, then he should always be a little tipsy. Life would be easier for him and everyone around him."

We waited nervously for news from the American Embassy. The instructions said we were not to begin selling any of our possessions until all the paperwork was completed. Hurriedly we went back to working on the house. We should at least have the lumber already purchased in place before putting the house up for sale. Saul nailed the boards with the help of the bigger girls. I put on the first coat of paint with Poju and Little-Sisko helping on the lower sections. Everyone had the America fever, but we said not a word to people we knew about moving to America.

After a few weeks, another form arrived for both of us to fill out. It contained fifty questions. Checking every question carefully, we realized that they all dealt with three basic subjects, but in different wording: "Have you ever been a member of the Communist Party?" "Have you ever used drugs?" "Have you ever been dependent on the county or the state for your support?"

Of course we answered all these questions in the negative. Again we had to wait for an answer, which came rather quickly this time. After that we were appointed a day for an interview with the entire family. *This is the final test,* I thought. *Now we have to look good enough to pass it. We can't afford to fail.*

We rode the train in, everyone looking neat and filled with expectation. The children had been told not to say anything except in answer to questions. Everything went well during the interview. The only thing left was to take an oath before signing the papers. An attractive woman official said, "Raise your right hand and repeat after me."

We were already halfway through the oath when I noticed that my left hand was raised. "What should I do now?" I thought, horrified. Slowly I began to raise my right hand, lowering my left at the same time. I don't know if anyone noticed, but I was relieved when I got my right hand up.

Now everything was in order, and we could pick up our visas in two days. The tension was over and the road to America was open. The whole family went to the Duck Pond to eat lunch, but most of the food went to the ducks.

On Friday we went together to pick up our visas. Only when I had the visas in my hand did I believe that we were really going. The date was November 22, 1963. Australian time was eighteen hours ahead of U.S. time. The next morning we heard on the radio that President Kennedy had been shot—on the same day as we got our visas.

In a few hours we heard the news that the assassin was an American and that he had been arrested. It was a sensational event and was in the news day and night. To think that such things happen even in these times.

Now, according to our papers, we had to be in the United States within four months. We really had to hurry. Christmas and the summer holiday were approaching, a time when sales in such businesses as real estate were slow. As to the trip, the cost was pretty much the same whether we went by sea or air. The difference was that the flight took only two days, and we could only take two suitcases with us on the plane. By sea we would rock on for twenty-two days, and we could take a lot of freight with us.

"We're in no hurry. No one is waiting for us," said Saul.

"Let's go by ship. We'll have a good three-week vacation with all expenses paid. We've earned it. A ship is leaving on January 22, 1964."

The children finished out their term in school. Tytti graduated the second in her class. We both worked until Christmas, when the summer vacation began, and received three weeks' vacation pay when we left work.

Before putting the car up for sale, we decided to make a day's trip to the Blue Mountains. We took a large basket of fruit and sandwiches with us, along with lots of water. It was the hottest time of the year.

The landscape was extremely rugged. Good Lord, if we should fall into a crevice! The idea had been to take the sky rail to the top of the mountain peaks known as the Three Sisters. "No, I'm not going to go dangling up there between earth and sky."

We decided unanimously not to try the sky rail.

"Something unusual is going on there," said Poju. We approached a gang of boys who were busy about something. They were startled at our approach. A creature about two meters long, which resembled a lizard, was lying dead on the ground before them.

"Conna, it's a conna," said Pia. "We read about it in school, and the teacher showed us pictures."

The boys looked at Pia in amazement. Of course they did not understand the Finnish. Then they explained that the creature had attacked them and that was why they had killed it.

The animal was quite thick at the mid-section, fully a meter around; it may have been about to give birth. The boys opened its mouth with a stick; its teeth were dull stubs. I had also read about the creatures, and I recalled that they were protected. That is probably why the boys were frightened when we approached.

"Let's get out of here. You're not allowed to kill those things. If they find us here, we'll be fined fifty pounds," I said.

"Have you seen any snakes yet?" one of the boys asked.

"Not yet. Are there snakes here too?" asked Saul fearfully.

"There are. We killed a black one. They're very poisonous. It was only about so long." The boy spread his hands a half-meter apart.

"Let's get out of this brush," said Tytti. "If a black snake bites you, you can die in a few minutes. We read about them in school. You find them in and around old houses."

We hurried over to the parking area and took our lunch basket to a picnic area where there were tables for visitors. It was cool in the shade of the eucalyptus trees, and the view of the craggy mountains was dizzying. A few of them jutted upward by themselves, like rotting, crumbling pillars. Everything was so peaceful and untouched. Here the rush of the world had not yet been able to disturb the peace of the wilderness. Only a few people had come to the mountains. In the summer most of them went to the seashore.

"A Finn in Queensland got very drunk, so drunk that on his way home he toppled over into a patch of brush. You can guess that he had a headache when he woke up in the morning. When he went into the shower at home, he noticed that his arm was swollen. His wife began to check and saw two small marks, which looked exactly like snakebites. The man panicked and rushed to the doctor, who examined him. A blood test revealed that he had been bitten by a black snake. The only conclusion the doctor could come to was that the man had had so much alcohol in his blood that it counteracted the effect of the venom. Otherwise the snakebite would have killed him."

"Sometimes liquor has its benefits," I said. "It's used as a base in may medicines."

"Maunula told a funny story one day," Saul began. "A Finn started driving north from here one day to a mining town named Mount Isa. Once he had to wait two days while a farmer drove his sheep across the road. When the flock had finally crossed, a bulldozer came to open the road because the pile of dung was so high."

"That sounds like a lot of crap," I said.

"They said at the hostel that it was the absolute truth. Someone got a letter from the man. He had quite a trip. As you know, you have to make a hand signal for a right turn here. The traffic drives on the left, and the man was making a right turn. Someone came barreling up from the opposite direction so close that he cut the man's arm off. The other driver didn't even stop, and the Finn had to drive many hours to get help because the place was a total wilderness."

"Take a look at this landscape; we may not pass this way again. We've seen all we're going to see of Australia."

Everything was going according to plan. Real estate sales were in a real slump during the summer vacation, but we did have a buyer for the house, although at a low price because we had no alternative.

"What will we do with Miki?" I said one morning as the cat washed its face on a kitchen chair.

"Do what you like. It's your cat and the children's. You remember that I didn't give you permission to buy it," Saul said, annoyed. "Just leave it here. It can take care of itself. It's always warm summer here."

"No, my conscience won't let me do that," I said. "That would be abusing an animal. It will die of thirst, even if it did find something to eat. It may not even be able to eat mice, since it has always had prepared food. We should find an animal shelter and call; maybe they would take it in. I hope they have a place for Miki and can come and get him since we no longer have a car. Leave him here to die of hunger? Never!" I said angrily.

A few days before leaving, we told the Lehvistös of our plans. They bought our refrigerator and some other things. The couple was already living on their third lot and getting rent from six dwellings. Their plan was to live in Australia for ten years, then sell everything and move back to Finland. They had been very enterprising, had worked very hard, and had succeeded in all their efforts. They had already built two homes in six years.

We were facing departure the next day. The Lehvistös came to fetch their goods early in the evening. "Thursday I'll go and tell the Saarnos that you went to America. Let's see what kind of face they make," said Kerttu.

"Yaah, you can tell them when we're really gone, but no earlier," I said with a laugh. "They keep talking about going, but you don't get there by talking. You have to get busy, and the paperwork is a big job. It won't be as easy for them to go now when there are three of them."

"But what are you going to do with the cat?" asked Kerttu.

"I'm not sure yet. I'm not going to leave it here to starve in this heat."

"What about trying rat poison?" said Kerttu.

"Listen, I tried it a few days ago. It didn't bother the cat at all. And she looks as if she's going to have kittens."

"I thought it was a male cat?"

"That's what they told the children. I didn't check it."

"And now Miki is going to have kittens," Kerttu laughed.

"It's not the first mistake ever made in the world. Don't you want more cats?"

"Good lord, no! I have enough trouble with that dog. Listen, I always put pants on her when she's in heat. She doesn't wear them when she was inside, and once she slipped out and had pups again. I have to take her somewhere to be fixed. She's a good watchdog now that we have those building materials outside again. You can't trust those Greeks at all. Everything walks off if you don't keep an eye on it. Once they borrowed something and did not return it. I went and got it back. We no longer lend anything to them."

"Write your address here so we can stay in touch," I said.

"Of course. We'd like to know how things are going with you. I'll come to the ship with the children to see you off and make sure you leave. I don't know what tricks you might still be up to," said Kerttu, laughing.

Evening was drawing near, and I still had many things I wanted to give away. There was a large drawerful of Finnish magazines. Surely someone would be glad to have them.

"Saul, what if you were to take a walk to see the Maunula family? I'm sure they'll be glad to read these. They used to live right near here. Their boy was the same age as Poju, and they were good friends, just as we all were. We didn't get to see much of them after they bought their own house about a kilometer away."

Saul went striding off, and before long, he came back with the Maunulas in their car. We had told them nothing about our leaving either.

"Well, you are pulling a real stunt, leaving just like that. It's good that you finally told us about it. When you get a start there, we'll follow you."

While they were still sitting there, Miki peered in through the door and mewed piteously. My heart was aching—what would I do with that cat? It looked as if she would soon start to have kittens.

It was already late when the Maunulas left. It was dark outside, as it tends to be in the south when there is no moonlight. I went outside, sat down on the porch, and struggled with myself. I could not leave the cat here to yowl. We would no longer be here to feed her tomorrow night, and she would die of hunger with her kittens. Again she came toward me, walking painfully, and her voice sounded just like weeping.

I peeked into the house. Everyone was sleeping soundly. I went to an outbuilding, took a spade, and began to dig a pit into the soft ground, from which the last of the vegetables had just been pulled, with Miki beside me, mewing piteously. "It has to happen now," I told myself. I took the cat by the hind paws and struck her head sharply against the side of the building. She gave a heart-rending shriek and dug her front claws into my wrist. I forced her into the pit and pressed the shovel against her throat. Her hind legs were still kicking furiously. With my feet, I began to kick earth over her. Gradually her legs began to kick more feebly. I filled the pit with soil, even tramping it smooth with my feet. Sweaty and shaking, I walked to the steps of the shack, sat down on them, and wept.

Amazingly enough, my heart began to feel better. *It's done now, and Miki doesn't have to suffer any more*, a voice in my heart said. My mood began to lift. I knew I had done the right thing. Man was given dominion over the creatures, so says the Bible.

Feeling relieved, I rose, went to an outdoor faucet, where I washed my hands and cooled off my cheeks with the water. I noticed that there were bloody scratches in my wrists from Miki's claws. Wiping them off, I went inside, lay down wearily, and fell asleep at once.—What? What was that? I sat up in bed. I heard a cat mewing horribly—It stopped immediately, but I was sure I had heard it. I crept cautiously out the door and went to look at the place where Miki was buried. It was the same as before. It had all been a nightmare.

I had heard that cats cling tenaciously to life. I would go and get a couple of bricks to put on the grave to make sure the she would no longer rise. In the darkness, wearing a nightgown, I carried bricks to the grave. Now Miki had a memorial, I thought as I went in.

I could not sleep for the rest of the night, but still I felt fresh when the sun rose. First I carried the bricks back to the building. Saul came out at that moment and began to wonder, "What have you been doing with those bricks?"

I told him what had happened during the night.

"All that because of one cat!"

"Yes, and now the weight is off my heart because I didn't leave the poor thing to suffer. You mustn't say anything to the children about this. I'll make up something if they ask."

Saul left for the city early that morning. Only today would we get the money for the house. I stayed at home until the buyer of the furniture came and paid for it. We were to meet Saul at the ship, which would not leave until four in the afternoon.

"Where is Miki?" Poju asked as soon as he got up.

"Oh . . . Maunulas came to get her later last night," I said.

"Maunulas will take good care of her," said Little-Sisko.

"Oh, yaah, Simo always held Miki in his lap and petted her," said Poju.

"No way did Miki want to leave here," I said, and tears began to run from my eyes. I went out and sat on the half-finished porch of the house.

"God forgive me for lying to my children. But I can't tell them the truth now. When they grow up and can understand it all, I'll tell them. Then they will surely think I did the right thing."

Parents are not perfect. Remember that God had problems with Adam.

CHAPTER XI

January 22, 1964. The big ocean liner began to glide smoothly out of the harbor of Sydney. The Lehvistös were left waving as we disappeared from sight. It was the most beautiful of summer days, with not even the threat of thunder in the air.

Exactly six years before we had arrived here in the land of kangaroos with our minds filled with new hopes. During that time we had had to learn much that was new. There were three things I had not grown accustomed to: eating lamb, the coffee, which was roasted too black, and the tea, which was served everywhere with milk. For tea was the national drink; we were, after all, in a British dominion.

The ship was a British one owned by a famous steamship line and went by the name of *Oronsay*. It sailed all over the world, and it was completely different from our former refugee ship. The children shared a cabin with four beds, and we had a cabin for two directly across from them. Naturally we were below the waterline, and there were no windows.

Immediately after the first afternoon coffee, everyone was ordered to take part in a lifeboat drill. An unhappy feeling stirred in my mind. Was the craft just as flimsy as the old *Skaubryn*? This would be our only drill, we were told. Drills had been a weekly happening on the *Skaubryn*.

The menu was in French, and we understood nothing of it. The waiter was an old black man who did not understand my accented English. We were really hungry, and in our ignorance, we ordered double portions. The food was really good, but we ate too much. I was tired, but I tossed restlessly in my bed, hearing the miserable mewing of a cat. In the morning, there was a knock at the door. *Is it morning already*, I thought. *You come and bother a person in the middle of the night?* But I took the tray I was proffered and said thanks. Looking at my watch, I saw it was only six. That was an early hour to get up.

"Yaah, it's seven o'clock. Time to go and wash up so we'll make it to breakfast." said Saul, stretching his arms.

"But it's only six. There's your morning tea. The boy knocked at the door. I don't care for it, it's so black. And besides, it has milk in it. Your watch is slow. Don't you remember we had to set our watches an hour ahead?

"Oh darn, are we going to have to play that same game with out watches. Set them ahead an hour every night. Soon breakfast will be at midnight.

Next time I'm going to circle the globe in the other direction so I'll get to sleep an hour later every morning," I laughed.

"We'll find out today if we can get juice in the morning. This tea is really yucky."

At that moment Poju and Little-Sisko entered in their nightshirts.

"Aren't you sleepy any more?"

"No, I want to go on deck," said Poju.

"Wait a while for me so you won't get lost the first day," said Saul. "Did you get anything to drink this morning?"

"We did. Do you remember what it was, Sisko?"

"It was Fruitberry. It was awful, yuck," said Little-Sisko.

"What did you say, what-berry?" I said doubtfully. "Do they give it to children?"

"It wasn't wine. It was kind of like Coca-Cola," Sisko explained.

"Oh, I thought they all were Coca-Cola. I'm going to ask them to bring orange juice for all of us in the morning. It's a lot better."

The bigger girls joined us when we went up on deck. The waves were moderate and the wind felt chilly. There was, of course, no land to be seen anywhere. We were not on deck long before we had to go and get something warmer to wear. Someone was doing his morning workout by jogging around the deck.

Inside we checked our route more carefully. We were on the way to New Zealand. In two days we would anchor in Auckland on the northern island of New Zealand. How exciting!

The wind remained so chill that it was really no fun to be on deck. It blew from Antarctica, where it is always cold. Poju got a slight earache because he could not stand to be indoors all the time. In the evening we sat in the salon and listened to the orchestra rehearse. It was fine music. There were all the conveniences on board the ship: a library, a bank, a beauty shop, a store, and of course a bar. Two people acted as our entertainment directors, supervising all kinds of pastimes. We glanced at the list of passengers: there were no other Finns aboard.

The swimming pool was ready for use, but there were not many splashing in it. In the second-class area there was a volleyball court and other recreational facilities. We were allowed to make a guided tour through every nook and cranny of the ship. The children even got a chance to steer it. The ship was huge: there were two thousand people on board, including the crew. There was always some pastime going on on deck: throwing darts, ring tossing.

Early on the third morning, we already sighted land on the horizon. It was a narrow group of islands, a part of northern New Zealand. We arrived in the harbor during breakfast, and were given several advertising fliers presenting the sights of New Zealand. Bus trips to the more distant hot mud baths could also be arranged. New Zealand is basically volcanic land and there are frequent earthquakes. Fortunately they are mainly at the bottom of the sea, so they do no damage. It often happens that a new island will appear overnight. Hot lava pours out into the sea and hardens into an island. On this island there are fiery hot springs and mud ponds where the muck boils like a pot of porridge.

Half of the residents are English, or white, and the other half are the aboriginal Maoris. The main language is English, although the Maoris have preserved their own tongue. England sends a governor here, as it does to Australia. Otherwise the people choose their own representatives and decide their own affairs. The aboriginal Maoris have the same rights as the whites, and work side by side with them. In Australia the aborigines are still quite primitive. They live to themselves in natural surroundings and people look askance at them if they come into the cities. They live underneath trees, use their boomerangs to hunt birds, and light fires by twirling one piece of wood against another.

We went to walk around the city after breakfast. It was Saturday morning, and everything was quiet. The weather was suitably cool, and the streets were exceptionally neat. The traffic lights startled us: when we were halfway across the street, an alarm bell went off, and we dashed to the other side. We observed later that it was a warning not to begin crossing.

We visited a museum where authentic original tools were on display and could see that the island culture was age-old. The English explorer Tasman saw the islands for the first time in 1642, and Captain Cook was the first white man to land there in 1769. The island was then at a primitive stage. Now there are paper plants, agriculture, and sheep raising, along with mining as ways to make a living.

We spent the afternoon in a park with an open-air theater. There was a revue with song and dance. Whites and Maoris appeared on stage together in full harmony. The Maoris were rather brown, round-faced, with curly hair, and were somewhat smaller than average in build. What they were now presenting must surely have been their folk dances. The women were dressed in a white sleeveless blouse and an adorned jumper that reached down to the knees. Underneath was a skirt, and over it this jumper, which made a small, tinkling noise as they danced. The colors of the skirt were dark. The predominant color was red, and the shades blended well with each other. The men were bare to the waist, and wore brightly colored knee-length pants with a floral pattern. Around the neck was a leather thong, on which dangled the teeth of various animals. It created an impression of wild nature on the audience. The dance was wild compared to our folk dances. The dancers were all barefoot, so their steps made no sound on the grass. They had flutes and all kinds of rattles made from the shells of various fruits. The women danced quite reservedly; it was the men's dance which was wild, with leaps, somersaults, and now and then a loud scream when the drums banged.

The next day was Sunday. We walked around the other side of the city. Everything was so wonderfully calm and restful, and the weather was like warm milk. What everyday life here was like we did not get to see; our ship continued its voyage north that same evening. Beautiful and neat New Zealand remained in our memories as a haven of peace.

The next morning we were already in a tropical climate. The cold winds of the Antarctic lay behind us. The Southern Pacific deserves its name; only small waves rippled prettily on its surface in the sunshine. There a school of flying fish danced on the waves, reminding us of the mosquitoes at home.

The swimming pool was even too full now, especially in the afternoon. The clock had already been moved ahead three times, so that the regular wake-up time was already at the former four o' clock. We supplemented our lost sleep with little afternoon naps, which were really refreshing. Sunset on board a ship is truly a memorable experience. The ship was going east and the sun sank in the west. It would be shining full blast and suddenly it would begin to sink into the sea before one's eyes. Within a matter of seconds it was no longer even twilight. Sunrise is the same. The sun seems literally to pop up from the sea.

A stowaway was discovered on the ship, a fifteen-year-old boy who had managed to sneak aboard in Auckland. Another ship was coming toward us. A little motorboat that took the boy to the southbound ship looked fragile on the vast sea. And so the heroic young traveler's journey ended right at the start.

In the morning we awakened in the harbor of Suva, a city in the Fiji Islands. The air was anything but refreshing. We watched the harbor's morning activities from the deck of the ship. Some kind of antique orchestra was there to greet us. It must have been a great occasion when such a large ship came into port. We learned later that this happened only three times a year. The inhabitants wore practically nothing. The men had short pants or some kind of rag wrapped around them below the waist. The women wore a skirt of sorts, but above the waist they had only a piece of cloth tied in back with a cord.

The earth felt solid beneath our feet when we stepped on shore. Taxis were there seeking passengers, offering tours around the island at every imaginable price. Why bypass the sea to go fishing? There was a lot to see in this town, even though it was small. In the harbor was a huge building with sparsely boarded walls. It was probably a market of some kind. People in back of tables were selling all sorts of handmade wares. The competition was fierce, and prices were lowered quickly. There were the most remarkable objects made of seashells. It must have been a unique opportunity for the sellers to market their wares.

The children had saved up their money and bought souvenirs of the trip. It seemed as if the sellers would not let a customer leave empty-handed. They lowered prices, and even ran after customers to thrust their wares on them.

The only street in town was unpaved, that is, it was of sand. Car wheels had made ruts in it, and water from the previous day's rain still stood in those ruts. There were a few shops on the left side of the street. On the right side ran a brook, which gave off a disgusting stench.

From the door of one of the shops, a man dressed in a horrid costume darted out. We were frightened out of our wits. He wore a Fiji warrior's garb, and wanted to pose for a picture with us, for a fee. I shook my head, not wanting to have anything to do with a monster like that, not even in fun. His dress was a sleeveless cloak made from a hairy animal's hide decorated with large teeth and animal bones, and he had horns and colorful feathers on his head. His weapon was an ancient crossbow.

The shop doors were open, so that one could not miss them even accidentally. One of them seemed to be a "made to order" shop; two men sat at sewing machines waiting for customers. They sewed Indian saris while the buyer waited. The fabrics were beautifully colorful silk or blends, and the prices varied with the material. As I understood it, the sari was a straight piece of fabric of some fifteen to fifty meters in length. The more fabric, the finer the garment and the higher the price. The sari is wrapped skillfully around the body, and neither the arms nor the legs can show, only the ankles.

The weather was quite humid and heavy. We were so tired that we did not leave the ship after lunch. There was a feeling of a thunderstorm in the area, which added to our languor. After our daytime nap, it rained buckets. We heard that it usually did so every day.

In the morning we were far out at sea. According to the trip schedule, there would be two January 31sts. We had wondered about it, and now we would get to see it when we reached the International Date Line. Traveling east you gain a day, and traveling west you lose a day. "Of all the things they come up with," I thought in my simple mind.

A week's sea voyage lay ahead of us. Every day an interesting program was arranged. Today the captain had invited the passengers, that is, only the adults, to cocktails. The children had a party of their own.

"I'm not going," said Saul.

"Well I, at least, am going," I said. "It isn't every day that we're invited to a party like this. It is for all the passengers," I added firmly. "Let's enjoy life now that we have the chance. We're on vacation now. We've worked before, and we'll work again when the time comes. We're just as good as anyone on the ship. We've paid our fare with money earned by honest work," I kept babbling on as I got into my best dress.

Reluctantly Saul started getting ready to go. As we left he gave me a troubled look and said: "You really are fancy—earrings and all. You must have been free and easy with the money again."

"Well I have to doll up at least enough so that you won't be ashamed of me—since you went and married a gal from the country like me," I answered with a laugh.

"Of course you plan to vamp the captain," he said jokingly.

"Well, that's the idea. The captain's wife isn't always with him. We'll soon see." I caught him by the hand, and we went to find out where the cocktail party was.

I was surprised at my ability to joke about such a sore matter. I was freer now than I had once been and did not suffer as I had before. I had been a fool to weep in his claws.

Sisu Mother

I was pleased with my dress, although it had cost very little, since I had sewed it myself from some remnants of extraordinarily good fabric. It had little lacelike flowers on a black background, but was otherwise simple: narrow, a V-neck. and a large white-lace rosette on the left side. I had bought a set of beads and earrings to go with just this dress.

The secretary introduced everyone to the captain by name. He shook hands with all of us and welcomed us warmly.

"I can't tell from your name what you are."

"We are Finns," Saul said humbly.

"Ah, yes, Finns. *Sisu—sisu*—What does that mean?" asked the captain. Saul looked helplessly at me. I began to explain.

"*Sisu* and Finns. It means being tough, not giving in, being determined. For instance, if you decide to do something, you do it no matter how hopeless it seems."

"Good people, good people," said the captain, smiling and patting my shoulder.

There were travelers from all parts of the world at the affair, a few of them in everyday wear. Most of them, however, had dressed for the occasion. There were two women from India. One was wearing a beautiful royal-blue sari, the other a yellowish gold one, which surely must have been real silk. Their long, jet-black hair was parted and done up in an enormous bun on the neck. One had a lovely jewel just below the caste mark on her forehead, which hung from a chain in her hair. It looked like a genuine diamond. The caste mark was a deep red. They wore lovely rings on their fingers and also on their big toes, and wore only Indian sandals on their feet, tied with colorful thongs to their ankles. They were beautiful women, sisters perhaps. The men I took to be their husbands wore white, collarless shirts under Nehru jackets. They looked somehow colorless beside their beautiful wives.

There was also an Arabian couple. The wife wore a long, colorful floral skirt. On her head was a shawl-like hood of black cloth, which fell below her waist. It was gathered tightly around her face, with only the eyes showing. She clutched it tightly under her chin with one hand. The man was dressed all in white with a turban on his head and a loose collarless shirt. His pants were also white, wide pants which resembled golfing trousers, tied with a broad cloth sash at the waist. One end of the sash hung almost to his knees. On his feet were those Indian-Oriental sandals. His wife looked diffident, as if she were hiding behind her husband.

The dark-skinned waiters circulated skillfully among the guests, serving drinks and delicious hors-d'oeuvres. One of the Americans was like a hamster. He always took the glasses in both hands and drank them at one go, then turned away to find another waiter and repeated the performance.

The orchestra had been playing in the background all the while, and a few couples were already on the dance floor.

"Hey, this is really great. It would be fun to see those Indians dance," I said to Saul. He seemed to be enjoying the situation. A couple of drinks had done him good.

"That sounds like a perfectly familiar waltz. Shall we go and try it?"
"Of course," I said, and emptied my glass.

"This is wonderful," I said, between dances. "They dance in deck every evening, but we are always so tired."

"These time changes get everything messed up."

"Are you still sorry you came?" I asked when the number was over.

"No, this fun. It would be a shame to miss it."

Most of the partygoers seemed to have unwound, and a few were going wild to a rock-and-roll beat. Most likely the continual emptying of glasses had something to do with it. Only the Easterners continued to look gloomy. Were they ever able to relax and enjoy life at all?

Now a Spanish couple was out on the floor. This was undoubtedly a rumba, an exotic tropical dance. The girl was dazzlingly beautiful in a long, flowing dress. Her white blouse was cut quite low. The man was wearing black tails, white trousers, and a white shirt with a bow tie under his chin. The dance was an artistic exhibition. Someone behind us whispered, "They are professional dancers and travel around the world."

"Oh, how smoothly they dance. They are a joy to watch."

When the dance ended, there was a tremendous round of applause. Now the orchestra struck up a samba. The couple began to dance again; they seemed to be thoroughly enjoying themselves, and their performance was marvelous and charged with temperament. At times the man dipped the girl's upper body so low that her jet-black curls grazed the floor. When the dance was over, they tossed their sweaty heads and disappeared from the room.

We were dancing a waltz again. What was that? The captain was tapping Saul on the shoulder. "May I have this dance with your *sisu* wife?" he asked, bowing. Saul looked as if he had been struck over the head, and so did I. Noticing my confusion, the captain began to lead me slowly in the dance. It was more like walking than dancing, with no attention to the music. I felt my cheeks flushing.

"How do you like the party? Are you enjoying everything being served?"

"Yes, yes. Wonderful party," I said in my halting English.

"Do you have a family?" asked the captain.

"Yes, we do. We have four children."

"You are a *sisu*-mother," he said laughing. The dance ended and he escorted me back to Saul.

"*Sisu*-mother. *Sisu*-wife," said the captain, taking leave by shaking hands with both of us. He was a very pleasant person.

The party was beginning to break up, and it was time to leave. The American hamster was so limp that the steward had to be on one side and his wife on the other in order to take him to his cabin.

Often we sat by the pool in the afternoon and watched the funny competitions. If laughter lengthens life, we must have added years to ours there. The most fun was when a smooth, round log was laid across the pool. Two competitors sat astride it and tried to knock the other off with a sack the size of a pillowcase. Even without the battle, it took skill to stay on the slippery log. There were many other amusing pastimes as well.

Our family was sitting on deck one day chatting in Finnish. A voice said, also in Finnish, "Well, goddammit boy."

We looked around to see who it was. A man laughed loudly and began to explain in English. "I was with the Finns in Queensland, working in the sugar-cane fields. I learned a few words from them. They were *sisu*-men, hard-working and hard-drinking. Cutting sugar cane is goddamned tough work. Boys can't keep up there. Half the newcomers quit and went looking for better jobs. And it's damned sooty on top of everything."

"Why is that?" asked Saul. "I know nothing about the work."

"The field is burned over first, to get rid of the snakes. The dry leaves burn well, and it doesn't harm the stalks. Come evening, a man is all sooty. The sugary juice that drips from the stalks hardens on a man's clothes. It's disgusting. Many a Finn has sweated in the fields of Queensland. There are lots of Italians there too. We're *sisu*-boys too." The Italian showed his stout arms. From then on, whenever he saw Poju, he stroked his thick hair and said "*Sisu*-boy."

The Italian was a lively companion and a good talker. He was on his way to his native country for the first time since leaving it.

"What are those triangular things moving in the water?" Pia would ask.

"Oh, sharks. How come they're swimming so near the ship?" Saul wondered, rising to his feet, as did our new acquaintance, the Italian.

"They are big, at least fifteen meters," he said.

"Ooh, what if you should fall in," said Tytti, horrified.

"I heard that an American died of a heart attack last night," said the Italian.

"Is that so? How old was he?" asked Saul.

"A little over forty. He had been sent to Australia by some company. He was a heavy drinker."

"Could he be the same man who was so drunk at the party?" Saul wondered.

"The very same, if you mean the one who wasn't able to walk."

"That's just who I mean. Well, I'll be damned."

"You never know when you might go. Well, at least he had a good party. The sharks will get to eat that food, if they haven't already," said the Italian, with a carefree laugh.

"Ugh, it's sad to think of such a thing happening," I said softly. "You get to know someone who lives so close to you and eats at the same time. Every now and then we chatted a little to pass away the time."

That evening the American's wife was not at dinner. It must have been true then, although I had doubted the Italian's story. We really do not know which journey will be our last. But I would really rather not die here and be dumped into the sea. As for my ashes, they might as well be thrown there, for I had no homeland now that Karelia was gone, nor did I really want to be buried in the ground to become food for worms. When ashes are thrown into the sea, they settle to the bottom and become earth, as the Bible says.

Today we cross the Equator and Neptune climbs on board the ship. I don't even want to go and watch, it's such a wild happening.

"He tried to grab me," shouted Poju, running into the cabin in a panic.

"What are you talking about? Who and where?"

"That—that Neptune. Many of them climbed on board the ship. One had a pitchfork in his hand, and a sailor put a crown on his head. Then they started throwing people into the pool."

"Don't tell me . . . But why?" I pretended ignorance. Poju had seen nothing of what had occurred six years ago on our way to Australia.

"I don't know, but the women were screaming, and there was a lot of racket, and the water was splashing."

"Did you see the girls there?"

"They were there, but I don't know what happened to them because I skipped away as fast as I could," said Poju, his eyes wide.

The girls came in, looking stupid. Tytti was soaking wet, but the others had only been splashed.

"They weren't tarred the way they were then," said Tytti.

"Thank God. There would have been a lot of wash to do. That devil on the *Skaubryn* was all tar. I had to throw a whole dress away because I couldn't get it clean."

"Why do you go poking your nose into every place?" Saul said nastily.

"Well, it was fun to see that merrymaking. What's the use of going around the world if you sit in your cabin the whole time and don't see a thing? It would be cheaper to sit at home in your living room."

One morning Poju came racing into our cabin when we were still in our nightclothes. We had turned our watches ahead again—I don't know how many times it was now. We were slightly tired all the time, but we could always fall asleep to the rocking of the ship no matter what time it was.

"Come on deck, quick, we've docked. An orchestra is playing down below," the boy said breathlessly.

"Yaah, we're in Hawaii now," I said sleepily. "Famous Honolulu."

"Come and see," shouted the boy, and disappeared quickly out the door.

A warm breeze wafted toward us on deck setting the palm trees to swaying gently. Down below a small, colorfully dressed orchestra was playing. The musicians wore no shirts, but a broad red band fastened to their knee pants ran over one shoulder. Their skin was a golden brown, probably because of the abundant sunshine. They looked like a mixture of Philippine, Chinese, and Japanese.

One of the musicians sang a solo, accompanying himself on the Hawaiian guitar, the ukulele. It sounded charming and peaceful. I could not hear the words clearly and would hardly have understood them. The Hawaiians have their own language, although English is the official language of the islands. There are seven islands, all of them volcanic in origin. Apparently they have been formed in this manner over thousands of years. The name of this island is Oahu. Honolulu is its largest city and the main center of the islands. We were spending three days here, so we had to think of how we would see the most and get to know this world-renowned island, its nature, people, and culture.

After breakfast we started out. Passports were being checked, but we had none, only a visa to enter the U.S.A. as immigrants. Saul had to get out our entire bundle of official papers for checking. We were taken into a separate room where the entire family would be checked.

"Is there someone there to take responsibility for you?" we were asked in a very official way.

"No, no one," said Saul.

"How could they have sent you here, without guarantors and with no one to receive you?' The man was sweating and scratching his head. "Six people. A huge family. Where will you go for the night? I don't understand how they let you start out."

"We thought Los Angeles was a city where there are hotels and motels we could stay in until we are able to rent a house," I said, somewhat troubled. "We have learned that there are plenty of places to live available."

Saul jerked at my hand angrily and whispered, "Shut up!"

"Oh, there are places to live, but they cost a lot for families like this," the man said quickly. "I have to consult with others to see if they will let you go on," he added, then rose and left the room.

"Damn it, you've gone and made him mad. Now there's the devil to pay if we have to go back to Australia," said Saul, his fists clenched in anger.

"We won't be sent back just for that. Our papers were in order when we left Australia. He looked only at the first page. When he comes back, Tytti can talk to him and explain that we have resources. We are not going there to be supported by anyone. It looked as if he didn't really understand us."

The man returned to the room with another official.

"Would you look at those papers a little more carefully?" Tytti said. "We have enough money to get started on."

The man began to leaf nervously through the papers, stopping to read one of the pages. He gestured to his companion to come nearer. "Yaah," they mumbled to themselves, nodding their heads, and then adding, "Okay," still to themselves.

"Excuse us for getting excited too quickly. Everything is in order. When you get to Los Angeles and have a permanent address, go to this office and let them know. It's something you have to do if you want to stay in the country. I wish you all the best in the future," the man said, shaking hands with all of us in farewell.

"That was really annoying," said Saul. "Remember to keep your mouth shut in public places, woman. It would have been your fault if they had sent us back." To top it, he glared at me angrily.

All was forgotten when we walked down the gangplank. Before us was a colorful sight. Young Hawaiians, the girls in colorful muumuus in large floral prints which reached midway to their calves, and the boys in shorts of the same colors. They put a wreath of flowers called a lei around our necks and planted a kiss on our cheeks. I saw Saul get red to the ears. Flash bulbs blinked, so we were being photographed. Someone stuck a card in my hand.

"This tells you where you can get the pictures in the afternoon."

"Well, it's just business," said Saul, relieved. "I thought we were so famous they would put us in the papers."

"Did you see those young people? They were barefoot. And the boys didn't have any shirts on," I whispered softly.

"I didn't see anything. I was so darn shocked. Do they welcome everyone so royally?" he added.

"They must. We were the last ones to come onshore, since we had to go for the questioning. It looks as if some late sleepers are still coming off the ship. Yaah, they put flowers around their neck too," I said.

We decided to see Honolulu on foot at first. After seven days at sea it felt good to have solid ground under our feet again. On the first street corner, three taxi drivers offered us a ride. We had leaflets with us to guide us to the most notable places we wanted to see.

"It's eternal summer here," said Saul. "According to the calendar, the third of February is still winter, but the weather is like midsummer."

"They don't need fur hats or felt boots; they can just pad along barefoot in that muumuu that looks like a nightgown. People have it easy here in this land of summer. Look, we should have found out more about this place and gotten permission to stay here," I said admiringly, hearing the sighing of the palm trees in my ears.

The street names were in Hawaiian, but they sounded perfectly familiar to our ears. There was Leilani Street. Why, that was Finnish. Iolani Palace, a large, three-story building of clay tiles. There was an idyllic garden around it, with trees and shrubs in bloom although it was February. What a calamity that it was only open in the evening. We rested for a while on a bench in this royal garden. It seemed as if the word haste was unknown here.

"Look at those flowers. They look just like a bird. The leaves are exactly like a lily's. The flower is reddish-gold, in the shape of a bird. It is blue under the imaginary wings and breast."

"The name of these flowers is 'Bird of Paradise,'" said the dark gardener.

We came to the Chinese section of the city. Delightful buildings with broad, upward-arching roofs. Advertisements in that picture-writing which is read from top to bottom. There was a genuine Chinese man with a braid and a peaked cap. Pants and collarless coat were of some dark-checked material. No shoes of course—that seemed to be the custom here. Some shops had their wares out on the street in order to sell them better. Poju bought a bamboo flute, which we noticed later was "Made in Hong Kong."

In the afternoon, we took a bus to the famed Waikiki Beach. On the way we saw an enormous pineapple. It was about five meters high and two meters in diameter. There were shouts of astonishment, and the bus driver began to explain. "A lot of pineapples are grown here, and that is a canning plant. You can also go there to visit. A bus that goes from Waikiki will take you there for nothing. Sad to say, no children are allowed."

Waikiki was a lively place. People walked around in bathing suits, even on the streets. The road we were on led to the international market. There were many kinds of sales stands, some with roofs of reeds, and others merely open tables. There were ornaments made of rocks, seashells, and other materials. And there was Hawaiian clothing, of course, and every kind of trinket one can imagine. Many kinds of craftsmen made their wares while the customer waited. Woodcarvings, totem poles, animal images—anything the mind could conceive.

We watched in amusement at a place where one could fish an oyster from a half-barrel of water for a half-dollar. People opened the shell excitedly, and a cheer went up if a pearl was found.

On the shore some of the people were lolling on grass mats. A few tried to swim, but soon came out of the water blue with cold. Although the air was warm, the water was quite cold.

A surfboarding school was in session. First they practiced the techniques, one teacher to five pupils. Now they charged running into the waves. It wasn't easy to stay on the board even while lying down, not to mention standing up.

Often during the day, we had seen people walking around with grass mats rolled up under their arms. We had thought they were on sale somewhere. Now it dawned on us that they were used for lying on the sand. What a good idea. Just beat the sand off, and there was no washing to do. The children were annoyed at not having bathing suits with them. Since they were at Waikiki, they at least had to go wading. "It isn't as warm as it looks," declared Pia.

"You can swim on the ship when we start off again. It's so hard to bring everything here with us and change," I said.

There were showers in the open air at the beach. A water pipe in the center, with a ring of concrete around it, where four to six could shower at the same time.

The following morning we went by bus in another direction. First we stopped at Pearl Harbor, an American naval base during the Second World War.

On December 7, 1941, the Japanese made a surprise aerial bombing attack on the base. Within two hours, eighteen ships were either sunk or damaged. The largest ship, the *U.S.S. Arizona*, had just gotten ready to leave. In all, over three thousand men were lost in this bombing. On the *Arizona* alone, eleven hundred and seventy-seven. Oil was still leaking from this ship and rising to the surface. It had just been fueled for a voyage with six million liters of oil. A monument was being built over the *Arizona*.

It was a sad subject upon which to reflect. I still had scenes from wartime and the bombings in my own mind. The cruelty of war was everywhere, even on this faraway, peaceful island.

The guide explained to the travelers that this island, like all the others in Hawaii, was the result of volcanic eruptions, although there had been no eruptions on this one for hundreds or thousands of years. But on the larger islands there are constantly open craters, and several eruptions occur annually.

The famous Diamond Head was the result of an eruption from the side of a volcano. It is now a national park. Visitors can get to the crater through a tunnel. Years ago there were gleaming stones in the crater walls. People came to dig them out, thinking they were diamonds, although they were probably fool's gold. But it was from them that Diamond Head got its name. Trees and shrubs grew in the park, and there were many paths, on which we saw quite a few joggers.

The bus made a loop on the craggy shore, where hot lava had shaped many freaks of nature. One was called the Blowhole. Water entered it from under the ground and then spurted up some ten meters into the air. The sea was a lovely blue, and from it "Blue Hawaii" has gotten its name. The Pacific Ocean covers a large area of the earth's surface.

We stopped at the Punchbowl Crater. Here we found the monuments to Hawaii's dead of the First and Second World War and the Korean War. Nearly 20,000 dead and as many missing. Impressively wide steps led up to a beautiful monument, with low structures to either side into the marble walls of which every hero's name had been carved. Higher up on both sides was a map of the world, with the places where battles had been fought marked. High had been the cost of freedom for the United States, although no battles have been fought on her soil for a hundred years.

The winding road led to the edge of a crater, from which an eye-filling view of Honolulu and Waikiki opened up.

"Hey, I can see our ship there on the shore," said Little-Sisko.

"Where, where?" cried Poju excited. "But why is it so small?"

"Because we're so high up and so far away," his father explained.

The bus took us back to the harbor. That was all we could manage for the day. Its yields had been rewarding, although sad, but history cannot be changed.

"Hey, wake up." I shook Saul. "We have a reservation for a luau tonight. I forgot all about it."

"What luau? What are you babbling about?"

"Don't you remember? We made the reservation on the ship already. It is something especially Hawaiian."

"I'm not going anywhere," he said, and turned over.

"Well, I am going. I want to see everything there is to see. The bus is leaving in a half-hour, at six, that is. I've already spoken to Tytti, and she'll take care of the smaller children. They can get along here by themselves. I promised to take them to the zoo tomorrow. We'll have supper at the luau."

"Why should we go and pay to eat somewhere else when we get free food on the ship? You keep coming up with ways to spend. It's just throwing money away," he muttered, and began to dress.

"There's a long program that goes along with the dinner. It may be quite late when we get back."

We sat in the bus, with Saul looking grumpy. The first thing the guide advised us to do was to "hang loose." We had some thirty miles to go, but a good party had been arranged for us at the destination. There one could eat and drink (alcoholic drinks included) as much as he could hold. We had a bus driver to get everyone home safely.

"Look at the street names, Saul. The Lualualei radio station. Kokohahi village. Pohokupu Street, Hihimani Street, Aina Haina village, Punaluu district, Makua village. This Hawaiian language is absolutely catching; it feels as if it were related to Finnish. It has only twelve letters. That's why it's so easy."

Even Saul was beginning to laugh at the guide's funny stories. He started asking how far from home everyone was. "You two there, you haven't raised your hand," he said, pointing at us. "Where are you from?"

"From Finland," I said shyly.

"Finland, Finland. Why, that's the polar bears' land. You really are far from home. I've never met anyone from so far away. You must really like your vacation in this warm climate."

When we reached our destination, the guide placed a seashell necklace around each woman's neck and kissed her on the cheek. He also gave them beads to put around the men's necks, along with the admonition: "Don't forget the kiss."

This was all taking place on a lovely white sand beach. We were urged to get something to drink. There were booths (*keitas*) everywhere, so no one had to stand in line or go thirsty.

Long tables and benches were lined up on the sand. An area some eight meters square was fenced off in the center, where a pig was roasting under the sand. Just as the sun was setting into the sea, someone requested silence —the royal ceremony was about to begin.

First the king, queen, and their guards entered, all in the most colorful of costumes. Red was the predominant color—beyond that, the costume was difficult to describe. Many brilliant feathers. The men's breasts, calves, and feet were bare.

A hula-dance pair stepped forth, the girl wearing a skirt of actually living tea-tree leaves. They were followed by all the dance couples who would appear in the evening's program. Samoa, Tonga, Tahiti, Fiji, and the New Zealand Islands, all in different costumes, or should I call it full dress. They stationed themselves in an arc within the fenced-off area. From the loudspeaker came a prayer in Hawaiian.

Two men dressed only in red shorts came in, carrying on their shoulders what looked like a baking tin some meter and a half long and wide. Setting it on the ground, they began to dig up the sand with shovels. First broad, black tea leaves came into view, which they removed carefully. Next there was a coarse sackcloth. Under that was the roast pig, enclosed in chicken wire. Slowly and carefully they lifted the pig onto the tin.

The royal party and the dancers began walking away in pairs. Last came the pig tin, borne on the shoulders of the men. It had been buried the previous evening on red-hot rocks. The pig had been roasted head, hoofs, and all—only the innards had been removed and the cavities stuffed with spices.

Now we moved over to the long tables, which had been reserved for twelve to fourteen people each. I kicked my shoes off like the others because they were full of sand. The drink *keitas* were open all the time and in diligent use. Performers were already beginning to sing on stage, and the hula girls began to dance. "Attention! attention, men! We have all relaxed in the Hawaiian way. Now get up, circle your table, and kiss every representative of the fair sex."

I gave Saul a teasing nudge in the side. "Well, I'm not going anyway," he said, and headed for a *keita*. Most of the men obeyed the announcer's urging.

The women were not ignored either. Two girls from each table were urged to go up on the stage and learn the hula. There were eight women at our table, and no one was eager to go. Lots were cast. Good Lord, I had to go. I took a good swallow from Saul's glass to give me courage, and he gave me a nasty look. It didn't bother me a bit. I just gaily went along with the crowd.

This is neat, I thought on stage. I wasn't even blushing at the thought of performing in public. I swayed my body to the sweet music of the ukulele. One could soon learn this. The hand movements were something new, since they had a verbal meaning.

"Attention—attention, men. Line up on either side of the stage. The girls have danced beautifully. Men, you have to thank them now by hugging each girl as she comes off the stage. I felt myself being hugged hundreds of times. Saul was not among the huggers, but nevertheless he seemed to be enjoying the situation.

"I want three handsome men up on stage. You can dance with the hula girls. The best dancer will get a special prize." Men began running to line up by the stage.

A handsome man from California won the competition. The prize? He got to kiss the prettiest hula girl. But the kiss seemed endless. The announcer had already cleared his throat many times, but the lad merely went on enjoying his prize. Fortunately the lights dimmed, and the pair were lost to sight in the moonlight.

The supper was served buffet style, with a large number of serving tables. Everyone filled his plate, and the serving went without a hitch, although there were six hundred diners. There were so many kinds of food. One's plate was soon filled to overflowing with too many delicacies, with that roasted pork, of course, and many other combinations of meats. Raw fish in the Polynesian style, which tasted a little like salt salmon in a tomato sauce. There were fresh, tasty salads, and the vaunted Hawaiian poi, made from the inner shell of a coconut, dried and ground into a powder. It is a sort of porridge, a gray-green in color. I have to admit that it didn't taste good to me.

The program went on, with different kinds of hulas to the glare of flash bulbs, and with the drink *keitas* always open. Everyone seemed to be relaxed. And why not? A warm breeze swayed the palms restfully, and a full moon had risen in the sky. There was romance in the air. Saul squeezed my hand, just as when we were young. I was happy.

It was time to gather at our bus for the trip home. Just as we were getting on, Saul remarked, "Where are your shoes?" We found them under the table where I had left them. On the way home, the guide struck up many songs, but everyone was so tired that they all fizzled out.

"What did you think of it?" I asked Saul.

"Oh, it was a real party. It's good that I went. We saw how they celebrate. They had so many kinds of entertainment."

"Yaah, you only live once. Why keep counting money all the time. And I'm not afraid to go to the United States. We'll do all right there," I said.

In the morning we were on the way to the zoo. How extraordinary it was—all those big and colorful southern birds. "That one has such a big beak it can hardly lift it up," said Tytti.

"He does have quite a nose," said her father.

"Too bad we don't have any food with us," I said. "The people over there are throwing pieces of bread to the elephant, and it catches them in the air."

"We won't be on time to eat on the ship again," Saul grumbled.

"Yaah, it is mealtime there. Let's get a bite to eat now. We can have a fuller meal in the evening, when it won't cost as much."

"It will cost something. We could eat free on the ship," Saul said.

"I have enough in my pocketbook for a meal. It's not worth quarreling about," I said casually.

There was a free hula presentation near the zoo on a few square meters of grass surrounded by benches. These were older girls in long muumuus, their heads and necks wreathed with flowers. Some sang and played the ukulele while others danced. Afterwards they circulated among the crowd and placed wreaths of flowers around the men's necks. Now one of them came toward us. Somehow or other, Saul wound up with a wreath around his neck and a kiss on the cheek. He flushed a bright red. This Hawaiian friendliness was too much for a Finnish man. I tried to smother my laughter. People here knew how to take things in an easy and natural way.

On leaving, we stopped at the pineapple cannery. First they showed a movie on growing the pineapple. Children were allowed in. I had always thought the pineapple grew on trees. What next? The green tuft on the fruit is cut off and planted, and from it there grows a pineapple. Most of them produce only one fruit, but some produce two or even three. It takes them a year and a half to grow. On the ship they were often served as dessert.

On our last night in Hawaii, and the program called for a hula presentation at eleven in the evening. Everyone wanted to see it, and even the children did not go to sleep. We had good seats in the second row of the benches, which surrounded the performers. In front of us sat an elderly man, whose eyes followed the limber movements of the dancer avidly. Little by little, the dancer took off her clothes and was left with only red bikini panties and a few golden buttons on her breasts. The man was hypnotized by the dancer as she came closer and closer, wiggling her fanny right in front of him. On her last turn, the dancer blew a kiss to her admirer in passing, The man tried to clutch at her, but she was already on the other side of the floor. The audience broke out into thunderous applause.

Poju had dozed off during all this hilarity. Hula dancers meant little to an eleven-year old. The ship left Honolulu that night, and ukulele-playing hula dancers were a thing of the past.

The first night back on board there was a dance at which people were urged to wear what they had bought in Hawaii. It was a motley group. The women wore mostly muumuus. A few men wore grass skirts, with nothing above the waist. There were, however, some poor people, not just us, who wore their ordinary travel clothing. Everyone agreed that Hawaii was a nice place.

Day by day, the weather grew colder. We were traveling northeast, and it was winter, after all, in the Northern Hemisphere. The swimming pool was no longer in use. Now the Scottish dances began. They were practiced as a pastime under the direction of a real instructor, and reminded me very much of Finnish folk dances. One could not really do anything else on deck when it was so cold.

Every evening there were movies and dances below deck.

We did not see land for several days, and the wind blew very cold, probably from the North Pole. The ship arrived in a port, and we read on a wall somewhere: "Vancouver, British Columbia." The air was humid, and the drizzle falling became more and more moisture-laden. An orchestra tried to play a welcome for us from underneath a temporary roof. Suddenly the wind snatched the roof and carried it up into the air. That ended the music for the day.

"The usual weather at home," said a woman we had gotten to know. She was from nearby Vancouver Island and had been our table companion since New Zealand. Her son was waiting below in the shelter of an umbrella.

"I don't feel at all like going ashore. It's so wet and windy," I said.

"Let's wait and see of the weather changes for the better. We'll be here until tomorrow. The ship doesn't leave until one in the afternoon," said Saul.

In the morning the rain had let up and the sun shone from a clear sky. We went to see the city, but the wind felt cold.

"Hey, you can see snow on the side of the hill," said Tytti, delighted.

"That's why the wind is so cold. We've been in the land of eternal summer for so long that it's hard for us to huddle up here in the North. What would it feel like to live in Finland now?" I said.

"I don't know. We've been where it's warm for too long. Being warm feels a lot better," said Saul.

"Well, to tell the truth, I haven't missed the snow at all the whole time. We don't even have winter clothing."

"According to books, Los Angeles, California, is just as warm as Sydney, so we won't have to get anything warmer," said Saul.

Two days later, we awoke in San Francisco, California. The air was noticeably warmer than in Canada. But it happened to be a very windy day nonetheless. We set out for the city in the evening. The land was very hilly. Down below, the houses looked poor and rundown, but the higher we climbed, the larger and more handsome the houses became.

The Chinese district of the city seemed quite crowded. Tiny, tiny shops, with most of the wares out on the street. We heard Chinese on all sides. I wondered if they could speak English at all.

"They have to know the language of the country," Saul said.

"That one, at any rate, didn't understand my English," I said.

"They speak a different kind of English here than in Australia," said Tytti. "I spoke to an American girl on the ship. This is American English, but we'll soon get used to it."

The next morning we looked at the sights from on deck. There were many bridges, bays, and hills. In the morning sun, the whole city shone gleaming and white. It was a beautiful and varied city. The high bridge to the west was the Golden Gate Bridge, the pride of the city, which was spread far and wide because of the bays. The blue water is what gives the city a tinge of color. Perhaps because the city is on the West Coast, there are many Japanese and Chinese here. During the Gold Rush, many foreign nationals arrived, chiefly Italians. They left their own stamp on the development of San Francisco.

Most of the passengers were on deck when we left the harbor. Everyone wanted to see the Golden Gate as we passed under it. This was our last day on the ship, which had been our home for twenty-two days. The next day our everyday life would begin again.

A person's life is no laughing matter,
but can you imagine a life without laughter.

Love does not just sit like a stone.
You have to make it like bread, over and over again.

Great Spirit. Don't ever let me condemn anyone
unless I have walked for two weeks in his moccasins.

(Sioux Indian prayer)

CHAPTER XII

We were in the harbor of Long Beach, a part of the city of Los Angeles, California. This was the goal of our voyage. We checked a map of the city. Where would we find a home for ourselves in this strange metropolis?

"We should get closer to downtown; the job possibilities may be better there," Saul conjectured.

"This is a huge city, some five to six million inhabitants. Our family will be lost in it, like a fly in the Baltic. But where should we go? Tytti can do the talking for us. It looks as if I don't understand them, and they don't understand me," I said.

"But what should I say?" asked Tytti doubtfully.

"We'll be sure to tell you when the time comes."

After breakfast, we stood in line with our suitcases. While waiting for our papers to be checked, Saul said: "We have freight on board. What shall we do, when we don't have an address or a place to live?"

"We have the address of a storage place here. The luggage can stay there for ten days for a small fee. I hope we can find a place to live by then."

We stood at the curb, all six suitcases neatly piled atop one another. Saul wanted to take a picture so that we would remember what our arrival in Long Beach, California, on February 13, 1964, was like. *Will this thirteenth be our lucky or unlucky day?* I wondered.

"Where are you going?" a half-black cabby shouted to us.

"We've just got off the ship, and we'd like you to help us find a place to live. It may take a few hours."

"No, I can't help you. I have to pick up another fare in an hour."

In a few minutes another taxi pulled up. The same explanation from Tytti, who added: "It may take the whole day, but we are ready to pay for the ride and for your trouble."

"Let's see how we can get those suitcases to fit," said the driver.

"We'll have to put some of them in the back seat," the driver muttered to himself. "You grown-ups can sit up front with me. And the bigger children in back. It looks like the boy will be left over. What will we do with you?" The driver laughed. Poju was hopping around, ready to go.

Sisu Mother

"What's going to happen to me? Are you going to leave me here in the street?"

The driver began to rearrange the suitcases. He took one of the smaller ones, put it in the trunk, and tied the lid shut with a rope when it would not close.

"Let's see if we fit now," he said hopefully. He loaded the children onto each other's laps; there really wasn't room for their feet. Nevertheless, we were on our way.

The driver began to ask for a better explanation of our situation, and we explained how things were.

"There are plenty of places to live available. Of course, everyone steers clear of families with children. It helps when there are girls. I'll try to think of where it would be best to take you."

"If there is a separate black neighborhood, we don't want to go there."

"No, of course not. I won't take you to a colored district," the driver assured us. He himself was a mixture of some kind, probably Mexican, I thought. We had heard there were a lot of them here.

"The buildings all seem to be low here," I said half to myself as we passed low, private houses along the expressway.

"Yeah," said the driver. "The only concrete jungle is downtown. There are a lot of earthquakes here, so it's safer to build a one-story house."

"Earthquakes!" came a chorus of voices from the back seat.

"Yes, but there hasn't been anything big for a long time. Sometimes the pictures on the wall swing a little bit."

We came onto a regular street, into stop-and-go traffic. Its name was Whittier Boulevard. The driver turned into a real-estate agency.

"All of you come out and stretch your legs while I go in and ask about the situation," he said, opening the door and helping the children out of the cab.

"It really is a tight squeeze," Pia complained.

"My legs are all numb," said Tytti.

"Will we be in our own house soon?" asked Poju.

"We're on our way there now," I said. "We were lucky to get a driver who promised to take care of us."

"How big a charge will he slap us with when he leaves?" Saul worried.

"Well, if we get a place to live right away, we won't have to go to a hotel. That would be expensive," I said.

"I wouldn't like to stay here. It's such wrecky neighborhood," said Little-Sisko.

"All of you come into the office," said the driver, bustling out. "They want to see the whole family. All your children are well behaved and neat. I don't think they should have anything against you."

The office was small. They tried to find chairs for everyone, but without success.

"We have a furnished house for rent in Bell Garden. You do know where that is?" The man nodded toward the driver. "You'll have to pay ten dollars now. Here's the address. The key is under the leg of a bench to the left of the kitchen door. Go and look at it now. If you decide to take it, call this number after six this evening. If you don't like it, come back. We have others to offer."

The woman handed a slip with an address on it to the driver, and Saul dug some money from his pocket. The driver told us to get a receipt for the money. *He's on our side when he takes care of such things*, I thought, pleased.

The driver checked his map before starting out. "It's about five or six kilometers; we'll be there soon," he consoled the children, who were packed like sardines in a can. "I think there's a store nearby. That's the first thing you'll need, in any case."

Two wrong turns and we found the place. The house was in a rather messy condition. The water was turned on, but there was no gas or electricity.

"What do you think of it?" asked the driver. "The rent is 110 dollars a month. That doesn't seem high to me. It's a big house, and you have a large family. It's hard for children with families to find a place to rent. There's still time to get the gas and electricity hooked up today."

"Well, yaah, I think we'll stay. At least we'll have a roof over our heads here," said Saul. "Let's go and bring in the suitcases."

The men carried the things in. Saul went with the driver to see what the bill was.

"The meter shows thirteen dollars," said the driver.

"I want to pay for all your help and the time you spent with us," said Saul. I had followed the two out to the cab.

"I have spent some time with you. It's two o'clock now, and it must have been about ten when I picked you up."

Saul took out twenty dollars and asked: "Is that enough?"

"Yeah, yeah," said the man and put the money into his pocket. I had taken out a five-dollar bill and slipped it secretly into his hand, putting a finger to my lips. We shook hands good-bye, and the driver wished us luck in our new country.

Indoors, the children sat silent in the gloomy-looking house. When they saw me, they all said at the same time: "We're hungry."

"Let's see," I said, digging into my bag. In it, there was a small sandwich made with a roll for each one. In the morning everyone had been so excited they had no appetite, and I had made the lunch without their noticing. I had saved some oranges from the day before, which now tasted good as dessert.

Now I really began to look around the house. There seemed to be even too much room, compared to the little shack we had left. Here there were three bedrooms, a living room, and a large kitchen. The place was supposed to be furnished, but there was nothing in the living room. In the kitchen there were a table and four chairs. The children decided among themselves that if Father and Mother ate first, and then they did, that everyone could eat sitting down. That's some decision, I thought.

There were spring mattresses on the beds. They seemed quite cold, with only a cloth cover over them. Was that what Americans slept on? I would much prefer a rye-straw mattress. Oh, well, when in Rome, do as the Romans do, or leave. Later we learned that these were only the box springs, which were supposed to have a thick, soft mattress on top of them.

"Hey girls, let's start cleaning up here. The water is cold, but what of it. We can't eat from such a dirty table, and we can't go hunting after gas and electricity any more today. Poju, tell Father to clean up the yard outside. There's all kinds of junk around both doors."

The kitchen was already beginning to look a little better. "We won't unpack our clothes from the suitcases until we get warm water and wash out those closets."

When the clock was nearing six, we went to the store to buy food and call the owner of the house. "Perhaps it's best that Tytti come along, since the language sounds so odd to me. Maybe they won't understand us," I said. "You others stay here in the house and be good. And you mustn't open the door for anyone, no matter how much they knock."

The distance to the store was longer than we had estimated. When we came in the cab it had seemed quite short. "This is at least a kilometer and a half," was Saul's guess.

"It'll be some job to carry food from here every day," I said, disappointed.

"The girls will have to help. They have time to walk."

"That depends on where the school is," I said.

We tried to call the owner of the house, but there was no answer, so we began to make our purchases. It was a small, privately-owned, self-service store. There were only a few customers. I noticed that the storekeeper's wife was following our actions curiously. Finally she began to ask questions, and we explained the situation. She spoke English with an accent and told us that she was Polish.

"Listen, that place is too far away from everything. I'll give you an address closer to here. There's a house for rent there. Don't call about the other place until you go and look at this one. Go right away this evening."

We bought only the cold food that we absolutely needed, and went back "home." Saul and I decided to go and look at the house the Polish woman had advised us about after we had eaten.

The sun was already quite low when we left. The place would have been easier to find in daylight, but we did find it, and knocked on the door. No answer. We knocked again, louder this time. A short, plump woman appeared in the doorway.

"We heard you have a house for rent," I said. The woman pricked up her ears. My poor English must have sounded odd to her. Now she caught on.

"Yeah, yeah . . . we have. There. Wait and I'll get the key and come and show it to you. Go around to the back door. I'll come out that way."

The lot was long and narrow. In back of the first house there were two others besides the one we were going to look at. It was an old building, just painted and very neat. It was unfurnished, with one bedroom, a medium-sized living room, and a large kitchen.

"We'll take this," we both decided, without even asking the price.

"Let's go inside and we can talk more," said the woman.

"What is the rent?" asked Saul.

"Sixty dollars, and always in advance."

Saul paid the rent, and she wrote out a receipt for him.

"Do you have a lot of stuff? My brother can come and get you with his truck tomorrow morning."

"Yaah, we have six suitcases. The children can walk," said Saul.

"Children," said the woman, taken aback. "Do you have children?"

"We do. Didn't we mention them earlier?"

"You didn't. How many are there?"

"Four. Three girls, and the youngest is a boy."

The woman turned pale and was speechless. We all looked at one another, stunned. How would we get out of this quandary?

"We didn't deliberately try to hide anything. We can back out of the deal if you don't take children. I'm sure we can find a place somewhere else. Everything has to be done in good accord," said Saul gravely.

"Let's try it. You've just come from the old country, and I don't think children there are as undisciplined as they are here. But the rent will be ten dollars more. Is that okay?"

"Yaah, it's okay with us." Saul paid the woman the extra ten. "You don't need to give me a receipt for this. I'll walk here in the morning, and then your brother and I will go and get the stuff. What time can I come?"

"Let's say at nine. Is that okay?"

"Right. It's okay. Good night."

It was totally dark when we arrived "home." The children were sitting in the dark around the kitchen table with their coats on, shivering with cold. The night was dank, and the house had been empty for a long time, so it felt damp. Was this supposed to be a furnished house. Weren't window shades a part of furnishings? There was a constant hum of cars from the heavy traffic on the street, the lights of which shone directly in through the uncurtained windows. We went into the room farthest back, where there were two wide beds, with nothing but two thin blankets for covers and that bedspring under us. The girls went into one bed, and we and Poju into the other. Everyone kept their coats on, with only the thin blanket for a cover.

Nevertheless, I heard someone fall asleep after a while. But I was so cold that I did not sleep the entire night. On top of everything, motorcycles roared by continually. Often I heard their tires squeal directly in front of the house. Perhaps they had seen that there were new dwellers in the house and were trying to frighten us.

Everyone was already awake in the dim light of dawn. We were so cold that we began running from one room to the next. Even here in the land of summer, the houses needed heat. There was gas heat in the house, but we did not have it hooked up, since we were not going to rent the place. All the food was cold, for we had nothing but bread, butter, milk and cereal flakes. The long morning dragged on. Finally Saul went to get a truck. We tried to play every imaginable game while waiting. Sometimes we sang in English and Finnish.

The waiting finally ended when Saul arrived with the landlady's brother. In a few minutes the house was empty and the key back under the leg of the bench outside. Poju got to ride in the truck with the men; the girls and I set off on foot, stopping in at the market on the way to get something for lunch. I knew I couldn't cook since I didn't even have a stove.

Poju, accompanied by the lady of the house, came to meet us before we reached our destination. She invited us in for a while and offered us coffee. It tasted really good after the cold night.

"The children can stay here while you go and look for furnishings," said the woman in a friendly way. "You can't even sit down in that empty house. There is a sale within walking distance of this place," she added, trying to speed things up.

"Are the stores open? Isn't this Valentine's Day?" They were already advertising it in Hawaii, and I thought it was a big holiday."

"Pooh, that's just sales talk—to sell chocolates and flowers. It's a day for lovers. Poju is my valentine. He's such a nice boy."

Leaving the children in the woman's care, we went shopping. We showed the salesman a flier and asked to see the bed it advertised. He hemmed slightly and headed for the rear of the showroom. On the way, however, he started to show us a bed costing three times as much.

"But we only want to see the one in this paper."

"They aren't any good," he said.

"Then why do you advertise them?"

The man was nonplussed, but, nevertheless he said: "Look at this." He sat down on the bed, and the bottom fell out. "You see. Do you want to buy something like this?"

"Of course we don't want to buy junk that you can't even sit on. What else do you have at a reasonable price?"

The man began to show us other beds.

"What do you think of buying just a mattress?" I asked Saul.

"Yaah, that's a good idea. I can make the beds later."

"We'll buy mattresses, a table, six chairs, and a stove," I said. "We want them delivered today."

"I don't know if we can get them there today."

"If you can't, then we'll go to another store," said Saul decisively. "Our house is empty, and we can't sleep on a bare floor."

The salesman gestured to us and went to consult with some other men.

"Yes, they will be delivered to you today," he said.

Life seemed lighter as we walked back to the house.

"We've really been lucky on this trip," I said. "Everything has gone better than we expected. The second day in this country, and we can already set up housekeeping."

"Yaah, it looks as if we're off to a good start. Last night I asked Eddie if he has time to get the stuff from storage tomorrow."

"Right, we really can't get started cooking until we get those packages here. We can manage on cold food for today. The most important thing is that we have heat and warm mattresses under us."

"Remember that we have to go and report to the immigration office tomorrow the way they told us to," Saul said.

"Oh, yaah, I forgot all about it. That's on Monday. On Tuesday I'll go and find a school for the children. Then I can start looking for work. This is going so much better than we hoped," I said.

The lady of the house had prepared a lunch for the children and offered us coffee and sandwiches, too. She invited us to stay with her until our purchases arrived. What would we have done in the empty rooms anyway?

"Your children are very well behaved and considerate," she said, in praise of them. "They're a little shy, but once they got started, it was a delight to hear about your adventures. You are brave and enterprising people. It isn't easy to move from one country to another and with such a large family. I can see that you are sure to get along anywhere. You say that you had a job, too?" she asked.

"Yaah, I was a seamstress. When we get everything organized, I'll start looking for work. On Monday we have to go to the immigration office in the city."

"You have to get the children into a school," she said.

"Of course. But since we had no one to vouch for us here, they were angry. They were going to send us back. That's why we have to obey all their orders."

"I see. I see," said the woman, sounding puzzled. "But are your papers for coming here in order?"

"They are. It's all perfectly legal, but since there was no one to vouch for us, we had no address to give. It was only a question of that."

"I see. All is well then. You've gotten off to a good start. I'll bring you the Sunday paper, and you can start looking for a job. There is plenty of work for seamstresses here, but it's really high-pressure work in factories. Have you worked in a factory?"

"Yes, in a factory. I was in a clothing factory at first, but for the last three years I sewed athletic shoes. I should think I could get that kind of work here too. It was contract work, and it was rushed, too, but I earned well."

"Yeah, there is that kind of work here too. I think your husband can get work too, since he's in the automobile trade. The cars have to keep running, as you can see."

In the morning we rode the bus some twelve kilometers to downtown Los Angeles. The immigration office had been moved to another location. We did not know the city, so we had to take a taxi. Now everything was in order as far as our immigration was concerned. Saul went to the designated bank to which the money for our house had been transferred, while I sat outside on a park bench waiting for him. I was not thinking carefully about the matter, and only later did it dawn on me. He had deposited all the money in the bank in his own name.

"Was everything okay? Did you get the money?" I asked.

"Yaah, yaah, everything was as it should be," he said.

We both got jobs within only ten days of our arrival in the country. I worked in a swimsuit factory and earned quite well. Often I had to work Saturdays, but for that I was paid more. The girls helped with the housekeeping.

"We should start looking for a house of our own," I began suggesting.

"What? We've got plenty of room here, and the rent is cheap. There are expenses in your own home too," Saul replied, annoyed.

"That's true, but we can afford to buy our own. We have a good down payment in the money from Australia. The children could have their own home at last, and there isn't much room here either. Do you plan to sleep on the living room floor for the rest of your life? What's the use of working if conditions at home don't get better? I'm already getting tired of doing the washing for six people by hand. We live like Stone-Age people. No matter how much money you have in the bank, it doesn't wash these dirty clothes."

I was in a bad mood because I had expected a change in our relationship with regard to money. I was buying the food and clothing for the whole family from my wages, while he paid the rent, plus the electricity and gas bills. We did not have a joint bank account. Where was he putting his money? I knew that he was not squandering it on anything. He never even bought anything for the children.

"If we buy a house, I want it to be in my name only," he said in a monotone. I did not reply, but walked angrily out of the room.

Every day on my way home from work, I passed a law office. The next day I stopped in at it. I wanted to clarify a few things about one's rights in this country. The secretary went in to ask if the lawyer had time to see me.

"Yes, he said he would see you. This way, please."

The room was dimly lighted. I introduced myself, and the gentleman pointed to a chair, arranging papers on the table at the same time.

"Ahem. How can I help you?"

"We came to this country a few months ago and are looking around for a house to buy. Now my husband wants to buy it in his own name. I would like to know if I have any right to the house in case we are divorced later."

"How long have you been married?"

"Lets see, how long is it now? It's over twelve years."

"You are certain to get at least half of the value. Are there any children?"

"There are four."

"You have no need to worry, for in that case the house will be entirely yours. The children will not be driven from their home, since usually the children are left with the mother. A mother has to be a real tramp to have the children taken from her. I can tell from your appearance that you're a good mother."

"Thanks, that makes things easier," I said, as I rose. "How much do I owe you?"

"Nothing," he said, patting my shoulder as he opened the door.

"Thank you, thank you," I mumbled as I left. I felt relieved. Now it was only a case of getting Saul to buy a house before he disappeared with the money. He didn't really care for the children. The only thing he could think of was money. At least that was better than the insane jealousy I had had to suffer before. I knew I would be able to manage with the children as long as we had a roof over our head. Wages were higher here, and food was cheaper. I could buy fabric from the factory at half price to make clothes for the girls. I had sewed clothes for Poju earlier, but now I searched for them at sales. And besides, boys wore jeans here. I wanted the children to be dressed like the others. They were already being subjected to a severe trial, having had to start school under entirely new circumstances.

We received an invitation to a "Welcome" festival at the International Institute and wondered who and what was in back of it.

"We're not going. They've made a mistake. Who would be inviting us anywhere?" said Saul.

"This is clearly our name—it's addressed to Mr. and Mrs. There's no doubt that it's meant for us," I said.

"We have to look at the map to see where it is so we can think about it."

"Friday evening. We don't have to work on Saturday. It's perfect for me. It says Mr. and Mrs., which means no children."

"We wouldn't drag those brats there anyway."

"Are you ashamed of your own children? You're some father. Damn it, I'd be willing to take them to speak to the president. But in this case, since only we have been invited, they can stay at home," I said angrily.

On Friday we were actually on the way to the festival. It was not far off, but we had to take two buses. The building was low, with many wings. It was in a lovely park through which a small brook babbled. A few ducks swam in a calm bend of the brook. We had arrived too early and wandered through the park. It was totally peaceful, although the highway was only a few blocks away. Primeval oak trees cast long shadows. There were azalea bushes on which the buds were just opening, which reminded me of Finland, where I grew the same plant on the windowsill. There it did not even bloom every year. The sun here had a remarkable power. Of course the plants were constantly in the fresh air, since they were growing outdoors. Plants, like people, need oxygen. No wonder I sometimes saw a giant person. He had enough oxygen and nourishing food, I thought childishly.

Indoors, we were given a friendly reception. A man and woman came up to us immediately and asked what country we were from.

"Come and have coffee. The program will begin as soon as everyone has arrived." We did as we were prompted. A few dark people who looked like Indians were already seated there. They smiled and said something we did not understand. More couples arrived, some Italians and a blond couple who stepped before the audience and welcomed us all.

"Now everyone will introduce themselves in turn and tell us their nationality."

We were from here and there: Mexicans, Germans, Italians, Indians, Hungarians, Poles, Scottish, Norwegians, and two Finns—us.

"This is a miniature picture of America," the speaker began. "This is how the American people began and developed. Perhaps we have progressed farther than many other countries because only the bravest dared to leave their homelands and face the challenge of a new and unknown future. Here we are fused into one whole nation. I don't mean that you have to give up your former customs and traditions. On the contrary, I hope you preserve your respect for your old homeland and that your heritage will survive in the customs of your grandchildren. It is the heritage of different peoples which lends color to American life. Be proud of your old homeland. That is the purpose of this house, where people of every country can gather to foster their own traditions. I know that homesickness sometimes afflicts you, but this is a gathering place for all languages. We are a voluntary organization which organizes these parties for all new arrivals, and we want everyone who has sacrificed so much in leaving his homeland to feel that he is welcome to America."

There was tremendous applause at the end of the speech. How well he had struck the right chord. Those of us who had just arrived needed this kind of support. Now an extraordinarily tall and husky man stepped forth to perform, a Scotchman wearing a plaid, knee-length skirt with all its adornments. Of course he was carrying the national instrument, the bagpipes. He walked slowly around the room playing the pipes. It was nice music, which I had never heard before, except on the radio. Now when it was presented in all its splendor, it seemed really remarkable. Actually I had heard nothing about the Scotch, except for jokes about their stinginess. I found it hard to believe all this was real, and pinched myself to make sure that it was.

The next person on the program was an American woman, who explained about all the organizations which housewives could join, giving their names and addresses. I was hardly interested, for I knew I would be holding a job, and it was work that concerned me. It was psychologically easier for me to work and earn money than beg for it and give an accounting every day of where the money had been spent. Nevertheless, I kept a record of earnings and expenditures so that I could estimate the financial differences between Australia and the United States.

The program continued. An American Indian entered the room in all his regalia. His dress was colorful indeed, the predominant color being red, and he wore a huge feather headdress that reached to the floor. He danced the well-known rain dance. It was really appropriate here, where the rainfall was so very scant. We had been here almost three months, and it had not rained a single time.

"Here we see a Native American, and he has not lost his traditions or his culture. It is 472 years since the whites began to conquer America. So I urge you newcomers to hold on to your traditions and culture as a lasting memento of your homeland. You will become Americans, but don't forget the place you came from, and don't be ashamed of your nationality. We all have our good and bad sides, and we all need each other. Try to bring forth new trends and ideas. You are now a part of America."

We were urged once more to socialize with each other over a cup of coffee. The organizers of the program circulated among us like old acquaintances. I marveled at how spontaneous and pleasant the Americans were in all situations.

They began to shift the chairs to the sides of the room, and the orchestra started tuning up. Everyone danced the first waltz with his partner, but then we were urged to change to new acquaintances. The Scotchman in his full regalia was coming to find a partner. Oh, my, I was totally nonplussed and must have blushed to the gills when he bowed to me. He led me so slowly and protectively that I calmed down. He was a tall man—I did not even reach his shoulders—and he said not a word during the entire dance. I doubt whether I would have understood him. The Scottish dialect is quite difficult.

Later the organizer of the party danced with me twice. He was able to make everyone feel at home. He was lively and talked a lot.

"I think there are Finns practicing folk dances in one of the rooms. I'll find out during the intermission. Have you met any of your fellow-countrymen here yet?"

"No. We haven't met a single Finn here."

"Is that so? Didn't you have someone to come and meet you?"

I told him the whole story. The dance was already over, but he continued talking to me. Saul came nearer to listen.

"You have an interesting story. It takes a lot of courage to set out for a strange country with such a large family. We need people like you here. Thanks for coming."

During the intermission he came and introduced a man to us. He was a Finn named Jussi.

"We're practicing folk dances. My mother teaches them. We have five couples. I dance with my wife. Let's get together before we leave. I have to go now."

The dance continued. The Scotchman came to ask me again. He gazed so deeply into my eyes that I felt actually felt weak in the knees. Naturally everyone danced the last waltz with his or her partner.

"That Scotchman liked you," said Saul. "I saw how covetously he looked at you."

"I can't help it. He didn't seem to have a partner. An odd type. He didn't say a word either time we danced. He must have thought I didn't speak a word of English."

Our program was over, and we went to seek out the Finnish dancers. They were just dancing the "Säkkijärven Polka." At the end of each session, they always did a regular dance. The folk-dance teacher, a warm, middle-aged woman, came to greet us. She asked what was new and what part of Finland we were from.

"And you haven't met any Finns yet, after three months here? There are lots of us here, some two thousand in the Los Angeles area. Our Finnish club is very active. In a couple of weeks we'll have a dance in that big hall there, with an enjoyable program. Do come. You can get to know more Finns. I can take you home today; it isn't much out of my way. It's better than waiting for the bus on the street in the middle of the night."

"Thanks, really, but that's too much," I tried to object, but still she took us home. We and our families became lifelong friends.

One night Saul came home and began to speak enthusiastically. "I saw an old house for sale. There's one in front of it and another in back. It must be rented. It looks as if there are two tenants in the house in back. There are five garages. It looks as if someone planned to build an apartment above one of them, but gave up on it."

"It sounds good. Are there stores nearby? With a large family, we have to have them."

"Yaah, the store is only two blocks away, and it's on the main street. You know it; you pass it every day in the bus on your way to work."

"Oh, that one. Hey, I'll wait for you on the corner there tomorrow evening. I'll leave work an hour early so that I can look around that part of the city while I wait."

"Good idea. The agent's name is on an ad there. We can't get in, but we'll look around the neighborhood and see if there are schools nearby. We're too far away from them here."

The next evening I walked around that part of the city. It was large, and there were stores of all kinds. No need to go far for any shopping, and so close to where I worked that I could walk the kilometer or so: it would be good exercise. And the place where Saul worked was only a few blocks away.

"Not bad," said Saul. "Of course an old house always needs little repairs, but I can do them evenings and weekends. The backyard looks like a jungle."

"Just start swinging an ax," I laughed.

I took down the telephone number, and we decided to call in the morning. We walked a few blocks farther and found a handsome brick middle school.

"This is for Tytti now, and in a few years Pia will transfer here." We continued walking, and found three schools within a radius of one kilometer. The school for the youngest children was the farthest away, but it was still within walking distance.

"It looks really good. How will it go? Can we get a loan since we've just come into the country?" Saul said doubtfully.

"We won't know unless we ask. We're both working."

"Yaah, and we'll get rent for two of the houses. That should help. I want to buy them in my name only," he said.

"Whatever you like, but then you'll be responsible for the loan too," I said, thinking it was good that the money would be tied down to the houses, rather than in some other crazy scheme.

On Sunday afternoon, the agent came to get us to look at the house. The larger one was also rented out, and the owner lived elsewhere. It had three bedrooms, a spacious living room, and the kitchen was large enough to fit a small table. The interior of the house needed painting; otherwise we were satisfied with what we saw. The agent assured us that we could certainly get a loan. He asked if we would call his office at the end of a week, since we had no phone.

Everything went well. We got the loan, and in a month the deal was concluded. The tenants had been asked to vacate the house as soon as the loan was approved. They were a Mexican family with many children, but they apparently had no intention of moving. I called the agent to ask what we should do.

"It's none of my business, the deal has been closed," he said coldly, and slammed the receiver. We would not really have been able to move yet, because the children still had two weeks of school, and we were in another school district. On Saturday evening we went to talk to the tenants. They received us hospitably, and the woman even asked us to sit down.

"Would you like a cup of coffee?" she asked.

"No, thanks. Have you found a house to rent yet?"

"No, we haven't found one that's suitable."

"How so? When I ride the bus I see lots of houses for rent."

"We can't find one that's big enough. We have a large family."

"We bought this house so that we could come and live here ourselves," said Saul. "We want to move in within a week. Otherwise we'll have to pay another month's rent there for nothing," he added.

"You get rent from us. You won't lose anything," stormed the woman.

"I don't understand that you can't find a house when you live here. We found one the first day, even if we had just come into the country."

Saul jerked at my sleeve and said angrily, "Let's leave before they throw us out." It was touch and go. The woman slammed the door on us as we left.

On the following day there was a sale of some sort at the place where Finns gathered. We went there on the chance that we would find someone who could give us advice.

We were in luck and got the number of a Finnish lawyer. Saul arranged to meet him within a very few days.

"You won't have to go to court with this, which is good, because that is very expensive," said the lawyer. "It will cost a bit, but the police will take them an eviction order. If they haven't moved within two weeks, the police have the authority to carry their furniture out onto the street."

"Yaah, that is complicated." Saul wondered at the procedure.

"I hope, though, that you won't have to go that far. Mexicans are sometimes very troublesome afterwards. They might even come to exact revenge. I'll take care of the matter right away, and if they haven't moved within a week, let me know."

Every evening on the way home from work, I walked a little loop around the house. School was out already, so we were ready to move. A week had gone by. On Friday evening I noticed some boxes on the veranda. It was a good omen; perhaps they would move this weekend.

On Sunday evening, Saul and I went to investigate. The house looked empty; there was no longer an automobile parked in front of it. Saul had the keys, and he approached the door cautiously.

"What? It isn't even locked," he said astonished as he tried the door. We crept in on tiptoe. Who knows? Someone might be lying in wait to attack us.

"Anybody home?" I called out. We waited in silence, holding our breaths. Not a whisper.

"They seem to have left," Saul said, opening the door to every room, even peering out the back door into the yard. Everything was deserted.

"Hurrah, hurrah?" I shouted, doing a dance on the floor. For a wonder, the rooms had been left in a fairly neat condition. Only the kitchen counter was in an awful state. Its surfacing was so worn that the soggy, rotting wood showed through in many places.

"That has to be fixed before we move in. I'll come after work and clean up for a couple of hours every evening. Then on Saturday we can move in. Our rent is paid for ten days yet."

"I'll get what is needed for that counter-top and fix it during the week. But there is a bus strike in the wind, and if they don't reach an agreement, the buses won't run tomorrow. How will we get to work then?"

"I'll have to ask Edith, just in case. I'm sure she'll take us if we pay."

"Why did this have to happen just at the wrong time? If the strike had started next week, it would have been no problem. We could both have walked to work from here."

The bus strike began. We got a ride from Edith every morning, spent several hours working on our new home every evening, and took a taxi to get home. One day when I had just begun cleaning and was shaking something outdoors, the wind slammed the door shut. It was locked, and of course the keys were inside.

"Now you've done it," I scolded myself. What a stupid thing to happen. I hoped the back door would open, although I had never opened it. Of course it didn't.

Now I had to wait for nearly an hour before Saul arrived. There would have been plenty of work for me to do inside. I was really an idiot, the most idiotic of idiots. Would I be able to finish the cleaning by Saturday, sitting here idle the whole evening with my arms crossed?

I sat with my head in my hands, letting my thoughts roam freely. It calmed me down, now that there was no need to hurry. I could think and reflect on matters in complete peace. It's good for the nerves, I thought. There's is always such a rush at work that I can't really think of anything else. Just one piece of fabric after another before my eyes, with only one thing in mind: the more you get through the machine, the more dollars you get.

Ha, ha, the expression on that old maid's face when I finished my box before she did. She got a really black look on her face and did not say a word during the whole afternoon. Just before quitting time, she snapped out, "You don't have to go to work. You have a man to support you."

It was the jealousy she felt speaking, which always appeared whenever I was faster than she was. I searched for the right words and then said, "I happened to marry such a poor man that he isn't able to support me. You are still free and can pick out a rich man so that you won't have to come into this rat race."

She really did fly off the handle. Was I becoming a nasty person because I enjoyed it? But she had started it out of envy; I defended myself. I had heard her ask many times why I had come here to eat her bread. That day I could no longer stand her harassment. From then on I would be deaf to what she said, no matter what it was.

The hour passed quickly as I sat there. Saul arrived and lectured me on my stupidity, but that did not affect me one bit. The hour's rest had done me good. I got a lot more done that night than usual.

We walked homeward in high spirits. There were no taxis in sight. One or two drove by, but they were already fully loaded. The distance was some five or six kilometers, but it was summer, and the weather was beautiful. We admired the beautiful yards we passed, their glorious shrubs and flowers, thinking of the kinds of people who must live in the different houses.

"An ambitious and well-to-do family must live in that house. Everything is so neatly arranged. The children's playthings are all lined up beside the steps, and there are two big, well-polished cars in front of the garage."

"A different kind live here. Playthings scattered here and there all over the yard. A tree here and there, and an old wreck parked in the yard."

"Not everyone here is rich," I said. "It depends more on the people themselves. Some may of course have bad luck, or illness, or some other misfortunes."

"A man can make out well here as long as he works. Some are so lazy they can't stand to do anything, or they drink too much," said Saul. "One of the men often comes to work with his eyes as red as a roach's, and at least once a week he's absent. I'm sure it's when he can't get up. The boss was shaking his head angrily yesterday when Jim didn't show."

"The bad thing is that here you can buy liquor in all the stores. A few of them are even open at night."

"I think it's the right system," said Saul. "It's up to the people themselves how much they want to drink. In that saloon they'll give you as little as a thimbleful if you don't have the money for more."

"We're close enough to home so that it doesn't pay to get a taxi. Tytti has made food for the others; we'll eat whatever we can find. Tomorrow is Friday, and I'll have the house all cleaned up. Let's talk to Eddie in the morning about picking us up. This is too far to walk every evening."

"Yaah, that's best. Do you think we'll be ready by seven? I'll tell him to come at that time."

"Sure, we'll be ready by then. If there's time, I'll do tomorrow's shopping."

"Right. There's only one more day left. Let them stay on their goddamned strike for the rest of their life. It won't bother us," said Saul angrily.

Finally the hoped-for Saturday arrived. Moving day. It was of course Eddie who moved us. Everyone was full of enthusiasm, but it was hard to leave our kindly landlady, who promised to come and visit us when we were all settled.

"Is this really our very own home?" Pia shouted in delight.

"So big and clean—now we girls can have our own room," Tytti added.

"Yes, this is our own now," I said proudly. "I'll get curtains on the windows as soon as I can. We might even use sheets to cover them till then. I didn't have time to get everything as ready as I would have liked."

We were all tired that evening and went to bed early. In the night I was awakened by something cool and damp that fell on my face. I felt it move and snatched it into my hand. Then I sprang up like a shot and turned on the light.

"A cockroach!" I cried shrilly. "A cockroach on the ceiling and it fell on my face. Good God, what kind of a nest is this?"

Saul opened his eyes, too, and began to look around.

"There are two of them over there on the wall. Give me a rag so I can kill them. Where the hell do they hide out during the day?"

"It's weird to find cockroaches in the bedroom." I ran into the kitchen and turned on the light. There were two of the insects on the counter, but there were none at all in the cabinets. I sighed with relief. Checking carefully, we moved the mattress into the living room, and I shook out all the bedclothing. But I could not sleep at all that night.

During the following weeks, we fumigated all the rooms one at a time and succeeded in getting rid of the nasty insects. I could not understand how cockroaches could be allowed to spread through an entire house these days when there are so many poisons to kill them.

"We should go and look for a refrigerator," I said casually one day. "It would make food preparation a lot easier, and we have to buy one sooner or later. We can't do without one in this hot climate."

"I suppose so. And we should buy a washtub too," said Saul.

"It's time we got a washing machine," I said pleadingly. "Some of the neighbors had them even before we left Finland."

"Oh, no. They wear out the clothes too much."

"Buy new ones then. I'm not going to start scrubbing clothes by hand in modern-day America. I have other work on the weekend besides just washing clothes," I said hotly. "There's no point in my going to work if we can't get improvements for the house. It's time this household moved out of the Stone Age."

"Well, I'm not going to start buying a washing machine."

"Well, there will be no washtubs in this house, and that's that."

"Well, if you can't stand to wash clothes, then buy a machine. But you won't find it easy to get money for it from me," Saul said, and he walked out.

We went to a used appliance dealer. Saul paid for a refrigerator and a television set. I bought an old-fashioned washing machine.

"If you think your pants will wear out too much in this machine, you can wash them yourself wherever you like," I said nastily.

Life here in California was very different from that in Australia. There were black people everywhere, a few even where I worked. They were well dressed and polite. There were Mexicans everywhere too; the place was swarming with them. They acted as if they owned the place, that is, they were very bold. In addition, they did not want to learn English, but expected that everyone would learn to speak Spanish. The people who lived in the house in our back yard were Mexicans and Cubans. Each of the houses had only one bedroom, a living room, and a kitchen. In the Mexican family there were man and wife and four children plus the grandmother and other relatives. Their housecleaning was haphazard. I saw the lady of the house dump table scraps from a plate directly into the yard. It was nauseating in that eternal summer and warm climate. One can guess at the stench that emanated from the yard, and the flies had a constant buffet.

We wondered why the clotheslines were constantly full; only on Saturday was there room for me to hang out my wash. We knew that the man of the house worked in a laundry. We were flabbergasted when we got our monthly water bill. It was for 136 dollars.

"Goddamn, there is something wrong here. Our monthly income from two apartments is 130 dollars. That doesn't even cover the water bill. How can water be so expensive?" Saul shouted angrily.

"Something is really rotten here," I said. "I'll ask the neighbors what they pay. There are fewer of them, but they have a tenant; they can give us some idea of the cost of water. And if water is so expensive, then how did our landlady rent to us so cheaply? There were six of us, and I did the laundry there too."

"I can check the meter—or maybe a pipe is broken, and the water is leaking constantly."

"That's a good idea," I said, my mind busy. "Our neighbor is out in his yard. I'll go and talk to him. They were very helpful when we were moving in."

"Good morning, Mr. Miller."

"Good morning. How are you doing? Are you settled in yet? You have a good-looking family, and the children are quiet, too. To tell the truth, we were a little scared when such a large family moved in, but there's no problem. A rowdy bunch lived there before."

"I hope we don't disturb you too much. Are you retired?"

"I started loafing years ago. But I go and take turns at the Esso gas station there. That's where I worked for twenty-five years, but I sold it last year. I'm getting to the age when I should retire. My wife has never worked, and her sister has lived with us since she was widowed a year ago. The children flew from the nest long ago. It won't be many years before yours will too."

"It's true, they grow up quickly. Too quickly. Listen, we've been wondering about our water bill. We have no idea what it costs. What would you estimate it should be with the two houses on the same meter?"

"Ours is about four dollars. You have a lot of people living there. Lord knows what it might be, but it shouldn't go over fourteen dollars."

"We really wondered. Just think—it was 136 dollars!"

"Oh, no! That's absolutely impossible. Does all that wash have something to do with your water bill?"

"Saul checked to see if it was leaking anywhere, but it wasn't."

"You have to be strict and go and check the meter every evening. No one is allowed to run a business here, especially at your expense."

"Thank you Mr. Miller. It was nice talking to you."

The evening the two of us went to knock at the Mexicans' door. The man of the house answered and asked what we wanted.

"We came to check if you needed anything repaired," said Saul.

"No, we have nothing that needs repairing," said the man, beginning to close the door.

"Still we want to check the rooms," said Saul, and we went inside. The man looked at us suspiciously.

"I think there is a broken water pipe somewhere, so I want to look in every room."

"No, no. We haven't noticed anything like that." The man disappeared into a bedroom. Saul looked first into the kitchen and then into the bathroom. The bedroom door was closed during that time. Rubber hoses ran from the water pipes in the bathroom into the bedroom through holes bored in the bottom of the door. Without saying a word, Saul opened the door. I saw the man clench his fists and the black look that came over his face. I was afraid he would attack Saul. I had been standing in the living room all the while, following what happened. Saul gestured for me to come into the room, and lifted an old piece of tarpaper to reveal a washing machine.

"We have a large family and we get a lot of wash," said the man, stuttering. We couldn't find another place for it—we had to put the washing machine somewhere."

I went out first, thinking that if a fight started, I could get away. Saul and the man followed me out.

"Why isn't there a laundry room for the tenants?"

"Look at this bill. You're running a laundry in this room."

"It's not all ours, there are these two houses," the man tried to defend himself. "And maybe it's leaking somewhere."

"This is how things stand. You are to be out of here within a month. This place is too small for your family anyway. Why don't you buy your own place where there is more room for the kids to run around?"

"Yeah, sure." The man had trouble speaking, he was sputtering with such rage.

"Good night," we both said at the same time. There was no answer.

That was the end of the laundry business. At the end of the month the man came to us and said humbly: "Can we stay a few days more. We've bought a house, but the papers aren't ready yet. I'll pay a week's rent, and if we have to stay longer, I'll pay more. We don't want to move somewhere else for such a short time."

"That sounds good. Of course you can live here until the deal goes through. When you get into your own place, no one will have anything to say, and the children will have their own yard," said Saul.

In time, the family left. We began to clean up after them. The corners of the kitchen were so thick with dirt and food scraps that after soaking them for some time, I found spoons and other objects in them. We needed a lot of insecticide for the cockroaches, for we had to apply it evenings room by room for two weeks. The next evening I swept away the corpses. Saul painted and repaired until the rooms were in good condition.

In the other end of the house lived a middle-aged Cuban couple with their dog. I was astonished when I heard the man's first name: Jesus. "We really have sacred tenants," laughed Saul.

"Yaah, he's a kind of Jesus I don't know what to do with," I said.

"They want to pay only a half-month's rent at a time. They both work. I don't know what kind of darned trick they're up to. I think I'll ask them to move, too. I don't want to start begging in my own house," said Saul. "I'll get a form that says the rent must be paid a month in advance. They treat us like fools because they see we've just come to this country. I'll find a law to fit them. It's best that they move out; we'll be sure to find tenants."

Jesus, Jesus, I repeated to myself. *How can one give such a name to a child?*

"There are all kinds of sacred places here," Saul said. "A few kilometers away are the Bethlehem Steel Works. It would be interesting to hear how many Jesuses work there. They call it José."

"It would be gross to hear someone shout 'Jesus' on the job."

The word soon spread that we were Finns. On Saturday when I was weeding a flowerbed, an old man stopped on the sidewalk.

"Good day, Ma'am," he said in pure Finnish.

I was so astonished that my jaw dropped, and the hoe fell from my hand as I stood up.

The man noticed how shocked I was, and began over again, "Good day, Ma'am. I'm not a ghost even if I'm old."

"Good day. Excuse me. I couldn't believe my ears. You hear Finnish so seldom here," I managed to say. I wiped most of the soil from my hands on a bunch of hay, went over to the man and extended a hand.

"My name is Elsie. We moved here about two months ago."

"They call me August. I live a couple of houses down on the opposite side of the street, in that old house in the shade of the trees. I heard that you were Finns and decided to come and find out. I haven't had any contact with Finns for at least fifty years."

"Well, let's go in and have 'coffee and . . .' in honor of the occasion."

"Don't start bothering with coffee now," said August, but, nevertheless, he followed me inside.

"I made *pulla* today. It must have been in your honor."

"I'm just plain August. You don't have to be formal with me. Here in America, every one is casual. We don't bother with polite formalities."

"Well then, let's forget the formalities and shake on it." I squeezed both the old man's hands in mine.

"Yaah, I came to Chicago first. I was a tailor there, for a tight-fisted Jew. Then when I found Ida, we came out here to L.A. And I haven't seen any Finns since."

"Well, that's amazing. We ran into them by chance. They say there are some two thousand here. They even have some organizations, and there's supposed to be a church somewhere, but we don't know the city very well. Where in Finland did you come from?"

"From central Finland. Saarijärvi."

"Really. 'In the frosty wilds of Saarijärvi / there lives the farmer Paavo . . .' I began to recite. Children, go and see if Father has time to come for coffee. He's making repairs in the back of the house."

"The *pulla* here looks very good, but so does the lady of the house. You could have entered yesterday's 'Missy' competition. Did you watch it? That Finnish girl was pretty, but almost too blond, which is probably why she didn't win. (He was referring to the "Miss Universe" competition.)

"Yes, I watched. And she did win one of the prizes."

"I haven't had such good *pulla* since Ida left this world. It's been twelve years already."

"Do you live alone? Don't you have any children?"

"I do have a son who lives on the other side of the city. He comes to see me now and then."

Saul came to have coffee with us. After being introduced, he mostly listened to our conversation.

"How old are you now, August?" I asked finally.

"Oh, I carry a number of years on my shoulders. I'll soon be eighty-six."

"And you still move around so lightly without a cane."

"I manage to amble along by myself. It's good that the store is so near. The boy comes to get me on the biggest holidays, and my sister comes for a couple of weeks every summer. I arranged for her to come here way back when. She is a few years younger than me."

"Here are a couple of pieces of *pulla* to go with your morning coffee. I'll be sure to keep you supplied with Finnish *pulla*, since you think it's such a delicacy," I said as I escorted the old man to the door.

"I'll have these in the morning with coffee," he said, holding his gift gently and carefully.

"Remember to come again," I admonished him once more.

"I will be sure to."

After the old man left, Saul confronted me. "You are stupid. Such a country bumpkin that I'm ashamed of you," Saul began to upbraid me. He was really angry.

"Well, what have I done now that's so stupid?" I asked innocently.

"You don't have an ounce of manners when you talk to an old man so casually."

"Oh, so tha . . . that was the stupidity," I said, dragging out the word. "August is so used to this country that he asked at once that we speak as friends. No one here stands on formality."

"You still shouldn't talk that way to an old man."

"But since that is exactly what he wanted, I didn't want to hurt his feelings. It's a wonder that he still speaks Finnish so well. He tended to slip into English now and then, but that's no wonder since he hasn't spoken Finnish in twelve years."

"Does his son know Finnish?"

"August laughed and said that the only thing he knows is 'shit-pants.' He says it's the only word he remembers."

"Well, our own kids can't speak it properly even if they were born there. They shouldn't forget it. Who knows—we might even go back there some day."

"Don't talk nonsense. I, at least, am not going anywhere until every one of them has finished school. It's not easy for children to change schools every year. In the fall they'll be in another school again, and will have new schoolmates."

"We should go back soon before they become completely Americanized."

"What's gotten into you now? You wanted to leave because it was so cold. Finland hasn't gotten one bit warmer since we left. If your dream of getting by with just a fig leaf here crashed, nothing can be done about it. And now you've just started heaping up the money while I'm supporting you and the children too, and the tenants are paying for the house. You could put the bank account in my name, too. Wouldn't I help it grow, too?"

"There's no income from the house in back. On the contrary, it's an expense, since I've been repairing it for two months," snorted Saul.

I must have hit a sore spot, I thought, and left the matter at that.

School began in the fall. Saul and I too began to study English at night in a nearby school. American English was much different from what we had previously learned. Mexicans made up most of the class. We had to study three separate things in English: speaking, reading, and writing. Neither of us had any basic schooling, so we had to hammer things into our heads almost word by word.

Life continued to be hectic. In the winter, I had to work on Saturdays, too. Three evenings were taken up by the school, and other evenings I sewed clothing for myself and the children, if there weren't other things to do. I no longer sewed shirts for Saul but thought he might just as well buy them. It was enough that I bought the food and clothing for the whole family. I didn't take up the question of money with him, although I knew that he was putting all his wages into the bank account. The rent from the houses covered the loan payments, as well as the electricity and gas. I had a telephone put in at my expense, since I considered it a necessity. He refused to pay a penny toward it.

He had again gotten the idea that he was ill, but refused to go to a doctor. "Why complain then," I asked him, "if you don't want to go for a checkup. You must expect me to pay for that, too. We have no medical insurance for the whole family. Thank God the children have stayed healthy. It would be a problem if we had to take them to the doctor. I've been able to pay for their dental care by working overtime, but don't expect me to pay your doctor bills too," I said sourly.

He did not go to the doctor, but studied all kinds of books and decided that too much eating was not good for him. We were in the habit of eating fish once a week, but now he demanded to have it every day, even for lunch. I had to go and buy it daily, to be sure it was fresh. The rest of us tired of eating it after a few weeks, and I began to prepare separate food for us. I began to hate the very smell of fish.

I noticed that Saul was growing thinner bit by bit. The eating of fish had gone on for a year and a half, and I kept waiting for him to tire of it. He went diligently to work, and was otherwise ambitious. Astonishingly, he began to take care of the flowerbeds outside. Until that time he had done only the lawn-mowing. I think the man next door had dropped hints to him about it.

One evening an insurance agent came to the house, from the same company from which we had purchased the fire insurance. He began explaining new types of coverage to us.

"This type insures the debt on your house. In case something happens to the head of the house, it pays the debt, and the house is left debt free to the family. For example, a family took out this policy a year ago. After a few months, the husband fell ill of cancer and died in six months. Now the family was left with a house that was paid up, and that helped a lot when the wife was left alone with the children." The agent kept on talking about all the good points of the policy.

"That sounds good," said Saul when he finally got a chance to talk.

I nearly dropped from the shock. Why was he so willing to agree now, when he was usually so resistant to any kind of sales talk?

"It's good that you understand the matter. Just sign your name here. At least your wife won't poison you for this insurance," the agent said jokingly, as he gathered up his papers and left.

"Of all the things they think up. Now we had to go and take that," said Saul.

"You didn't have to take it."

"I didn't? I thought we had to, since we have a loan."

"Don't you understand anything? This had nothing to do with the loan, except that, in case you die, the insurance will pay it off."

"Well, damn it all, I took it by mistake. We have to cancel it. I'm not going to pay for anything so useless."

I said, "Is everything that's for the good of the family useless?"

"Take out insurance, and you might even poison me like the man said."

"Now you are going crazy," I said, looking at him sharply. I thought at first that he was joking, but now I realized that he was dead serious.

"Cancel it immediately so that you won't have to start fearing for your life because of it," I said scornfully, but yet I was thinking, *Oh, my God, if that man goes crazy, it will really confound me.*

On Monday morning I had to call the agent from work since I left home before his office was open. In no way did the man want to give up on the policy, but finally I said, "Don't ever mention such a thing as a wife's poisoning her husband in hopes of collecting insurance money. My husband took it seriously, and now he wants to cancel the policy."

"N-no. But that was only joking," said the agent, agitated.

"Of course, it was a joke, but my husband has delusions," I said.

"Oh, no. Do you think it would help if I came to talk to him this evening?" the man asked courteously.

"It wouldn't help. I only told you so that you would be careful of what you say from now on. You never know what kind of people you may run into."

I noticed that I always had to go to talk to the tenants if they needed to be reminded of something. I was like a cur Saul would set on them to remind them of unpleasant truths. It bothered me, but I did my best to maintain good relations between him and the tenants.

He bought an automobile, for cash of course. He did not want me to go with him to buy it, but when they jacked up the price, I had to go to a lawyer to explain the case. I asked once if he would teach me to drive, since I would be so happy to learn. He happened to be in a good mood and promised that he would.

We went to try it out in a narrow alley in back of the house. We drove back and forth for ten minutes. I was extraordinarily enthusiastic.

"No, you'll never make a driver, everything tells me that. You'll never drive, at least not my car," he said tonelessly.

"Well, you didn't learn in a few minutes either," I said angrily. "You promised," I added, on the verge of tears.

"That kind of jerking will ruin the car. There's no point in it. You can see that—you can't even find the brakes."

At that moment I was boiling with rage, and I vowed to learn how to drive to show him I could learn as well as others.

In a nearby school there was a course in the basics of driving. I took it even though I was told the course would not result in a driver's license. I would at least learn more English there. Saul continued to go to the other course. I learned a lot about the handling of an automobile, and we even got to practice sometimes in the parking lot. When I had completed the course, I contacted a driving school. It was quite expensive, so I decided to try to complete it in the least possible number of hours.

"I think six hours will be enough for me," I said to the instructor.

He asked my age, and then he said, "Six hours isn't enough for a forty-year-old. You'll need at least twelve hours. And that may not be enough," he conjectured.

"Let's arrange for six hours now, and then we'll extend the contract if necessary," I said decisively.

Saul looked on suspiciously when the driving instructor picked me up for the training. I knew the look, and it boded no good, but I had already gotten used to that. My life was badly on the rocks, and there seemed to be no escape from it, at least not yet. I had to learn to drive before I was too old. I knew that I was alone every day, that I could not stand to have this kind of

Sisu Mother

pressure continue to the end of my days. At the end of the six hours, I felt that I still wasn't ready for a test drive, so we added another two hours.

"I just don't believe that a person your age can learn so quickly. It usually takes twelve to sixteen hours, and still some don't have the nerve to go for the test," said my instructor after the last hour.

I asked Saul if he would give me the car for the test. I would save a considerable sum of money, but this was the answer I got: "You have the money to pay. Or the man could go with you for nothing, and take it out in trade."

"You have a sick imagination, you poor old man," I said coolly. "Do you think someone as stupid as me could learn to drive in eight hours if she had been fooling around in the back seat? You've seen me come home on the dot every day. And they're so concerned with money that they won't give one free minute."

"You haven't got your license yet, so don't brag ahead of time. They don't give it to every dope," he said nastily.

I had no difficulty with the driving test. I was even able to go to work in the afternoon. That evening Saul asked maliciously: "How did it go?"

"No big deal. There it is," I said, tossing my license onto the table. He stared at me open-mouthed and turned pale. Without a word he walked out, slamming the door shut with a crash.

If he were a proper husband, he would have praised me for my progress, I thought. On top of that, it was almost three weeks before he said a word to me. Nor did I bother him. I worked, played, and chatted with the children, but he was rigidly silent.

Two months had passed, and things seemed to have settled down. It was a Friday evening. I was tired and went to bed about ten. I woke up to find him shaking my shoulder. I opened my eyes to find him glaring at me fiercely.

"You have to go and sleep somewhere else. I want this room for myself. I know why I've been getting thin. You've been poisoning my food, but that's over now."

I was so frightened that I didn't have sense enough to get up. He looked strange, really insane. He pulled me up by the hands and literally thrust me out of the door into the living room. The pillows came flying out after me. I sat on the edge of the sofa, still not really aware of what had happened. However, I was aware enough to realize that if he attacked me, I would run into the girls' room.

He closed the door, and I heard him shove something in front of it. After a while the lights went out in his room. I sat there on the edge of the sofa with a pillow in my lap, thinking that at least this was mine, bought with my own money, since he didn't even want to buy furniture. I made up a bed on the sofa and stacked up the chairs around it. If he were to get a fit of insanity in the night, the clatter of the chairs would awaken the children.

It was a futile idea. I couldn't sleep a wink the whole night, and I had promised to work on Saturday. As tired as I was, I went anyway. In the afternoon my head began to spin, and I saw black spots before one eye. I left for home early and sat on the bus in a daze. I sensed that someone came from behind and sat next to me. I was not even able to open my eyes to see if it was a man or a woman.

After a while I felt a hand stroking my knee. Opening my eyes, I shoved it away. A fairly young man was sitting next to me, wearing a suit with a white shirt and tie. In a few moments, the hand again began to stroke my knees. I thrust it angrily away, but it was back immediately. I pressed my knees firmly together so that the hand was caught between them. Rising, I grasped the hand firmly, kicked the man in the shins, and sprang into the aisle. I could feel the hot blood rising to my cheeks. Luckily there were few passengers on the bus. There was nobody in the back seat, and no one had noticed what had happened. I sat in the first seat behind the driver, where I felt safe. Why did everything aggravating have to happen to me on that one day?

At home Saul was especially friendly and began immediately to talk of his plans.

"I brought a bed for you from the garage and put it in Poju's room, where there is enough room. You can sleep with him. From now on I'll make my own food, and don't you come into the kitchen while I'm doing it. The poisoning stops here."

Tired and hopeless, I listened to it all, then went into Poju's room, which was the smallest one in the house. Somehow two beds had been crammed into it. Between them was a twenty-centimeter crack, by which one got into the beds. I threw myself onto the bed and wept with all my heart.

"What's wrong, Mother?" The voice woke me up. Apparently I had dozed off.

Sisu Mother

"Are you sick?" asked Pia.

"No, not really." I began to get up, but again I saw only black spots before my eyes. "I'm a little tired. I'll get up soon, and then we'll see what to make for supper." I closed my eyes again for a moment.

Saul had suggested that we say nothing to the children about his latest wild notion. Finally I got up and went into the kitchen, feeling weak. I advised the children on what to cook.

"Shall I go and get Father to eat?" asked Little-Sisko.

"No, no. He promised to prepare his own food. Let's leave him alone." No one paid any attention to my words. Their father had kept very much to himself in the past. The children sensed his moods and very seldom asked any questions of him. Cleaning up the kitchen that evening, I let slip these words: "I guess I have to get a divorce from him."

"Don't do it. It's so ugly," said Pia, who was only fifteen.

"I would get one," said Tytti, who was nineteen. "I wouldn't like to live with someone like Father.

Tytti started to attend a technical school that fall. She also worked a couple of hours when she got out of school. It was always quite late when she got home. I always put some food in the stove for her. Saul would often look at it and say, "Who is that for?"

"For Tytti. She leaves early in the morning and has only a small lunch with her for the whole day. She's hungry when she gets home."

I might as well have been talking to a wall. One night after work I went to water the flowers. Suddenly things went black before my eyes, and the hose fell from my hand. No matter how hard I tried to pick it up, I could not hold on to it. I staggered in, told the girls to take care of the food, and went to rest on the bed.

"Okay, Mother, come and eat," I heard the children call. I was feeling a little better and got up.

"I think it's some kind of heart attack because I couldn't get the hose to stay in my hand," I began explaining to Saul.

"It's no wonder, when you're carrying on all night and feeding those visitors of yours."

"What are you saying?" I pricked up my ears. The children were all around us, and seemed stunned.

"Haven't you children seen your mother carrying on with those strange men every night and even feeding them? She puts food in the stove every evening to warm up for them."

"What are you saying?" Tytti began. "She keeps the food warm for me, and it does taste good. I don't have time to eat when I go from school to work. I have to get through the whole day on the sandwiches I make in the morning. You're mixed up in the head, Father."

"I wouldn't be one bit against Mother's getting a divorce from you now. No one can live with you," added Pia.

"Keep quiet, you kids. No one has asked you anything," Saul said.

"You asked us," said Pia. "You asked us if we saw Mother going out. I know we haven't because it's never happened. She's often in bed before we are. It's lucky she's stayed as well as she has so far, with the long days that she works. It would be your business to take her to the doctor. It's your fault if she gets a heart attack, the way you torment her with your crazy imaginings."

"You children don't understand anything about the ways of the world. Of course you're on her side when she buys you anything you ask for, whatever pops into your heads."

"If it were up to you, we would have no food or clothing. You don't care at all what kind of rags we go around in. Why did you bring us into the world? Tell us that," said Tytti, who was furious.

"Who knows who your father is. What do you know about your mother?"

I burst out into inconsolable weeping, sobbing with my head in my hands and my elbows propped up on my knees.

"There, you see. Your mother wouldn't be crying if she were innocent."

"Let's leave. Don't listen to him," said Pia. "Take hold of my elbow." Tytti took my other arm, and we went into their room.

"You can't stand this any longer, Mother. Get a divorce, tomorrow even."

"We're on your side. It's a wonder you were able to put up with it so long. Have you ever told anyone about his delusions?"

I shook my head. Things were black before my eyes, and I lay down at once.

"Why haven't you even told us?" asked Tytti.

"You were still such children. I thought you wouldn't understand such things. Sometimes years have gone by without his saying anything. I've always hoped that he would come to his senses. I think this is that men's middle-age madness. He's already over forty."

"What is that?" they both asked.

"When some men reach that age, they change somehow. Some of them go crazy over young women. I think your father has been driven insane by his imaginings. There's no remedy but to get a divorce, even though I hate the thought of it."

Day after day passed without my starting the divorce proceedings. Saul seemed to have calmed down somewhat. I tried to be careful not to go into the kitchen when he was preparing his food. Most of it seemed to come from cans.

Once by chance I came into the back door and through the kitchen, not knowing that he was cooking. He came into the kitchen and dumped all the soup into the garbage container. That told me he had only gotten worse. We said very little to each other. Once, to my astonishment, he started to speak: "If you want, we can eat together on Saturday. It would be better from the children's point of view."

"Whatever you say," I answered indifferently. I guessed that the canned food had lost its attraction. I couldn't even laugh, but only pitied him. We had meatballs with gravy in a bowl. It was the custom for Father to serve himself first. He dug out the ones that were on the bottom of the bowl because he believed I had poisoned the ones on top. It never occurred to him that if there was something in them we could all die when we ate them. The poor man—he could never think of anyone but himself. How bad might he become if he would never go for help? I had heard that such delusions could not be cured, but could be controlled with the aid of medications. But he did not believe that there was anything wrong with him. That was the crux of it —there was no way to get him to a doctor's office.

Tytti had found a boyfriend and was often out on Saturdays. The Christmas vacation arrived. One evening Tytti came home with two boys and introduced her boyfriend and his brother to us. It was only natural; Tytti was already nineteen. To her father it seemed absolutely crazy. "The brat has a boyfriend already." He spoke very little to the boy. The lads were in no hurry to leave, and Saul gestured to me to come into the kitchen.

"You have to tell them to go home."

"Well, why can't you go and tell them," I objected.

"I can't speak to them as well as you can. Just go."

"You treat me like a dog to sic on people, but this will end some day," I said angrily. Nevertheless I went and said courteously to the boys, "Listen, it's late already. Wouldn't it be better if you went home? How far is it to where you live?"

"At least eighty-five kilometers. A good hour's drive."

"Come during the day sometime. Good night."

It was no temporary acquaintanceship. The boy came again one Saturday evening in January.

"We've gotten engaged," said Tytti shyly.

It was like being hit by a thunderbolt. It seemed such a hare-brained idea. Getting married. I was sure nothing would come of it.

"Engaged," I finally managed to say. "Isn't it too early? You're only in the first year of school, and you have to think first about graduating. You don't know how to set up housekeeping together. Tytti doesn't even know how to cook. She's never been interested in it." All kinds of objections kept occurring to me.

The engaged couple appeared deeply disappointed by my reaction. Rudy began to explain that his mother would be glad to teach Tytti how to cook. They left the same evening to visit Rudy's parents. Later Rudy's mother called to say they were spending the night with them, that there was no need to worry. I also talked briefly to Tytti.

I was still sleeping in Poju's room; there wasn't space anywhere else. We always kept the door leading to the hallway open. One night I awoke with the feeling that there was someone in the room. I could hear that Poju was sound asleep. I opened my eyes and froze with fear. In the dark night I could see a pale figure standing at the foot of the bed. Was it a ghost or a real person? It might be Saul, but what would he have in mind? Did he plan to harm me somehow? Why would he come to stare at me in the night? My eyes sharpened enough so that I recognized him.

"What are you doing here?"

"I heard someone snoring loudly. I came to see who it was."

"Well, which one of us is it?"

"I don't know. I can't hear it any more. He managed to slip away."

Who and what had managed to slip away, I thought sleepily. Did he imagine some visitor was here snoring? I began to pray with all my heart: "Dear God. You who are great and high. Look down on this lowly being. My need is great. Cure that man of his illness, or give me guidance or knowledge of what to do. I can't go on in this way for long. I ask forgiveness for not thanking you earlier for the many gifts you have given me. Thank you for the health that has enabled me to struggle on from day to day. Thank you for my bright and healthy children. Without them I could never have gone on. Thank you for leading us to America. Thank you for keeping us free of need. Oh, God, give me strength and the knowledge to make the right decision in this difficult matter, which will be an honor to you and a blessing to all of us. Amen."

A feeling of peace began to come over me. What a restoring medication. A moment before, every nerve cell in my body had been jangling, and now I felt the calm of nirvana. I slept peacefully the rest of the night and woke refreshed in the morning.

A few nights later, I heard creeping footsteps in the hall and saw someone peep in through the open door. I listened nervously to see if Saul would come in. The footsteps crept away. It even occurred to me that it might actually have been a burglar.

Rising carefully, I crept out to the hallway to check. I thought that if it were a burglar I could call the police from the hallway. I listened, but there was no sound. Then I heard the creak of bedsprings. It had been Saul again. What did he have in mind? One day I noticed that he had put a stout iron bolt on the inside of his door. I could hear him close it at night. The poor wretch, fearing for his life in his own home. I could not go on like this for the rest of my life. I was beginning to fear the nocturnal haunting.

My thoughts were a muddle. I couldn't sleep no matter how I tried. I had to work. How could I make it through the day? Often my head would ache around the eyes. It must have been because of the strain. I could not rest easy at night because I was afraid of his creeping around. I heard every time anyone went to the bathroom. I tried going to sleep early—often the girls were up late with their homework. That couple of hours was the only time when I could sleep peacefully.

In the morning I asked Saul innocently: "I heard footsteps last night. I thought there might be burglars in the house, but I didn't dare get up to look. Did you hear anything?"

"No. I didn't hear anything all night," he answered softly.

Tytti and Rudy were talking of getting married. I would not hear of it, and her father was even more opposed. One day when I came home I found a slip of paper on the kitchen table, which read:

Dear Mother,

> I'm sad to say I have to do this, since neither of you approves of our marriage. I rented an apartment near the school and work. We've picked April 22nd as our wedding day. We'll be married in Rudy's hometown. I hope you'll come, although it's eighty-five kilometers away. I hope to get your blessing on our marriage.

I collapsed onto a chair. This had to happen now too. Why did all the blows come at the same time? Rebellion rose in my heart. "Why are you tormenting me, God, if you do exist? What have I done that you should punish me so? Why, why, why? You are supposed to be mild and merciful. Why did you give me this burden to carry?"

Of course, I was to blame in all this. Why hadn't I been favorable to their plans? Rudy was from a good home, although they had a large family. I had let Saul influence me too much in the matter. I should have been able to think more clearly after the first fright. Why hadn't I thought for myself and understood the young people better? My thoughts were wildly chaotic.

I was still sitting there when Saul came home. I threw the letter down before him and saw him turn pale as he read it. For a time he said nothing.

"Well, let them go. They'll see that living on their own isn't as easy as they think. Are they living together?"

"I don't think so. Rudy seems to be a decent boy. I think they are both nice kids. I don't think they've gone too far. But they want to get properly married. There are still six weeks until the wedding. It's up to the father of the bride to stand the expenses of the wedding. It's the custom in this country."

"Well, you can if you want to. I don't have the money for such nonsense. Weddings yet, pooh."

"I don't have the money, but you do. That's the truth and no lie. You haven't touched your bank account for months. I know it," I snapped. "You must be planning to buy the keys to heaven from St. Peter with all that money," I added spitefully. Nothing more was said on the subject for a few weeks.

About a week before the wedding, Tytti and Rudy came to see us, bringing an invitation to visit Rudy's home on the next day. It was for what they call a wedding shower here. Neighbors, relatives, and friends get together and bring gifts for the wedding pair. There is something to eat, and simple games are played. Our whole family was invited for supper.

"We're not going," said Saul, looking at the invitation and turning it over in his hands. I said nothing. Tytti left the room in tears, followed by the younger children. Saul too followed them out, and I saw him talking to them. When he came in, he said nothing.

I thought about the matter alone that evening when I was trying to get to sleep, and decided that I would go there with the youngsters, even if we had to take a bus. We could not punish the young couple, for they had done nothing wrong.

When I first saw Saul in the morning I began talking quietly to him. "I've come to the conclusion last night that we are going to that shower today. If you won't come, we'll go by bus."

"I thought so, too. It would be ugly to act this way."

"You're going!" I shouted joyfully. I came close to hugging him. "I wouldn't have believed it." I danced around the room like a calf let out in the springtime."

"I'll go to the store with the girls to buy the gifts. We have to call them so they'll know we're coming," I said, all business now.

"You don't have to call them. They'll see us when we come."

"The invitation says to call if we're coming. There will be five of us. I think courtesy demands that we call."

"What next. There's no point in it. Now you have to call all over the place," he added.

I didn't dare fuss at him further, although I knew it was wrong not to call.

I went with Pia to a store where they sold all kinds of household goods. I picked out sheets, pillows, pillowcases, and blankets, although I had no idea of the sizes of American bedclothing. Only later did I learn them. (I heard later that Tytti's mother-in-law had gone to exchange them for sizes that fit.) What can an ignorant person do, when customs differ in this large world? Pia looked in amazement at the huge pile of goods and asked, "Are you going to buy them all? They'll cost a fortune."

"They need them since they have nothing. When you're a bride, I'll buy them for you too."

Pia blushed in confusion. She was only fifteen. She was very good around the house and diligent in school. I remember that she saved her weekly allowance of fifty cents and bought a camera. It took her four months, and a few weeks more to get film. She was an energetic and persevering girl. I was proud of her.

We sat soberly in the car during the ride north. All of us were excited. I felt a pang in my breast—why hadn't I called anyway? Why did I always have to listen to him, although I knew that he wasn't right? This was the last time I would obey his commands. We were sure to be shamed by this. From now on, I would do what my conscience told me to. Five people popping in on them without advance notice. It really griped me.

We found the place easily. A map had been drawn on the back of the invitation. I saw faces in the window, and someone came out onto the steps. Everyone was surprised and curious.

"Hey, there's Tytti," shouted Poju, waving. "At least we're in the right place."

"You did come, even if you didn't call," said Rudy's mother.

I was ashamed.

"Didn't Saul call? He promised to when we went to the store." (God, forgive me for this lie.) The men carried the packages into the house.

"We didn't hear anything. Men so easily forget," said the woman. "We can fit you in easily. Let's not say anything to him about it."

Now I saw an American kitchen with all its devices. It was a little lacking in neatness and organization, but our arrival had been a surprise. The dishwasher had not yet been loaded that morning. They had a large family—

nine in all. The woman of the house asked me to sit down in the kitchen as she put some food into the oven. The electric can opener was under some things on the kitchen counter. She took a while in finding it. It did work nicely, though, when it was plugged in.

A large, round table had been set with fourteen places. The oldest of their seven children was in the army in Germany. We all held hands in a circle as the man of the family said a prayer for the meal. It was an extraordinarily pleasing custom. The father carved the meat, which was an American roast beef.

Later the mother of the family showed us the house, which had seven bedrooms. The largest bedroom belonged to the parents, of course, and from it, sliding doors opened onto a blue swimming pool a few steps away. Everything indicated that the family had no shortage of means. The husband must have been well employed, since the signs of prosperity were so evident. His wife was a nurse by profession, but had not worked in years because of all the children.

The other shower guests did not arrive until twilight. We were accepted in the group like old friends. The evening went by pleasantly. At the end, we were served coffee and cake. We noticed that no one even smoked. It was quite late when we got home.

As I lay in bed that night, the day's events unreeled before my eyes like a film. They were a delightful family and had received us warmly in spite of our being strangers. I felt as if they had gotten an impression of us as a close-knit family, although we were on the point of breaking up. I had spoken to none of the outsiders about our family problems. We had no relatives or close friends in whom I could confide, and if we had spoken to others, the result would only have been empty gossip. Everyone has his own troubles to bear, and if he has no big ones, he'll magnify the small ones.

It was a week until the young couple's big day. We went to rehearse at the church so that everything would go according to rule. The whole family was there, and everyone had a part in the ceremony.

At the wedding, everything went smoothly, as it had in the rehearsals. Pictures were taken, and juice was served in the church clubroom. Now I was a mother-in-law. I hoped I wouldn't be a bad one.

It would have been proper for us to take the new relatives to dinner, but I did not have the money for it. I mentioned it to Saul, but my words fell on deaf ears. He did give the young couple a gift of money.

We were very tired as we drove home in the afternoon. Before we reached the yard, I said: "Wouldn't it be better to go and eat at that Swedish smorgasbord place. It's right over there. I'm too tired to go to the store and start cooking."

"Well, let's go, but you pay," said Saul.

"I don't want to start arguing about money on a day like this. You can pay for yourself or not come. We'll walk home."

For a wonder, he drove to the restaurant and came in with us. The food was very homey, with many kinds of delicacies. The bread, a round rye loaf, was still warm from the oven.

"I haven't had such a good supper in years," said Saul.

"We have to come here more often. It's right in our neighborhood, too. We could even walk to it."

Our daily life went on smoothly and monotonously. I talked to the children in the evening. Sometimes days passed without a word between Saul and me. He was shut up in his own world, sometimes withdrawing into his room quite early. I could hear the bolt snap into place inside. Things were too calm, I thought, recalling old experiences. His mind is brooding on some lunacy. I became more careful in all my actions. I slept poorly, and I heard every footstep if someone was moving about the house. My eyes felt tired, and I had to go for a checkup. I knew that it all resulted from the tension and from too great a strain. I got a pair of glasses for work and reading purposes.

"Of course they want to sell glasses when fools like you go there." That was his reaction when he saw my glasses. I did not want to start a discussion and left the room.

It was about the middle of May in 1967. I awakened again to the sound of someone creeping softly to the foot of my bed. I opened my eyes carefully without moving a muscle and saw Saul standing at the foot of the bed with his hand extended toward me. In the dark I couldn't tell if he had anything in it. I was so frightened that I broke out in a cold sweat. He lowered the hand to my feet.

"What are you doing?" I said in a hoarse voice.

"I'm just checking to see who's sleeping with you."

"Well go ahead and poke and prod through the whole bed," I said, starting to get up.

"Well, he was able to slip out again."

"Go and try that window. It's locked from the inside and hasn't been opened for the whole night." I sometimes opened the window on a hot night, but it was cool, and I had closed it before going to bed.

"I know someone was here. I was at the door earlier."

"Let's go to the other room so we won't wake up Poju." I started to walk before him to the living room. "You'll drive me crazy with your snooping around," I said angrily.

"Yaah, because you won't admit it. I have to get proof."

"I can't admit anything when I haven't done anything."

"You'll admit it, all right, when I get a gun."

"Gun or no gun, I'm not guilty of anything. I'm ready to die with a clear conscience, but I pity the children if they're left with a miserable father like you. Or to tell the truth, with no mother or father. Murderers are not allowed to bring up their children. Remember that," I said coldly, and left. I found a sleeping bag in a closet, got a pillow, and went softly into the girls' room. I spread the bag on the floor and got a little sleep.

In the morning I explained the situation to the girls. We decided unanimously to go to a lawyer after work and start divorce proceedings.

I got to speak to the lawyer that same evening. He promised to set things in motion and said that a mandate to live in separate quarters would be taken to Saul within a couple of days.

I no longer dared to sleep in Poju's room, but moved a mattress onto the floor of the girls' room. In the evening we braced the door shut from the inside just in case. Lately, Saul had been very good to Poju. He would take only the boy to ride with him in the car, and so Poju was not afraid of him and wanted to sleep in his own room. A couple of days later when I came home from work, Saul was already there. I saw from his face that he had received the court summons. I stayed close to the door in case I had to get out quickly. I saw that the girls were not home yet.

"Now we'll see when we go to court how fast you'll be thrown out of this house. Why did the police have to bring this as if I were a criminal? I would have believed it without them. You are a real witch. I should have gotten a gun. I would have been rid of you sooner. By God, when . . ."

I crept softly out of the door and went to sit on the swing in the back yard. One of our tenants, an Englishwoman well up in years, was sitting there. She saw the fear on my face.

"What's wrong? Why do you have to sit here at this time of the day?"

"It's stormy weather inside," I said.

"You don't say. What's it about?"

"I've mentioned something about it to you before. He was served with separation papers today. I didn't dare stay inside. He was so wild, I was afraid he would attack me."

"The man must have gone crazy. With a wife like you—they don't make them that way any more. He must be blind. Do you dare go in at all tonight?"

"I'll go only when the children come home, not before. He won't hurt the children."

"Come and spend the night with me if you're afraid. You can't know what that devil might do," said Ruby, and went in.

I entered the house with the girls when they came home and went straight into their room. We could hear Saul cooking something in the kitchen and then leaving in the car. He did not return that night.

In a couple of weeks we were in court, where all the details of the separation were mandated. Before that, Saul had asked, actually pleaded, on many evenings that I would cancel the case. He had insisted to his lawyer that he did not want to move away from home. To my amazement, I learned that under the law a divorced couple could live under the same roof if they had nothing to do with each other. In a sense we had already lived apart for nine months.

We were also advised to seek family counseling and to visit a psychiatrist. I promised that in that case, if he sought aid, he could live at home as long as he left us in peace. He was ordered to pay a small sum for the support of the children. In any case, he seemed relieved when we left the court. He chattered happily, as if nothing had happened. I had come there on the bus, but when he offered me a ride, I of course accepted, since we were going to the same place: home.

We went to family counseling, which was free, since children were involved. After two sessions, they advised us that they could not help, and urged a visit to a psychiatrist.

"I don't need any psychiatrist. My wife does," he replied immediately.

"What if you go together?" suggested the counselor, giving me a significant look.

"Yaah, I could go with her. I'll just drive her there. Why should a sound person like me go?" he said. "They would charge for two people for nothing."

"I'll arrange a session for the two of you anyway. Remember to go in, too," said the counselor.

Saul nodded and looked askance at the counselor, just as if he could not understand what he was saying.

He came into the psychiatrist's office without bidding. First we were interviewed together by the doctor. Then Saul alone, and finally I alone for a few minutes. The psychiatrist explained how I was to help Saul at home.

"He will never be free of these delusions, but with medication they can be kept under control. I hope you will do your best to benefit his peace of mind. I know you've suffered a lot over the years because of him, but try once more."

"I'll do my best," I said, with tears in my eyes.

The doctor wrote out a prescription for Saul's medication, which we could get at the drugstore nearest home. The doctor's office was in Beverly Hills, that is, in the film stars' section of the city.

Saul did not say a word, but drove home sunk in thought. We passed a drugstore near home, but he did not stop.

"Aren't you going to get the medication the doctor prescribed?"

"Not now. We'll get it tomorrow. There's no hurry," he said indifferently.

Two days later, I saw that he had still not gotten the medication.

"Do you want me to get the prescription on the way home from work?"

"Why did he give it to me? You're the one who needs it. I'm not going to start swallowing any poisons. And I'm sure they cost plenty."

"I'll pay for them, as long as you are willing to take them," I said.

"There you go again. You got the doctor to fall in love with you, and now the two of you are trying to poison me. I saw the way he looked at you. I wouldn't take that medicine if you brought it to me on a golden tray."

I broke out in bitter tears. I had had high hopes after the session with the psychiatrist. Now my dreams had come crashing down again. The situation seemed hopeless.

"We have a another session next week. Are you coming with me?"

"I'm not going there to waste money."

"What if you tried by yourself to find another doctor? One who doesn't know me, one you could go to by yourself. Just as a trial, to see if you need help or not."

"I told you I don't need anything. You've got the kind of a c— that needs stroking all the time. And you're not getting any better. The older you get, the crazier you get. You'll take any man who comes your way. That booze-hound has probably had you, too, the one who . . ."

I went out the back door. I could not stand to listen to any more. It was good that the children hadn't heard him. They were watching an exciting cowboy film on the television.

The next day I called the psychiatrist and told him how badly everything was going at home in spite of my hopes.

"To conclude from all this, he's a hopeless case. I feel sorry for you. I warn you not to live under the same roof with him. He's so mentally ill that you never know what might happen," said the psychiatrist, and hung up.

What lay ahead now? All this had taken up two months. The divorce would be final at the end of a year. I could not stand the pressure for so long. I went to speak to the lawyer.

"There are so many court cases that it would be at least three months before this is taken up. Is it possible that he could move into the rental house?" asked the lawyer.

"Well, I can try," I said uncertainly.

"I'll try to speed up this divorce case in the court. Sometimes it can be done. Perhaps we'll get it through faster than we expect."

I spoke to the girls about his moving, and they said it was a good idea. They too were afraid of their father, who hadn't spoken a word to them for a month. Poju was the only one he talked to, and he catered to the boy too much. In the evening I began cautiously to present the matter.

"Do you remember when it was arranged in the court that we could live under the same roof if you were in the care of a psychiatrist? You've refused care, and things are no better than before our separation. I've spoken to the lawyer, and he recommends that you move into the rental house. I think that would be a good idea now."

"Why do I have to move out of my own house? You're the one who has to go. If you don't want to live with me, you can move out tomorrow. The children can stay if they want to."

"I hardly think they'll want to live with you," I said scornfully.

I had a summer vacation, but had made no plans because of the situation at home. Nor did I have the means to travel with the children. Saul would not let me touch his car. Sometimes out of his good will, he took us to the beach. I realized, however, that I could not take much sun. It made me ill.

Now we took the bus downtown to see the sights of the city. The girls, who were already teen-agers, brought their friends with them. We had just come from rowing on a man-made pond and were walking in the park chattering happily. An oldish man stopped us and said: "I congratulate you, ma'am. Four such pretty girls and a boy to be his father's joy. You are rich to have such a family."

I was so dumfounded that I could say nothing. Actually there was a lot of similarity among the children. They were all tall, healthy, blond, and blue-eyed. No wonder the man had thought them brothers and sisters. If only our family were such a happy whole, I thought gloomily. No, our family was shattered forever—it had really never been whole and intact or sheltered. How had my life been tossed away in this fashion? I had forever been walking a round and slippery log like an acrobat, trying to stay on but afraid of falling off at any minute. Why had all this fallen to my lot? I didn't believe that everyone's life was like this—but what did I know of other people's troubles? I had heard that everyone was given his or her burden to bear. Perhaps I was not able to carry mine lightly. How could I be more laid-back about my life. A divorce was no run-of-the-mill matter. It was the last thing I wanted, but there was no alternative now.

I could not imagine the evening of my life with Saul. I had already lived in a state of insecurity for twenty years. I had done my best, or should I say all I could, but I had failed. I needed peace and security. As things stood, I had to be afraid day and night. The only safe place was at work. There I could be myself. I could talk and laugh, and that relaxed me. There I had friends, although no one so close that I could tell her my worries. I lived a day at a time, full of tension and fear every moment.

It was autumn, although here in the South there was little sense of the season except that the days grew a little shorter. Around five or six in the evening, it grew darker. During the days the temperature might rise to over eighty degrees. Nights it cooled off enough so that a heating system was needed. We had natural gas heat, which operated automatically. I sighed with relief at not having to chop wood and carry it in.

I still had to wait until April, the lawyer said. So it was six months until our divorce case would go to court. I could stand that. With heart and *sisu*, one can go far.

It was the last day of October. I was prepared for this American Halloween with all kinds of candies on a little table by the door.

"Let's eat early so that we won't have to run from the table to the door when they start knocking," I said.

"Oh, yaah, I promised to go with Carmen and watch her sisters while they go from door to door," said Little-Sisko. "They'll come here first and then we'll go."

"Remember to be careful when you come home. You know that anything can happen. Don't come home alone. You might even ask Carmen's brother to come with you."

Knock, knock, knock. "Trick or treat," we heard a chorus of voices. I hastened to the door. Outside were at least a half-dozen children in the zaniest of costumes.

"Trick or treat!" The voices were louder.

"You're so charming in those beautiful, elegant costumes," I said as I distributed the sweets. Each one was holding a bag or a small basket out to me. "Oh what a beautiful angel—and you must be a real princess. And who's inside that sheet."

"I'm a ghost," said a clear boy's voice.

"Ooo, I'm afraid of ghosts," I said in a trembling voice. "Here are some sweets for your bag, Mr. Ghost. And there's some for the tiger and the pirate. And a couple for that long-whiskered cat. You've really thought up some wild costumes this year."

"Thank you, thank you," we could hear them mumbling all the way to the street.

We were on a street where there was much traffic, so that the kids kept coming constantly. For fun I kept track of the number who came. Many arrived by the carload from another section of the city. Most of them were

Mexicans, accompanied by mothers and fathers who stood waiting on the sidewalk.

Oh, dear, now a little one got tangled in her skirt and fell on the hard walk. I ran out, and at the same moment her father was there lifting her up. Of course the child began to cry.

"She's bleeding from somewhere," said the father, a dark, black-mustached man.

"Come in and we'll see how badly she's hurt."

"*Gracias, gracias,*" repeated the man, and followed me in carrying the girl. I pointed to the sofa and he laid the girl down on it. I got some cold water and began to wash the blood from the girl's face.

"It doesn't look bad. Only a cut on her gum that she's bleeding from, but it will soon stop." I gave the man a Kleenex to wipe it if necessary. The father patted the girl's shoulder and said something to her in Spanish. The girl leaped to her feet, snatched up her small, pumpkin-shaped basket, and was on her way to the next house.

"*Gracias, gracias,*" the man repeated again before the door closed.

They kept coming all evening; only after nine did they slow down. There were very few sweets left. I was afraid they might not last. I had a bag of nuts in reserve, but I hadn't needed to tap them yet. We ate them ourselves— they were very healthy, and we always had a few around as snacks. I added up my list: 114 children had come begging.

I had heard that every beggar had to be given something, that it brought good luck to the house. If one gave nothing, the bigger children might do some mischief. Someone had had raw eggs and tomatoes splattered on his walls and windows. I asked what the origin of Halloween was, but no one seemed to remember.

Americans are warm-hearted and open people, but what happens today is forgotten tomorrow. They really live a day at a time, and not a day and a half, like the wife of old.

In the fall I began taking a home nurse's course, which met two evenings a week. I had already had the usual beginning English courses. I thought I would learn more English in the nursing course, along with a new occupation. Also, perhaps it would stimulate my weary nerves to think of something else besides my day-to-day existence.

The course was indeed medicine for the nerves. I learned so many new words that every night I made a list of them, kept them near my sewing machine at work, and tried to learn them on the side. The course was a pleasurable life saver. I made new and agreeable friends. Surprisingly I passed all the tests well. There were thirty-six students in the class when it began, some of them young as well, and in the spring when the course ended, only fourteen passed. I felt that I was something when I came out so well. I was the only one with language problems.

The six months passed more quickly than I had imagined. I had so many other things to think about that I had no time to brood over domestic troubles.

Usually I walked the couple of blocks from the school alone. Soon I became aware that Saul was never at home, but always came as soon as I had arrived. I mentioned it to the girls, and they promised to come and get me from the school. They were big and spirited girls; Pia would soon be seventeen, and Little-Sisko was fifteen.

Once Saul noticed that we came home together, he would already be home when I got there. The question of whether he had intended to do something to me or whether it was more of his delusional spying remained unanswered. I never asked him where he was going or where he had been.

Finally the date arrived: April 22, 1968. Our divorce case was scheduled for that day in the court. Saul paced the living room with a sneer on his lips.

"Today will decide how things will go for you, old lady," he said self-confidently. "Aren't you terrified?"

"Not at all. I've waited such a long time for this day. I think my life will be easier from now on."

He had asked one of our former tenants to testify, as well as our aged neighbors, who had been summoned and would have been fined had they not appeared. Saul had gone to fetch a widow, who was one of the witnesses, while our neighbors offered a ride to me and Pia, who was my only witness.

"There was no point in summoning us as witnesses. We can't say anything bad about you," said our neighbor's wife. "On the contrary, we could testify against him. If I have to speak under oath, I'll tell the truth, and it won't be to Saul's benefit. But we've only been summoned as supernumeraries, so I don't think we'll need to testify."

I had to take the oath first, and so I sat in the witness stand. Amazingly, I was able to tell my story in a calm and steady voice. I felt that I was doing the right thing. I had dismissed the idea of divorce so many times, thinking that there must be a better way. Now I felt I was on the way to finding relief.

Now it was Pia's turn. She told the truth about what had happened in recent years. The lawyer had learned the facts about Saul's bank account, where I had guessed that Saul's money would be. Saul had withdrawn all the money, a total of almost twenty thousand dollars, on the same day as he received the divorce papers. There was also testimony that he had, for example, put his entire wages for ten months into the bank.

Now it was Saul's turn to take the stand. He was pale and very agitated, and found it difficult to give a direct answer to any of the questions. His lawyer had made an elaborate account of where his money had been spent. For example, five hundred dollars a year had gone for family entertainment. The judge had proof from the bank that he had not spent even a penny on his own living expenses. Saul also demanded that the children be put under his care, to which the judge replied: "The girls are of an age to choose with whom they will live."

Saul's witness, our former tenant, said nothing either good or bad about either of us, so his testimony had no effect whatsoever.

Then it was Poju's turn, to whom Saul had catered for the last year and thus won over to his side. The question was whether he wanted to go and live with his father. The judge asked, "Why do you want to go and live with your father? Has your mother been mean to you?"

"No, never."

"Well, you must have some reason."

"Father lets me drive the car, and he told me to come here with him," said Poju, and he began to cry.

That ended the questioning. The judge and lawyers disappeared into a conference room to negotiate. In a few minutes they came out again. The black-robed judge began his official statement. "This is an easy decision for me. I've never seen such a dishonest man. He takes an oath, then every word he says is a lie. I am amazed that his wife has been able to suffer all this for so many years." Turning to Saul, he said, "Do you know that I could sentence you to jail for letting a thirteen-year-old boy drive a car. That is a violation of the law. A father as dishonest as you is not fit to bring up a child. As to the property, you have much more money hidden than the property is worth, so your wife gets the house, where she can live with the children, and also the car. You are to move from the house by the last of this month, and pay this mandated sum the first of each month for support of the three children."

Sisu Mother

He banged his gavel on the desk. The case was over as far as we were concerned.

Saul did not come home until several hours later. He sat silent on the living-room sofa as if he were stunned. I happened to have to get something from the room.

"Why didn't they take my life? They took everything else."

"What are you saying?" I responded. "Now you can live like a king. You'll have nothing to do but sit on your moneybags and enjoy life. You've finally gotten rid of the children, who've been a burden all your life. Time after time I've been ashamed when you've told others about how much our family costs you, when for the last seven years you haven't spent a penny on your children. And on top of all that, I've been supporting you, while you've just been fattening your bank account."

"I have been paying this last year," he said quickly.

"Only because the court ordered you to. Well, why keep mulling it over? It's all settled. Everyone has gotten justice."

I walked out, still feeling an inner tension after the days' events.

In the evening when the children were in their own room, I brought out a bottle of champagne I had stopped to buy. (In California one can buy alcoholic beverages in any food store.) I went into the living room where Saul was still sitting.

"Let's have a glass of champagne in honor of the occasion. We've earned it. There are the glasses—you can open the bottle."

"Where did you get that?" he said in surprise.

"From the store, of course. The shelves are full of all kinds of it. It's worth a toast, now that we have peace after almost twenty years of war."

He took the bottle and the glass and went into the kitchen. Having popped the cork, he rinsed out his glass and came back. He first poured his own drink, which he kept far away from mine, and then filled my glass.

"Cheers," I said, and clinked the glasses together. I drank from my glass frequently, but he barely sipped at his. When my glass was empty, I said, "This is really good. Try to empty your glass so we can have more. It will go flat if we don't drink it."

To my wonder, he emptied his glass in one go, and poured more.

"Yaah, here's to our divorce. Why not part friends? There are a lot of nice things about you—you even came up with this. Cheers, this is our last

Sisu Mother

drink together." I could see that Saul was beginning to thaw out. There was even a slight smile on his face.

"It's been a long trip since we first left the barn loft to get engaged, and now we're going our separate ways in California," he said, half to himself.

"We still have half a life ahead of us. Who knows what a happy man you may be when you find the right partner," I teased.

"Yes, and you, too. Everyone likes you," he said warmly.

"Let them, for all I care. I have too many other things to do. Men can go to hell. I'm not having anything to do with them."

"You've had enough of them," he said sneeringly.

"That's it. This is the last time I talk to you. Empty the bottle. I didn't mean for you to start dragging up the past and making me listen to your old delusions." I left the room without a word.

I felt bitter. It was pointless to begin any kind of discussion with him. I had heard enough of those insane accusations. They were a thing of the past for me. One more week, and he would be out of my sight. It remained to be seen when I would get the automobile. Officially it was supposed to be mine. I did not say anything in order not to set him off. As far as I was concerned, he could keep it to use for moving. He would be easily able to fit his things into it since he had no furniture.

I expected him to move on the weekend since Tuesday was the last day of the week he was given to move. But he merely kept on pacing the floor with his hands in his pockets. I didn't know if he had even looked for a place to live—there were plenty of them for single men.

"Have you found a place to live?" I could not refrain from asking.

"No, I speak the language so poorly," he tried to dodge the issue.

"If you like, I can call. I don't want to meddle in your affairs at all, but Tuesday is your last day in this house," I said firmly.

"Well, you can call, so that I can get started," he said helplessly.

I began to call in response to ads in the paper. The second call already yielded results. "There's the address. It seems to be about five or six kilometers away. The landlady is available at twelve, so be there then. Go and look at it; if it isn't good, we can call more places. And you may well see ads on buildings you drive by."

He came back in the afternoon. I could not tell from his face if he had taken a place or not.

"How did it go? Did you have any luck? I asked.
"Yaah, yaah, I got a place. The one you called," he answered negligently. "I'll move on Wednesday."

On Tuesday I thought it best to leave work early and go to change the electricity, gas, and water meters to my name, since it was the last day. I was told that they had already been changed. At the water office, I was told that a man had come in and ordered the water shut off.

"But we live in the house, and we need water."

"I don't know if we can get it back on today, since it's so late."

"How did you do it so quickly? We can't live without water. There are four of us," I pleaded, close to tears.

"The man came in yesterday already, and the water was shut off this morning. I'll try to call and see if there's still a chance of getting it turned on this evening." After talking on the phone, he said courteously: "They'll be there in a couple of hours. Be at home then. I explained the situation to them, and they'll stop on the way home from work."

"Thank you, thank you," I said, and began walking hurriedly toward home. I arrived just when the electricians were there and got them to stop what they were doing.

"I started to put the soup on as you told me to, Mother, but no water would come. And there was no gas either. What is this all about? And we can't reach anyone by phone," said Pia, troubled.

"This is your father. He's going to hear about this. Are his things still here?" I rushed to the door of his room and peered in. Nothing had been taken. "I'll have one more chance to let him know how I feel, and I'll do it from the bottom of my heart," I thought. I unscrewed the only lamp bulb from the ceiling. Since he wanted to turn the electricity off, he could go without it this evening.

I went to the neighbors to call the gas company, and they said they could arrange things that evening. We were not able to get the phone hooked up for three days. Why had he had to have the phone cut off, since it was in my name? He had not paid a single phone bill.

We had just gotten the water and gas back when Saul walked in. He took a couple of boxes into his room and began to pack them. In a moment he appeared at the kitchen door. I gave him a murderous look and shouted angrily, "What are you doing here?"

"I need some eating utensils."
"Why the hell did you have everything shut off here today?"
"They're not shut off. Everything's working."
"Yea, because I got them back on."
"I told them tomorrow . . ." he started to say.
"Don't lie," I shouted, and threw a wet dishrag into his face. "You can't fool me any more. I know you all too well by now."
"Goddamn," I heard from under the dishrag. He took it and threw it to the floor. "Aren't you a real she-lion."
"Yes, and an angry one too. You take nothing from this kitchen. If you don't believe me, I'll call the police. Nothing here was declared your property. Eat from your hands the rest of your life, you skinflint. It wouldn't bother me one bit. You keep pulling your rotten tricks to the very end. Damn, if only I could never see or hear from you again. . . . Take your things out of here right now, and if the car isn't out front here by tonight, I'll call the police."

At that moment the doorbell rang. I wondered who it could be on a night like this. Pia went to open it.

"Is your mother at home? We were supposed to write up an auto insurance policy tonight," I heard a man's voice say courteously. Oh darn, I had earlier arranged by phone for the agent to come. In the rush of things, I had forgotten all about it.

I tried to compose myself and went into the living room to meet him. We got everything ready so that when I had the car I would call him and the insurance would go into effect. But I didn't believe I would get it until I saw it there before my eyes. When the insurance man had left, Saul came in and began asking, "Why has the only light been taken out of that room? I need a light. I still have a lot of packing to do."

"Well, you're the one who told them to turn off the lights this morning. You got what you wanted now. I don't have any bulbs to give you."

He looked at me at me in disbelief, muttered something, went out, returned shortly with a flashlight, and began packing by its light. It was very late that night before he managed to get everything out. I did not go to bed until I was able to lock the door. But sleep did not come easily. The next day I had the locks changed on all the doors.

Sisu Mother

The weeks passed in total calm. Poju moved into his father's room. At last I had my own room and could sleep in my own bed. For seven months I had been sleeping on the floor of the girl's room. Life began to settle down, but I still slept with one eye open. I always heard if anyone was moving around in the backyard or around the building. I still hadn't gotten the car, and had been to talk to the lawyer about it many times. Finally, when almost a month had passed, I heard a knock at the door one evening. Little-Sisko went to open it. Saul was there. Without a word he thrust the car keys into my hand, whirled around, and went on his way.

"Hey, we got the car." Little-Sisko danced happily on the floor. She was overjoyed. "Where is it? Where?" We went to look from the steps. There was no car to be seen.

"Maybe he put it into the garage," I said hopefully.

We ran to the garage. It was empty. *What is it now?* I wondered.

"You go down the street that way and I'll go this way. We'll look around the neighborhood." I said.

I found the car two blocks away. It was thickly coated with dust, as if it had not been driven for months. The windows too were so clouded that I wondered how he had been able to drive.

Pia had gotten a driver's license a year ago, although she had never driven since then. I had not driven since I had gotten a license, and that was already two years before. We both were apprehensive about getting the car into our own yard, but Pia had nerve enough to drive it there. All of us worked on washing it, and then it looked brand new. It actually had not been driven much, and had been purchased new a couple of years before. Now then, how would we get it into the garage? The alley was narrow, and the place to turn around was cramped. Luckily there was no one around to watch and laugh at our efforts. Finally the task was accomplished.

Anger is a thief that robs you of moments of joy.

A person's life is an unrehearsed play.

One cannot live without a sense of humor.
You must be able to laugh at yourself; otherwise you will smother.

When difficulties arise, a positive person sees the opportunities hidden behind them.

CHAPTER XIII

It seemed as if at last we could begin our separate lives anew. Over the years I had learned to manage financial affairs on my own and to take care of everything that concerned house and home. I had learned to live economically, but not meagerly. Pia and I practiced driving the car a couple of hours after work every evening. One of our tenants gave us a lot of good advice on the use of a car.

"Now we can go to the shore on Sundays," Little-Sisko hopped around joyfully.

"Sweetheart, we don't dare go so far yet, but as soon as we learn to drive better, we'll go."

It was a few weeks before I dared to drive any distance from home. On Saturday morning when there was less traffic, I drove alone onto the expressway. This is the enchantment of speed, I thought, as I sped along with the others toward Long Beach. It was lucky I had gone to that driving school; otherwise I would never have gotten the car. And my income would never have been enough to buy a new one.

Poju disappeared every Friday evening and did not come home until Sunday evening. I asked him about it, but he did not answer. I realized that his father was behind it. I could not get Poju to help mow the lawn, not to mention clean his room. No matter how much I asked him, it didn't help.

The girls and I joined the Finnish church where they had earlier attended confirmation school. It provided us with a good deal of enjoyable activity. Our weekdays were hurried, often full of cares, but when I sat in the church pew, all that seemed to melt away. I enjoyed the beautiful hymns; their words touched my heart. Leaving the church, my mind was light. I was spiritually free to start a new day.

Saul's checks came regularly for the first two months, but then they stopped coming. Poju began to stay home on the weekends, but I could learn nothing from him. Where could I find things out—something was up again. I called the place where Saul worked. He had not been there for two months.

One evening we drove out to the place where he lived. No one answered the door of the apartment I thought was his. I went to speak to the landlady.

"He was ill and moved away about a month ago."

"So that's it. It's just that he's behind in child-support payments."

"He has only one boy."

"There are four children altogether. One is already away from home," I said.

"Ahaa. He was withdrawn. He didn't really talk to anyone. To me he seemed mentally ill," said the woman.

"Didn't he leave an address when he left?"

"None at all. He had a truck. He loaded his goods on it and left," said the landlady.

A couple of weeks later, the neighbor across the street told us: "I saw Saul walking around the house a few days ago. He tried to get in, but couldn't. It's a good thing you had the locks changed. I watched from the window as he went into the alley. You can't know what he has in mind: he might set fire to the house. Be careful. You can never know what a lunatic might do."

"I know. There's no one at home during the day, and he could do practically anything."

"It caught my eye when he tried to get in with the old keys and couldn't. I watched, and if he had gotten in, I would have called the police. I knew that he had no business there."

"Thanks. It's nice to know that we have such good neighbors."

Poju stayed at home continually and began to come along with the girls wherever we went, even to church. Finally he opened up to me.

"Father said early in the spring that he was moving. When he gets a place to live, he'll let me know where it is. I haven't heard anything from him since then," he said, sounding close to tears.

"Why didn't you tell me earlier?"

"Because Father told me not to say anything to you." The boy was crying.

"Then he lies to you, too. Oh, my little Poju," I said, hugging him. I would have taken him into my lap too, but a fifteen-year old is already a big man.

"Was Father good to you?" I asked.

"He was. We went to the mountains every Sunday, and he let me drive the car. I'm a really good driver," said the boy. "And then he gave me money."

"Didn't you ever have to do anything to earn the money?"

"No, he always asked if I needed money."

"You do remember that in my system money has to be earned. Listen, you have to learn that in this world you never get anything free. I've often thought of getting a new power mower. Do you want to earn money by mowing the lawn every other week? You won't have to do it as often in the winter."

"Yes, yes. When will you buy it?"

"I just saw in the paper that they will be on sale. Will you come with me if we go and buy one on Saturday? You probably know more about it than I do."

"Oh, yes, I'll come, Mother," said the boy eagerly. We hugged one another. We were friends again.

Poju's birthday was in July. Since there was no school during the summer, he and Little-Sisko were at home. Pia already had a summer job. There was no one at home when I came from work. I saw an open envelope on the sofa. It was addressed to Pia and was from Finland, but had no return address on it. Although the address was printed, I recognized Saul's hand.

Hurrah! I danced around the floor like a schoolgirl. Now I no longer needed to be afraid. Finally I was free of that nightmare. I have never in my life felt such relief as I did at that moment. I went to the phone and called my neighbor, Jane.

"Come over. I have a surprise. I'm so happy that I want to share it with you."

"I'll come right away. I'll just shift that kettle to the side of the stove."

"What is it? Tell me quickly," said Jane, breathless.

"Saul is in Finland. I'm free now. Now I can sleep nights in peace." We hugged each other joyfully.

"Good for you. I'm so happy for you."

"Look at that envelope. It's proof that he's there." I took two glasses from the cupboard, mixed us both a vodka-and-water and took one to Jane.

"We'll have a little drink in honor of this day."

"Cheers. There's good reason for it. I worked at a police station and got to see all kinds of criminals and lunatics there. To tell the truth, I feared for your life."

"I haven't slept in peace for years. I always had to be afraid of something. Now I can rest like Sleeping Beauty."

"How is it now? Is he making the child support payments from there?"

"He's paying nothing. I don't believe he will. As I told you earlier, I haven't gotten anything for half a year."

"How do you get along then?"

"We manage. I'd rather do with less than be afraid night and day. Cheers. I'm so happy I feel like going out into the street and shouting to the whole world, 'I'm free. I'm free.'"

"I saw Little-Sisko's picture in the paper not long ago. She's a pretty girl and has a good head on her."

"Yaah, she got a gold watch then," I said proudly.

"You were on the front page with Pia last spring too."

"Yes, it was a real accomplishment for her. She was the best in her class of three hundred. She starts college in the fall."

"You have some exceptionally good girls."

"I'll wait for the fall to take my summer vacation and drive Pia to the school. It's in northern California," I said.

"Isn't it awfully expensive?"

"Pia got a number of scholarships because her grades were so good. She also gets a state scholarship because our income is so low."

"That's one advantage in Saul's leaving. The children get state aid in school."

"It's like that old story. The children in a family thanked an insurance agent for selling their father insurance. He happened to die, and with the insurance money, they were able to go to the university. If their father had lived, he would not have given them the money to go there."

We had a good time, laughing whole-heartedly. Jane was a nice neighbor, as were all the others. Old August had been forced to go to a retirement home. His sons had taken him to the other side of the city, nearer to them, and I no longer had the opportunity to go and see him and take *pulla* to him.

When the children came home, I did not ask Poju anything. I saw, however, that he had a secretive look on his face. In the evening I showed him the envelope and asked, "Did you get a letter from your father?" He turned red.

"There wasn't a word in it. Only ten dollars in a sheet of white paper."

"Yaah, I saw that it was from him. I wondered. Couldn't he write a single word to you, not so much as wish you a happy birthday?"

The boy shook his head, looking dejected. He looked as if he could not understand his father. We hugged each other and both of us cried. The girls received the news happily. I realized that it was a relief to them, too. These last years their life had not been easy either. Where others had a gentle, loving father, they had a fearful tyrant.

I had been in constant correspondence with Saul's brother's family, and just to be sure I wrote and asked if they had heard anything about him. I got an answer saying that someone had got a card from him from Helsinki. Then it was true. Hurrah!

EPILOGUE

Once the youngest in the family had finished high school, I wanted to move out of smoggy Los Angeles. On weekends, we drove around the outskirts of the city to see what we could find. I managed to sell the house, and in 1973, I moved to Antelope Valley, about seventy-five miles northeast of LA. The air was fresh there, the sun shone, and the view was incredible, with mountains on every side.

There I bought a brand-new triplex and found work in a home for the care of the elderly. I enjoyed my freedom but felt the need of a hobby, so I joined a local rock club. We went around gathering stones that could be made into jewelry. It was an interesting activity. There I met my future husband.

Although I had sworn never to tie myself down again, we were married in 1977, when we had both reach the age of fifty. He was an engineer in the aircraft line and had even been in the Apollo space program for a time. When he was offered a two-year assignment in Iran, I, world traveler that I was, was eager to see something new again. However, we did not stay there the whole time and returned just before the revolution in Iran.

My husband did not want me to go on working. We bought an old farmhouse and repainted the inside entirely. Then he developed a skin cancer, and we were advised to move to a less sunny place. A job was arranged for him in the state of Washington. Two of my children already lived there, so I was ready to move.

There I made the aquaintance of two old sisters, whom I began to assist. They were already in their eighties and had no children, so they really needed help. We bought a bigger house, into which I took the sisters to care for them. Sometimes a couple of other Finns temporarily lived with us as well. I've always like old people and got along very well with them. My husband had to travel a lot, so the arrangement was quite convenient.

I cared for these elderly people until their deaths, and then my husband's back began to give him trouble. He was no longer able to work and got a disability retirement. That was fifteen years ago. At first, we traveled a little, but, for the last ten years, his condition has been rather poor. Five years ago, he had a cancer operation but has recovered. Lately, he has been able to walk around at home, but nothing beyond that. I am in quite qood health and can manage everything—caring for the house and yard, the automobile, and all the rest.

Lempi V. Wilson